The Work of Art in the Age of Deindustrialization

Post·45 Kate Marshall and Loren Glass, Editors
Post·45 Group, Editorial Committee

The Work of Art in the Age of Deindustrialization

Jasper Bernes

Stanford University Press
Stanford, California

Stanford University Press
Stanford, California

© 2017 by the Board of Trustees of the Leland Stanford Junior University. All rights reserved.

This book has been partially underwritten by the Stanford Authors Fund. We are grateful to the Fund for its support of scholarship by first-time authors. For more information, please see www.sup.org/authorsfund.

Part of Chapter 5 was originally published as "Art, Work, Endlessness: Flarf and Conceptual Poetry among the Trolls," in *Critical Inquiry* © 2016 by the University of Chicago. Reprinted with permission.

No part of this book may be reproduced or transmitted in any form or by any means, electronic or mechanical, including photocopying and recording, or in any information storage or retrieval system without the prior written permission of Stanford University Press.

Printed in the United States of America on acid-free, archival-quality paper

Library of Congress Cataloging-in-Publication Data

Names: Bernes, Jasper, 1974– author.
Title: The work of art in the age of deindustrialization / Jasper Bernes.
Other titles: Post 45.
Description: Stanford, California : Stanford University Press, 2017. | Series: Post '45 | Includes bibliographical references and index.
Identifiers: LCCN 2016046280 | ISBN 9780804796415 (cloth) | ISBN 9781503610088 (paper) | ISBN 9781503602601 (ebook)
Subjects: LCSH: American poetry—20th century—History and criticism. | Poetry—Social aspects—United States. | Capitalism and literature—United States. | Postmodernism (Literature)—United States. | Work in literature.
Classification: LCC PS325 .B47 2017 | DDC 811/.5409—dc23
LC record available at https://lccn.loc.gov/2016046280

Contents

	Acknowledgments	vii
	Introduction	1
1	Lyric and the Service Sector: Frank O'Hara at Work	37
2	John Ashbery's Free Indirect Labor	64
3	The Poetry of Feedback	84
4	The Feminization of Speedup	120
5	Art, Work, and Endlessness in the 2000s	149
	Epilogue: Overflow	174
	Notes	197
	Index	227

Acknowledgments

Writing a research-based book is at once the most solitary and the most collective of labors. Though I acknowledge my dependence on the writing and thinking of others with every citation, a list of references is only a partial record of influences and debts. Some contributions are so essential as to escape mention in the endnotes altogether.

The seeds of this project were planted at UC Berkeley, where Annie McClanahan and I together ran the meetings of the Interdisciplinary Marxism Working Group, many of whose members would go on to become some of my most important friends and interlocutors. This book is guided at every turn by the texts we read together and the conversations we had. Annie has for the last decade been a model of the kind of thinking to which I aspire, and I am delighted that our first books are proximate releases from Post•45 and Stanford University Press. Ted Martin, Chris Chen, Tim Kreiner, Maya Gonzalez, and Aaron Benanav also came to IMWG meetings reliably and helped this book develop in numerous ways, both direct and indirect. Celeste Langan and Colleen Lye, also IMWG members, have been enormously supportive, reading drafts and serving as informal advisers and mentors over the years. Joshua Clover was another IMWG stalwart, and his contribution to this book would be hard to overstate. I also received important guidance from other faculty at Berkeley—in particular Charles Altieri, Lyn Hejinian, T. J. Clark, and Chris Nealon.

Beyond Berkeley, work on this book was made possible by a postdoctoral fellowship from the Literature Department at Duke University and the mentorship of Michael Hardt and Fredric Jameson. Parts of Chapter 2 benefited from the expert revisions of Marshall Brown, and Lauren Berlant made crucial edits to Chapter 5. Loren Glass, Florence Doré, and Kate Marshall at Post•45 helped me see the way from manuscript to book. At Stanford University Press, my editor, Emily-Jane Cohen, has a been a vital supporter of this project and invaluable in her thoughts about revision. I am very lucky to have found such excellent mentors and editors.

Early versions of the chapters here were presented at the National Poetry Conference in Orono, the Society for the Humanities at Cornell University, the American Comparative Literature Association, George Washington University, the University of Minnesota, McGill University, Brown University, and UC Davis. At each of these occasions, I received important feedback. I am also very grateful for the opportunity to examine Bernadette Mayer's papers in the Archive for New Poetry at UC San Diego, as well as the Frank O'Hara papers at the Museum of Modern Art. I am also grateful to Bernadette Mayer for permission to quote from *Memory* in Chapter 4.

Other friends, mentors, and colleagues escape the previous categories but made invaluable contributions nonetheless: Margaret Ronda, Sianne Ngai, Michael Szalay, Sarah Brouillette, Michael Nardone, Brian Whitener, Anne Boyer, Juliana Spahr, Morgan Adamson, Jason E. Smith, Dan Blanton, Eric Falci, and Oliver Arnold. I apologize for any others I may have left out.

This book may owe the most to my wife, Anna Shapiro, who supported me in countless ways, material and otherwise, during my work on this project. Finally, I must thank my children, Noah and Astrid. I wrote most of these pages in the tight but intimate quarters where we have all lived together, and I am particularly grateful for their patience as I put on my headphones or closed the door to engage in this obscure adult labor.

Introduction

In the following pages, I argue that the *work of art* and *work in general* share a common destiny. Such a claim may seem commonplace, especially to anyone familiar with Marxist thought. It is perhaps such a truism, however, that it has rarely been demonstrated with adequate rigor, even if the works of Walter Benjamin and Theodor Adorno and a few others provide the rudiments of such argument. Most people on the planet spend the majority of their lives working, not out of choice but out of necessity. In capitalism, which now encircles most of the earth, this means performing unfree activities in exchange for money. The want of such money, and the means of survival it purchases, is what makes work unfree, even when people enjoy work or find fulfillment and meaning in it. He who does not work shall not eat, as the saying goes. This is the principle that organizes capitalist societies (and many other social forms as well), coming as close to a "human condition" as anything else we are likely to identify in the present world. Through a study of a particular time and place, the postwar United States, I demonstrate that, inasmuch as it is the dominant form of social activity in capitalist societies, unfree work affects the horizon of possibility for aesthetic activity.

This is not a relationship of simple reflection, where art is a mirror held up to some underlying economic "base" assumed to hold the truth of the world, much less one of homology, where art reflects some mystical world spirit distributed evenly across the whole of society. Rather, I argue for a complex set of reversible mediations between different social spheres. On the one hand, wage labor and other types of unfree work provide the social and technical *means* for art work. Artists and writers draw from the methods and means and techniques available to them, many of which come from the workplace, and in doing so respond to the world of work, recasting it, critiquing it, celebrating it, or constructing alternative social arrangements from it. At the same time, however, industry looks to art as a sphere that can be commodified and to art work as an activity that can be turned into waged labor. Finally, in searching out its own methods, industry looks to art for transposable techniques, means, and materials that it can borrow and put to work, so to speak. To Adorno and Horkheimer's notable examination of the industrialization of culture, we must add an understanding of the corresponding aestheticization of industry.[1] Additionally, we must understand both of these phenomena as dialectically entangled with an active, and sometimes critical, engagement by writers and artists with the methods and materials of capitalist work.

Neither compelled work nor wage labor is unique to capitalist societies. But capitalism is distinct in that it makes labor, and the conditions of labor, particularly central to its own development, constantly inventing new ways to make workers more productive, either by extending the time of labor (what Marx calls absolute surplus value) or transforming the means of labor through the use of more productive methods and technologies (what Marx calls relative surplus value). I follow Moishe Postone in arguing that it is only because of capitalism's drive to dominate, rationalize, standardize, and intensify labor, and in particular its drive to submit it to a common temporal measure under the pressure of intercapitalist competition (what Marx calls abstract labor time), that labor appears as an abstract entity at all. Because capitalism *abstracts* labor, in both senses of the word, it appears as a substantial entity, a category that is not merely ideal but real, a living, breathing abstraction.[2] Before capitalism, labor was entangled with a mesh of activities that made up a person's days and weeks, and not easily extricable from them. The division between free and unfree time, labor and everything else, emerges only with the wage. Activities that now fall under the purview of art were intermixed with the productive activities now organized as labor, so one might argue that it is, in part, as a result of the capitalist consolidation of labor that the work of art and the related field of aesthetic activity emerge as distinct objects and discourses. "Everything comes down to aesthetics and political economy," as Stéphane Mallarmé notes.[3]

In capitalism, therefore, the historical refashioning of labor and its conditions plays a major role in social transformation more generally. History in capitalism is always, to some extent, the history of work, and the violent transformations of the last few centuries are intimately entangled with an equally violent refashioning of labor—its methods, its materials, its distribution into different occupations, its subjectivities, and the corresponding balance of power between employers and employees. This book concerns itself primarily with the restructuring of labor that takes place in the already-industrialized countries of the global north—the so-called first world—beginning in the 1960s, a transformation of the conditions of labor that, as many will claim with some persuasiveness, puts into jeopardy the very nature of capitalist work and production and figures a new crisis of the capitalist system as a whole.[4] If capitalism *is* industrialization and *is* the mechanization of work, then there might be no possibility of a truly *postindustrial* capitalism, properly speaking. Hence, the doubleness of the prefix "post-," which indicates its dependence on an industrial moment that, as we know, persists as a dominant in the so-called developing countries and in a residual form in the postindustrial countries. I choose the term "deindustrialization" rather than "postindustrialization" for my title because it gives us the sense of a negation that has not itself been negated, an unending transition.

To understand the transformations of the 1960s and 1970s, we need first to understand something of the unique period that preceded them. As is widely acknowledged, the decades immediately following World War II were immensely prosperous, referred to in the historical literature as "the Golden Age of Capitalism," characterized by numerous "economic miracles" (in West Germany, Italy, Japan, and France).[5] By nearly every available measure—wages, profitability, investment—wealth increased greatly across the United States, Europe, and East Asia. Wages in the United States grew steadily during this period, particularly among white workers, facilitating the subsequent expansion of markets for new mass-produced consumer goods and the construction of numerous single-family houses to fill with these new products. There was, correspondingly, a massive growth in US productive capacity and blue-collar manufacturing jobs, and a particularly important part of postwar history is the story of increasingly affluent industrial workers who only a couple of decades before had been fighting for subsistence wages. The period likewise saw a vast increase in the white-collar workforce, an increase that occurred alongside rather than in spite of the increase in blue-collar work.

Capitalism during this period is often described as conforming to a "virtuous" cycle of investment and hiring, in which increases in productivity and wages were mutually constitutive, rising together. This allowed for a "compromise" between capital and labor, in which workers would relinquish control over the conditions of labor in exchange for a larger share of the proceeds. Capitalists could therefore institute a wide spectrum of techniques to rationalize and intensify labor in accord with the profit drive, and it was the success of such productivity-increasing programs that allowed capitalists to increase wages and still keep a handy sum for themselves. Typically, one speaks (sometimes interchangeably) of two types of managerial programs: Taylorism and Fordism. Taylorism refers to the "scientific management" techniques popularized by Frederick Winslow Taylor at the turn of the century, which involved an analysis of existing work practices ("time and motion studies") and an attempt to reconstruct such practices by way of precisely choreographed movements designed for maximum efficiency. Fordism, which often incorporated Taylorist management techniques, refers in particular to the automation of production through the establishment of assembly lines where workers at different stations perform a single task, notably pioneered in Ford Motor Company's factories.[6] Fordism also refers to a particular social arrangement in which workers are paid enough to purchase the products they make. Henry Ford famously paid workers five dollars per day so that they could purchase the very cars they had themselves built. Fordism thus becomes a particularly useful if also limited shorthand for the postwar order and its linkage of productivity and wages. Both Fordism and Taylorism typically imply processes of "deskilling" and "routinization" that allow workers to begin a job with no training and tend to increase managerial control over the pace and design of work. They also make it much easier to replace workers, since the years of apprenticeship that craft-based production required are done away with.[7] Since these processes required such large numbers of workers, and since deskilling meant that employers could expand their workforce rapidly, productive investment led to a favorable bargaining position for workers, whose unions emerged from the 1940s as powerful if also domesticated political forces.

Deskilling also affected white-collar jobs, especially in the years following World War II. By the middle of the 1950s, white-collar jobs outnumbered blue-collar ones; the rapid transformation of such positions meant that they were effectively split into two tracks: on the one hand, a class of managerial, professional, and technical positions that came with substantial privileges; and on the other hand, low-paying, Taylorized clerical positions.[8] This lower rank of clerical workers was, as we know, often but not always composed of women, which is to say that the division of labor was, in this case, also a gender division of labor (and a racial one, too, largely through the exclusion of nonwhites from the aptly named white-collar work).[9]

In an important study of post-45 fiction and white-collar work, Andrew Hoberek reads the novels of this period as doubly constituted. On the one hand, they feature a positive vision, "a fantasy of entrepreneurial labor in a white-collar world"; on the other hand, they are merely negative, "stylistic revolts" against the "ultimate proletarianization of mental labor."[10] Hoberek draws on influential contemporaneous accounts by C. Wright Mills, William Whyte, and David Riesman, all of whom emphasize or lament the "threatened individuality" of a postwar middle class no longer characterized by entrepreneurial property ownership but by white-collar mental labor in the managerial and professional ranks.[11] As it was for their blue-collar counterparts, prosperity for white-collar workers meant an erosion of control and deteriorating working conditions. My book picks up where Hoberek's leaves off, looking at the art and literature that emerged once this process of proletarianization was a step or two further along. But rather than treat these cultural products as ideological deformations of an experience of labor and class, as Hoberek does, I suggest we look at them as experiments with imaginary alternatives to the real problems that contemporary labor presented, for both white-collar and blue-collar workers. Associated as they are with the political and countercultural left of the 1960s and 1970s, or with various faces of the neo-avant-garde, the figures I examine do not imagine—as, for instance, Vladimir Nabokov does in Hoberek's account—forms of heroic individualism set against the routinized world of alienated mental or manual labor. Instead they typically imagine new forms of collectivity that might take the place of the bureaucratic, stultifying collective life of the postwar world. If, in C. Wright Mills's account, the transformation of modern work goes beyond the mere dispossession of the means of production, such that "rationality itself has been expropriated from work [along with] any total view and understanding of its process," the works that I examine try to form "total views" of a process they invent based on the real processes they observe. In other words, their total views are modeled in part on the economic world they actually have and in part on the economic life they wish they had.[12] However, unlike the notion of "economic fiction" that Michael Clune develops in his study of free market ideals in postwar literature, where literary texts provide not an "image of economic reality, but a space in which the economic undergoes a change,"

I am not afraid to make claims for the effectivity of the aesthetic sphere.[13] In the amalgam of realist and speculative modes I examine in the following pages, imaginative transformations of actually existing economic conditions become laboratories in which the emergent social relations, techniques, and ideologies of the future economy and future conditions of labor develop, in most cases, against the intention and conception of the artists and writers themselves.

Initial postwar accounts of the "new middle class" of white-collar workers tended to emphasize the "political indifference" that followed from their ambivalent class position, "powerless and estranged but not disinherited," as C. Wright Mills describes them. Mills connects the "apathy" of this class to a "larger problem of self-alienation and social meaninglessness."[14] But by the late 1960s, the vectors had changed a great deal, in part because of the ongoing proletarianization of the lower orders of this class, and even Mills, in his "Letter to the New Left," written during the last years of his life, would ascribe the end of "the age of complacency" to middle-class "students and young professionals and writers."[15] Similarly, Herbert Marcuse, as influential a 1960s figure as Mills, would reverse the grim assessment of the white-collar middle class that he offered in *One-Dimensional Man*. In that book, he suggested that because of "the transformation of physical energy into technical and mental skills," white-collar work was a form of freedom that actually entailed "masterly enslavement." In his account, both blue-collar and white-collar workers had been "incorporated into the technological community of the administered population," mastered by the machines that had liberated them from exertion.[16] Such domination held for the machinist as much as it did for "the typist, the bank teller, the high-pressure salesman or saleswoman, and the television announcer."[17] But within only a few years, with the publication of his *Essay on Liberation*, directed at the New Left of the time, Marcuse would, like Mills, soften some of his initial contentions, describing "scientifically-trained, intelligent workers" as a "'new working class' . . . vital for the growth of the existing society." The student revolt of the period was, therefore, a revolt of these future white-collar workers, one capable of "hit[ting] this society at a vulnerable point."[18] Though Marcuse's hopes ultimately lay with the urban lumpenproletariat in the industrialized countries and the rebellions of the developing world, he would acknowledge that despite the differences between "the middle-class revolt in the metropoles and the life-and-death of the wretched of the earth—common to them is the depth of the Refusal."[19]

Thus, by the mid-1960s, there arose the possibility that this partly proletarianized middle class (or "new working class," as others called it) might revolt against the alienating character of their routinized work, against the new forms of technocratic management and control that had come to administer even the administrators. At the same time, however, there was the promise of awakening rebellion among the classic industrial working class, as a new wave of discontent spread across the manufacturing sectors of the most developed countries. Rates of absenteeism, job turnover, and sabotage among blue-collar workers began to rise in the mid-1960s across most of these countries, followed by a global wave of strikes after 1968.[20] The US strike wave of 1970 still stands as one of the largest in US history, with over five thousand stoppages. In Italy and France from as early as 1960, various theorists and militants, breaking with Marxist orthodoxy, began to talk about a new "rebelliousness ... in large part incomprehensible from the classic 'protests and demands' framework" and an antagonism that was not a demand for better terms but "a refusal of the command of capital as the organizer of production."[21] The explosions that arrived with France's May 1968 and Italy's "creeping May," incomprehensible from a perspective that focused only on material prosperity but completely predictable by the lights of the new theories of alienation, only confirmed that something different was afoot. In the United States, toward the end of the 1960s, the mainstream press featured article upon article about the new "blue-collar blues" and the "new resistance to certain forms of work."[22] Alarm about this wave of dissatisfaction in the United States—which seemed to threaten that the revolt among students would spill into the organized working class, as had happened in Europe—spawned a now-classic government study, *Work in America*, which spoke of "the anachronistic authoritarianism of the workplace" and suggested, rather bluntly, that "[d]ull, repetitive, seemingly meaningless tasks, offering little challenge or autonomy, are causing discontent among workers at all occupational levels." This discontent, the study concluded, manifested in overt and covert ways, "as measured by absenteeism, turnover rates, wildcat strikes, sabotage, poor-quality products."[23] Whereas earlier analysts would speak of the auto industry as the central example of the so-called compromise between capital and labor, now it was "the *locus classicus* of dissatisfying work; the assembly-line, its quintessential embodiment."

Moreover, the report continued, "the dissatisfaction of the assembly-line and blue-collar worker is mirrored in white-collar and even managerial positions." The factory had spread, and the factory was a source of resentment: "The office today, where work is segmented and authoritarian, is often a factory. For a growing number of jobs, there is little to distinguish them but the color of the worker's collar: computer keypunch operations and typing pools share much in common with the automobile assembly line."[24]

In nearly every industrialized country, therefore, the so-called compromise between capital and labor began to break down, and workers were less willing to accept speedup, routinization, and deskilling in exchange for material prosperity. The struggles of the period put into question the very character of industrial work, not just the distribution of wealth between capital and labor. Qualitative rather than quantitative demands were the order of the day. If the goal of Fordist and Taylorist reconstructions was "the displacement of labor as the subjective element of the labor process and its transformation into an object," these struggles announced the return of that subjective element as a new terrain of struggle.[25] As the authors of *Work in America* contend, pay alone was no longer satisfactory: "[A]dequate and equitable pay, reasonable security, safety, comfort and convenience on the job do not insure workers against the blues."[26]

Such demands were difficult to articulate, or at least more difficult to articulate than a simple demand for better pay, since the changes they proposed were global and relatively structural. They usually consisted of calls for a greater participation in decision making, for a democratization of the workplace, for more varied and creative work, for greater autonomy, and even for worker's self-management. This maximalist latter demand was, of course, especially prevalent in the European case, in Italy and above all in France.[27] But in the United States, too, as Jefferson Cowie notes, a new wave of working-class struggles among miners and office workers, farmworkers and autoworkers rallied around "the 'new' qualitative demands of health and safety, quality of work life, and union democracy." Such struggles were leavened "with youthful energy, a sixties-style discontent, and an anti-authority mood created not by protesting the war but, more typically among the working-class, from actually serving in it."[28]

In this book, I argue that the various literary and artistic experimental cultures of the 1960s and 1970s helped to *articulate*, though certainly not to create, these new qualitative complaints and demands. In reacting against the same bureaucratic, "one-dimensional," conformist, and hierarchical society as their fellow workers, artists and writers participated in a widespread expression of countersystemic values (visible in the counterculture, in the women's movement, and in the antiracist struggles of the period). That artists and writers are quick to formalize, articulate, and transform these attitudes, visions, and values should surprise us only if we consider the sphere of culture as entirely abstracted from the contemporaneous transformations of the economy. Whether or not artists and writers themselves worked under these new conditions, where new attitudes and maladjustments were developing, is beside the point. They knew someone who did, or read about those who did, or partook of the products of such work. My claims therefore have to do with social experience rather than personal experience strictly speaking.

My argument, however, is not that artists simply registered, through the articulation of their own dissatisfactions, contemporaneous expressions of discontent. Though this did happen, many of the artistic articulations I attend to in this study precede, often by several years, the full flowering of the qualitative critique in the advanced capitalist countries. Though it would be absurd to suggest that artists and writers precipitated such rebellions—this discontent had been brewing, somewhat quietly, since the 1950s—what is more plausible is my argument that they provided some of its key terms and coordinates. When workers began to critique, in large numbers, the alienation, monotony, and authoritarianism of the workplace, they did so, in part, through the use of aesthetic categories, concepts, and ideologies. This is why Luc Boltanski and Eve Chiapello refer to the qualitative critique of work that comes to the fore in this period as "the artistic critique" (conceptually opposed to the largely quantitative demands of "the social critique"). Speaking of the French situation, they describe "the main themes of the artistic critique," which involve critique of society in general and not just work, as follows:

> On the one hand, the disenchantment, the inauthenticity, the "poverty of everyday life," the dehumanization of the world under the sway of technicization and technocratization; on the other hand, the loss of autonomy, the absence of creativity, and the different forms of oppression in the modern world. Evidence of this in the family sphere was the importance of demands aimed at emancipation from traditional forms of domestic control ("patriarchal control")—that is to say, in the first instance, women's liberation and youth emancipation. In the sphere of work and production more directly of interest to us, the dominant themes were denunciation

of "hierarchical power," paternalism, authoritarianism, compulsory work schedules, prescribed tasks, the Taylorist separation between design and execution, and, more generally, the division of labour. Their positive counterpoint was demands for autonomy and self-management, and the promise of an unbounded liberation of human creativity.[29]

"[I]nspired by Marx, Freud and Nietzsche, and Surrealism," this particular variant of the artistic critique "developed in the small political and artistic avant-gardes of the 1950s" before spreading through the various workplaces, especially white-collar ones.[30] My study observes a similar thematic convergence between artistic avant-gardes of the 1960s in the United States and the workplace struggles that emerge toward the end of the 1960s. I argue that these experiments pick up on a mood, a structure of feeling, about the alienation of modern work and give such a mood a set of themes and ideas from which the wave of resistance at the decade's end borrows. The story is a bit more complex and features a few more dialectical twists and turns, since these demands for autonomy and self-management, for more flexible schedules and routines, for dehierarchization, get instantiated in a particularly unsatisfying form with the emergence of new regimes of "flexible work" and "teamwork"—often described as post-Fordism or Toyotism. These new workplace regimes respond to the critiques of the period by instituting new forms of autonomy and self-management that are really regimes of self-harrying, self-intensification, and interworker competition disguised as attempts to humanize the workplace and allow for freedom and self-expression in work.

There is no single term or point of contact that links the aesthetic situation with the workplace; rather, the following chapters explore a network of terms, practices, attitudes, and values that link the two spheres. However, for our immediate purpose, perhaps the best introduction to my argument can be had by exploring the ideas that attach themselves to the concept of "participation"—or sometimes "collaboration" or "interaction"—in the art of the 1960s, a term that is also a fundamental part of the new qualitative demands and antagonisms that emerge in 1960s workplaces. In terms of art, we might think, first, of the "happenings" of Allan Kaprow and others, semiscripted performances where there were no audience members, only "participants." Brought into object-filled environments where they were sometimes given instructions, and sometimes not, the participants would become active producers rather than merely (or so the idea went) passive consumers of the artwork. As Kaprow writes, "[T]hough the artist sets up the equation, the participant provides its terms, and the system remains open to participation."[31] The participatory thematic of the period runs as much through the happenings of Kaprow and Claes Oldenburg as through its near cousins in Fluxus, as well as Latin American neo-concretism, Viennese actionism, the experiments of the Situationist International in its early artistic phase, and numerous currents of 1960s art, inasmuch as the entire field saw a move away from the strict production of objects and toward performances, conceptual elaborations, installations, environments, and earthworks. Indeed, we can take an even broader viewpoint and note that "Art and Objecthood," Michael Fried's famous (and in some quarters infamous) response to the minimalist sculpture of the late 1960s, which objects to the new art's reliance on what Fried describes as "theater," is really an objection to the participatory, viewer-oriented character of that sculpture. Fried is repelled by the "special complicity that [the] work extorts from the beholder."[32] In the same way that the happening is completed by the spectator-turned-participant, the minimalist work, for Fried, "depends on the beholder, is incomplete without him, it *has* been waiting for him. And once he is in the room the work refuses, obstinately, to let him alone—which is to say, it refuses to stop confronting him, distancing him, isolating him."[33] In other words, the minimalist object demands that the spectator become a *participant.*

In most cases, these strains of anti-illusionistic, participatory art are given specific political overtones, whether revolutionary or not, and connected both directly and figuratively to the political aspirations and tumults of the late 1960s. Much of this material trades on an older avant-garde politics that announces its opposition to the separation of art and life, intending to bring the technical means of art making to bear on life, and the social problems therein, with new force.[34] Indeed, proving that such boundaries were irretrievably blurred—so much so that avant-garde negations of them might be redundant—by the end of the 1960s the term "happening" had entered the mainstream vocabulary as an all-purpose term for political demonstrations, cultural events, or simple recreational gatherings. In particular, the technical methods of the participatory arts of the period were quickly put to use in the newly theatrical political demonstrations of the period, perhaps most notably in the case of the Dutch Provos, where theatrical performances by large groups of participants were engineered to provoke violent overreaction by the police.³⁵ There is an underlying equation here, which seems to suggest that the transformation of art practices into "life practices" through the use of participatory mechanisms is, in and of itself, a kind of revolutionary politics, or at the very least a direct contestation of the domination at work in capitalist societies. This is clear, as well, in the participatory "do-it-yourself" art of Fluxus—which often involved the creation of small kits ("Fluxus boxes"), filled with items and instructions nonartists could use to make their own "art" (or rather, experience). As George Maciunas writes in his "Fluxus Manifesto," by promoting a "NON ART REALITY to be grasped by all people, not only critics, dilettantes and professionals," Fluxus would "FUSE the cadres of cultural social & political revolutionaries into united front & action."³⁶ In Brazil, too, neo-concretist artists Lygia Clark and Hélio Oiticica proposed and elaborated forms of sculpture in which the object becomes "a mediator for participation" rather than a point of contemplation. Clark writes that such art forms would precipitate "the collapse of social preconceived ideas, of separations of groups, social classes, etc."³⁷ In Germany, Joseph Beuys took the participatory theme to its seemingly maximal limits, drawing out some of the thought underlying many of these examples with his typical grandiosity. Beuys insists on the ultimate identity of artistic and political projects, stating that "art is now the only evolutionary-revolutionary power." Revolution, in this sense, simply means the extension of artistic methods and principles across the social totality, a process he refers to as "social sculpture/social architecture," in which the liberation of the powers of creative self-expression and autonomy are "a politically productive force, coursing through each person and shaping history." In a society modeled on such principles, "EVERY HUMAN IS AN ARTIST." Acknowledgment of this fundamental baseline of creative potential is the foundation for numerous other forms of participation: "Self-determination and participation in the cultural sphere (freedom); in the structuring of laws (democracy); and in the sphere of economics (socialism). Self-administration and decentralization (threefold structure) occurs: FREE DEMOCRATIC SOCIALISM."³⁸

Perhaps the most sophisticated evocation of these themes can be found in the work of the Situationist International (SI), a group that Boltanski and Chiapello cite as particularly central to the articulation of the artistic critique in France. Guy Debord, chief theoretician of the SI, is perhaps best known for his development of the concept of "spectacle," or rather "the spectacle," which in his characterization is a total machine for the management of human activity through semiautomatic representations. What is important, for our account, is that the spectacle produces, and feeds off, nonparticipation. It presides over an "empire of passivity" where "the individual's own gestures are no longer his own, but rather those of someone else who represents them to him." The spectacle exists through "the spectator's alienation from and submission to the contemplated object" but also through the separation of subordinates from those who make decisions: "The specialized role played by the spectacle is that of spokesman for all other activities, a sort of diplomatic representative of hierarchical society at its own court, and the source of the only discourse which that society allows itself to hear."[39]

As the apotheosis of alienation, hierarchy, and nonparticipation, spectacle neatly encapsulates everything the figures we have been discussing so far fought against. Perhaps more important, the SI from its very earliest stages—long before Debord coined the term "spectacle" to describe late capitalism and its pathologies—had developed an anti-aesthetic politics, based on a reading of the historical avant-gardes and their failures, that conforms to some degree with the participatory thematics described previously. Against the enforced passivity and separation of modern life, they propose the "construction of situations":

> The construction of situations begins on the other side of the modern collapse of the idea of the theater. It is easy to see to what extent the very principle of the theater—nonintervention—is attached to the alienation of the old world. Inversely, we see how the most valid of revolutionary cultural explorations have sought to break the spectator's psychological identification with the hero, so as to incite this spectator into activity by provoking his capacities to revolutionize his own life. The situation is thus made to be lived by its constructors. The role of the "public," if not passive at least a walk-on, must ever diminish while the share of those who cannot be called actors but, in a new meaning of the term, "livers," will increase. . . . Let us say that we have to multiply poetic objects and subjects . . . and that we have to organize games of these poetic subjects among these poetic objects.[40]

Though we know that the SI thought very little of the projects of Fluxus artists and happenings, treating them as essentially spectacular reenactments of counterspectacular practice, the family resemblance between all of these projects is unmistakable, even if we acknowledge, as I do, that the SI presented the most serious and theoretically elaborated version of this project, allied in ways that were not merely figurative with actual processes of class struggle. If by the end of the 1950s the SI had resolved to "begin with a small-scale, experimental phase" dedicated to the development of "Situationist techniques" that would counter the false world of the spectacle, the actual course of capitalist restructuring would eventually put those techniques in the service not only of the art world they thought moribund but the capitalist order they opposed completely.[41]

The participatory thematic and the critique of the artist-spectator or writer-reader distinction is also prevalent in the literature and literary theory of the 1960s. Particularly notable here are theories of the "writerly" (*scriptible*) or "open" text, to borrow Roland Barthes's characterization and Umberto Eco's similar concept. Such a text does not impose an authoritative meaning like the "readerly" text but instead enjoins the reader to participate in the elaboration of its meaning. In the manifesto-like declaration at the beginning of *S/Z*, Barthes grandly claims that the age of the readerly text has passed: "what can be written (rewritten) today: the *writerly*." In the present "the goal of literary work (of literature as work) is to make the reader no longer a consumer, but a producer of the text." [42] Yet in the very next sentence, Barthes writes: "Our literature is characterized by the pitiless divorce which the literary institution maintains between the producer of the text and its user, between its owner and its customer, between its author and its reader."[43] This seeming contradiction, describing an age that is at once dominated by the writerly and readerly modes, resolves itself once one recognizes that the writerly and readerly are not so much categories of text, nor even modalities of reading, as they are possibilities within reading and writing as such, inasmuch as writing is an activity that can be undertaken by a certain type of active reader.

In North America, these distinctions, taken up by experimental writers, do end up as claims about varieties of texts rather than varieties of reading practices and become affirmations of the superior political, intellectual, and social effectivity of the writerly or open work. Particularly seminal here are the essays that emerged from the symposium on "The Politics of the Referent" that Steve McCaffery organized in 1976. His own contribution, published as "The Death of the Subject: The Implications of Counter-Communication in Recent Language-Centered Writing," gives a lucid articulation of the participatory thematic as it appears in the "language-centered writing" of the 1970s:

> Language-centered writing involves a major alteration in textual roles of the socially defined functions of writer and reader as the productive and consumptive roles respectively of a commodital axis. The main thrust of this work is hence political, rather than aesthetic, towards a frontal assault on the steady categories of authorship and readership. What it offers is the alternative sense of reader and writer as equal and simultaneous participants within a language product. At its core, linguistic reference is a displacement of human relationships and as such is fetishistic in the Marxian sense. Reference, like commodity, has no connection with the physical property and material relations of the word as grapheme.[44]

By stripping language of reference, reducing graphic marks to their material characteristics, the writer allows the reader to become a coproducer of meaning, a "participant within a language product." This becomes the instantiation of a communist principle in language: "Phonemes of the Word fragment! You have nothing to lose but your referents!' Non-grammatical emphasis is equal emphasis. Non-subordination. Non-hierarchy."[45] As Lyn Hejinian describes these ideas, in a later statement that is equally seminal and substantially more precise and modest in its claims,

> The "open text," by definition, is open to the world and particularly to the reader. It invites participation, rejects the authority of the writer over the reader and, by analogy, the authority implicit in other (social, economic, cultural) hierarchies. It speaks for writing that is generative rather directive. The writer relinquishes total control and challenges authority as a principle and control as a motive.[46]

The antiauthoritarian, proparticipatory character of the quote could not be clearer: writerly participation is a rejection of social and economic nonparticipation. As one of the most highly regarded experimental poets of her generation, Hejinian helped popularize the active reader theory, such that it is now almost accepted as a truism in the world of experimental poetry.

We might be tempted to sum up the preceding claims as follows: In the context of the rebellions of the 1960s and 1970s, resistance to the "anachronistic authoritarianism of the workplace" and the hierarchical relationship between those who command and those who follow commands finds its corollary in a critique of the enforced passivity of the arts, a critique, in other words, of the division of labor between artist and spectator, writer and reader, which condemns the latter to inactivity. Under the sign of participation, collaboration, and interaction, artists and writers imagine forms of art and writing that allow for reciprocal, "democratic" relations between artist and audience, or even, in the most radical version of these themes, a demolition of such distinctions. The problem with this story is that the timing is not right, or not completely right. Rather than merely seeing both the workplace and artistic manifestations of the times as expressing some underlying antiauthoritarian or libertarian spirit—a view that is certainly correct to a degree—my book asks us to consider the historical sequence of these struggles, in which the artistic critique in many ways seems to precede and prefigure the challenges that emerge in the workplace. I say "seems" because I do not want to make it sound as if such critique did not exist in the workplace before artists, writers, and intellectuals began their exploration. The artists and writers of the time provided tropes, motifs, and forms of articulation for a dissatisfaction that had its own vernacular expression. They thereby gave it a certain visibility and, perhaps more important, lent it a new conceptual vocabulary.

The diachronic story becomes more complicated, however, when we consider that this *qualitative* critique of work emerged at the same time as the postwar industries themselves began to encounter severe problems with profitability. Indeed, even though most histories identify the beginning of the economic crisis of the period as occurring in 1973, with the oil crisis, the corresponding inflation crisis, and subsequent recession, Robert Brenner has recently demonstrated that the high profit rates of the postwar boom really began to evaporate as early as 1965, once an "irruption of lower-priced Japanese and German goods" made it extremely difficult for manufacturers to pass on increasing costs through higher prices.[47] Since wage growth had already been limited from its highs in the 1950s, and pushing wage growth down to zero seemed difficult, the response by firms was instead to rely on the managerial prerogatives they had gained under the so-called compromise and to further Taylorize, speed up, and intensify work. The qualitative critique of work that spreads during this period, then, should not surprise us at all. The renewed workplace struggles that began in the late 1960s and early 1970s are a response to the attempt by capitalists to manage the crisis, first through various forms of intensification and then, once the crisis continues and worsens in the 1970s, by beginning to attack wages and defang the unions that were reluctantly pushed into the fray by an increasingly combative workforce. This is the opposite of the story that has often been told about this period—referred to as the profit-squeeze thesis—which suggests that the crisis of the period was brought on by rising wages and rising combativeness by unions. In a version of his account of postwar economic history that addresses in particular the workplace struggles of the period, Brenner argues convincingly against the idea that the crisis was caused by such struggles—a position that the data on wages and profitability do not support.[48] What these struggles did do, however, is make it more difficult for capitalists to solve the crisis through conventional methods, motivating instead a full-scale reconstruction of work and workplace relations, and the social relations of capitalism overall, undertaken during the long period of low growth and stagnation that lasted from the 1970s until the present (with a short period of affluence in the late 1990s), sometimes referred to as "the long downturn."

The new order that emerged in the 1970s is often described as "post-Fordism" (a term meant to emphasize both its difference from and continuity with Fordist and Taylorist methods), or alternatively "neoliberalism," "flexible accumulation," and "postindustrial society," where each of these terms stresses different aspects of the transformation. What matters for my argument is that—as Boltanski and Chiapello, Alan Liu, David Harvey, and many others emphasize—aspects of the artistic critique, such as the critique of work from the standpoint of participation, became essential parts of the restructuring undertaken by capitalists to improve profitability. This was done not only to respond to the critiques, neutralize them, and keep them from producing more problems in terms of absenteeism, low-productivity, sabotage, and strikes but also to allow corporations to intensify labor and trim costs, particularly administrative costs. Self-managing workers who participate in managerial decisions require fewer supervisors, as long as one can find mechanisms to keep the productivity of such workers high. The essential duplicity of many of these initiatives—responses to the resistance to intensification that are essentially new forms of intensification—was apparent to many commentators from the beginning. As Braverman writes, summarizing the early 1970s attempts to ameliorate worker dissatisfaction that often went under the banner of "job enlargement" and "humanization," "[Such reforms] represent a style of management rather than a genuine change in the position of the worker. They are characterized by a studied pretense of worker 'participation,' a gracious liberality in allowing the worker to adjust a machine, replace a light bulb, move from one fractional job to another, and to have the illusion of making decisions by choosing among fixed and limited alternatives designed by a management which deliberately leaves insignificant matters open to choice."[49] As the crisis intensified and the restructuring (a decades-long process) continued, these transformations increasingly became structural rather than superficial. Nevertheless, Braverman's basic point stands: Firms enlarge or humanize work, allowing opportunities for participation, only when it likewise increases worker productivity. Furthermore, as Boltanski and Chiapello note, transformations of the qualitative character of work often permit an erosion of pay and benefits—that is, concessions to the artistic critique allow for an attack on the material gains made by the social critique during the immediate postwar period.

The argument of this book is, therefore, that the critique of labor posed by experimental writers and artists of the postwar period became a significant force behind the restructuring of capitalism, by providing important coordinates, ideas, and images for that restructuring.[50] As David Harvey describes it, in what is still one of the best accounts of the transformation, the response to the "crisis of Fordism" pitted the rigidities of the old industrial system against a new regime of "flexibility." In opposition to the "rigidity of long-term and large-scale fixed capital investments in mass-production systems ... that presumed stable growth in invariant consumer markets," the new regime proposed decentralized production processes dependent on "a whole network of sub-contracting and 'outsourcing,'" an organizational form that "[had] the virtue of bypassing the rigidities of the Fordist system and satisfying a far greater range of market needs, including quick changing ones." Decentralized production processes could be linked together through computerized systems of ordering, shipping and receiving, using a "just-in-time inventory-flows delivery system, which cuts down radically on stocks required to keep production going."[51] Furthermore, the new post-Fordist plants and factories were often equipped with reprogrammable, multiuse equipment rather than the single-purpose machines of the Fordist assembly line, an arrangement that allowed producers to quickly change the goods they produced as market conditions changed, without new fixed capital investment. These new regimes of mutability in production and circulation required a new workforce. In opposition to the "rigidities in labour markets, labour allocation, and in labour contracts" of the Fordist system, with its "seemingly immovable force of deeply entrenched working-class power," employers introduced new "flexible arrangements" that meant an "increasing reliance upon part-time, temporary or sub-contracted work arrangements" and greatly weakened the power of unions and other institutions of working-class power.[52] Linked together by information technology, these new flattened, downsized, or lean structures were filled with self-managing "work teams" that participated in management decisions (managers became coaches and facilitators rather than directors and supervisors). Instead of asking workers to do the same thing over and over again, these teams would be filled with multiskilled workers who were flexible in terms of scheduling as well as tasks and roles.

A careful reader will have noted a slippage in the preceding discussion. Whereas I began discussing the change in occupational structure and the shift from blue-collar to white-collar work, I quickly changed the subject, talking instead about the transformation of the methods, means, attitudes, and social relations of work. These two topics are not easily disentangled, since these new regimes develop first in the world of white-collar work and then spread into other sectors, such that much of the manufacturing work under these new regimes increasingly resembles clerical and administrative activity, as automation shifts workers from direct contact with materials to an increasingly supervisory role. Nonetheless, the argument that follows is that the transformation of the kinds of things people do for work—a shift from an industrial, manufacturing-oriented economy to a postindustrial economy oriented around administrative, technical, clerical, and service work—has tremendous implications for the kinds of art people make and the kinds of literature they produce. That is, while artists and writers in the 1960s and 1970s develop a conceptual grammar that is important to the restructuring of work that follows, they do so under conditions where the horizon of possibility for art has already been deeply changed by the transformations in the initial postwar period (1945–1965). We can grasp this former change as a process of *deindustrialization*, one that means that people, by and large, turn from work based on making things or objects to work oriented around the performance of administrative and technical processes or the provision of services to customers. This process begins, as I have noted, in the 1950s but accelerates quickly from the 1970s onward. A central part of my argument, therefore, is my claim that, as workers in the United States turn away, increasingly, from the production of things, so too does art.[53] This is one way to contextualize Lucy Lippard's description of the late 1960s as involving a "dematerialization of the art object,"[54] which occurs alongside a more general dematerialization of labor. Though it is probably incorrect to think of art or work as immaterial—both involve physical activity and manipulation of matter even if their end goal is not an object—the term nonetheless grasps the importance of these shifts. This is why Benjamin Buchloh, in one of the best essays on conceptual art and its turn to institutional critique, has characterized this art as "an aesthetic of administration."[55] For Buchloh, post-Duchampian conceptual art, which follows from the nominalism of the readymade (capable of making any object into art merely by its placement in the museum or gallery), transforms the aesthetic such that it "becomes on the one hand a matter of linguistic convention and on the other the function of both a legal contract and an institutional discourse (a discourse of power rather than taste)."[56] Artwork in this case becomes paperwork, the production of documents that guarantee the art status of the work in question. Buchloh, too, identifies this work with the "newly established postwar middle class, one which came fully into its own in the 1960s." Positioned as it was "between logical positivism and the advertising campaign," the conceptual art of the 1960s allowed members of this class to "assume their aesthetic identity in the very model of the tautology and its accompanying aesthetic of administration."[57] But Buchloh mistakenly attributes to the entirety of this class privileges that had already been eroded. Though some of the conceptual art of the period might rightly be seen as "managerial" in its attitudes, much of it seems to match the standpoint of a mere functionary, an administrative assistant, a manager in name alone, or a cleric, idly shuffling and filing the papers of a routinized art industry. One notes, for instance, Sol LeWitt's description of himself "as a clerk cataloguing the results of his premise."[58] For, although Buchloh is correct to note that "this class's social identity is . . . one of merely administering labor and production (rather than producing) and the distribution of commodities," these administrators are often themselves administered and thus develop forms of antagonism toward their work that carry with them a will to experiment with and imagine new workplace relations.[59] I attend to the speculative dimension of the art and writing of the period more than its cynical dimension, which is not to deny the presence of cynicism.

As for the experimental writing of the time, much of which was actively aligned with the artistic practices of the period, the corresponding term might be "the turn to language," seen in the McCaffery passages quoted previously as an emptying out of the referential or expressive capacities of language and a focus on its material characteristics, functions, and conditions. Encompassing as it does the "chance-based" compositions of John Cage and Jackson Mac Low, the collage techniques of New York School writers, and the radical fragmentation and agrammaticality of "Language poetry," the turn to language seems at first pass the exact opposite of conceptual art, its emphasis on linguistic *materiality* contrasting sharply with the immateriality of conceptual art. As conceptual art was turning the visual object to little more than words on a page, or words on a canvas, poets were either attributing to language a kind of sculptural immediacy and heft or attempting to fill out the words on the page by transforming poems into performances and installations.[60] Despite this seeming opposition, art and the poetry were also beginning to look increasingly similar, such that it was difficult, at the time, to tell whether someone was an artist or a writer—and indeed, many of the figures I discuss inhabited both worlds seamlessly, which is one of the reasons I borrow from art criticism and literary criticism equally.

Seen from the perspective of the independent histories of poetry and visual art, this merger might appear perplexing. Seen, however, as a response to and reflection on deindustrialization and a reflection on the increasingly routinized character of white-collar clerical and administrative work, it makes a great deal of sense. Like clerical work, both the art and the writing of the period treat language—or symbols, more generally—as a kind of material medium, or substance, to which one applies a series of techniques or processes: rearranging, sorting, cataloguing, parsing, transcribing, excerpting. For conceptual art and experimental writing, what is happening is dematerialization or materialization only in the sense that some things that are not really material—verbal and written signs—are treated as if they were. The only difference is in the angle of approach. The name for this partly materialized and partly dematerialized object is, as discussed in Chapter 3, information. Information is a sign that behaves like matter, or is treated like one, as in the case of binary code, which maps exactly (rather than merely approximately, as in the case of the written mark) to the physical arrangement of transistors in a chip. Such materialized signs were the object of an increasing amount of workplace activity and, for a time, important strains of art and writing.

Consider, for instance, Jackson Mac Low's seminal proceduralist poems in *Stanzas for Iris Lezak*, based in part on the techniques behind John Cage's chance-generated music. Mac Low's poems use a "chance-acrostic" method, in which a word, name, or phrase becomes a tool for extracting language from a particular text.[61] By applying the phrase "Call me Ishmael" to *Moby Dick*, for instance, Mac Low produced a poem spelling out the phrase acrostically. He would extract the first word beginning with *C* on the third page of the book (since *C* is the third letter in the alphabet), the first word beginning with *A* on the first page of the book (since *A* is the first letter) and so on, until the whole phrase was spelled out:

> Circulation. And long long
> Mind every
> Interest Some how mind and every long[62]

By treating a literary text as a mass of material—or information—to which one applies an algorithmic process, Mac Low's poetry of the period bears a remarkable resemblance to the actual activities that made up contemporary clerical and administrative white-collar work, much of which involved the translation of one set of materials into an alternative notation system—whether the translation of speech into stenography, stenography into typescript, or invoices into punched cards using keypunch machines. Mac Low's textual manipulations also bear a strong resemblance to that old standby of clerical work, filing, inasmuch as they recategorize material according to alphabetical indices.

In one of the most referenced pieces of writing about the art of this period, "Notes on the Index: Seventies Art in America," Rosalind Krauss claims that a distinguishing feature of "post-Movement art" is its adaptation to the "formal character of the indexical sign." This means "jettisoning . . . pictorial and sculptural codes," producing instead a "message without code," where the relationship between sign and referent follows the logic of "the physical cause, the trace, the impression, the clue."[63] This gives photography a privileged place in the new division of the arts, since the photograph is indexical in a special kind of way, produced through a physical-chemical process. She is careful to note, however, that the index emerges in all kinds of artistic media during the period, anywhere that "truth is understood as a matter of evidence, rather than a function of logic."[64] For Krauss, indexical art takes extraction or selection as its technique rather than active construction or formation, much less symbolization. It is therefore at the very least analogous to (when not identical with) the photograph, which displays a "dependence on selection from the natural array by means of cropping."⁶⁵ Even though Mac Low works with verbal rather than visual signs, his chance-acrostic poems are equally dependent on cropping, or what counts for cropping in the realm of the verbal, an abstraction of bits of language from the source text. But we can go further than Krauss, who never really explains *why* the "logic of the index" comes to dominate in this period. If she notes a waning of art's powers of symbolization or logical articulation, I would argue that this should be referred to the general enervation of intellectual work or symbol-based work, which increasingly asks workers to treat written signs as a kind of *material* to be manipulated, processed, extracted, shaped, collated, cut and pasted, and transcribed, irrespective of its referential content.

In terms of occupational structure, deindustrialization means more, of course, than the rise of proletarianized clerical and administrative work in inverse proportion to manufacturing jobs. Typically, sociologists and historians speak about the rise of the service sector, or tertiary sector, a vaguely defined section of the economy that includes the white-collar office jobs described earlier but also health-care workers, educators, store clerks and cashiers, barbers, flight attendants, waiters, baristas, and massage therapists. We might, however, usefully distinguish between those service-sector jobs that involve direct contact with consumers, customers, patients, students, or the like and those that, like clerical work, involve instead the administration and distribution of information, goods, or other people. Jobs where the contact with other people, the service, is treated as a commodity (waiting tables, nursing, teaching) tend to feature a routinization and commodification of human feelings, attitudes, and personalities that mirror the cognitive routinizations of clerical work. Robert Reich has proposed describing these jobs as "in-person services."⁶⁶ As Arlie Hochschild notes in her seminal study of "emotional management" by flight attendants, *The Managed Heart*, this work involves a kind of "deep acting," where one's very character and personality are overtaken by the protocols and demands of the job.⁶⁷ Sianne Ngai links this type of work—"affective labor," as it is sometimes called—with what she calls "post-Fordist performance," a category that includes performance art and happenings, as well as contemporary film and types of writing with strong performative characteristics.⁶⁸ If the turn toward certain types of conceptual art and experimental writing has as its horizon the routinized cognitions of clerical work, then the emphasis, in other forms of art and writing, on immediacy, interactivity, and intersubjective relationality has as its horizon the forced conviviality of the service sector.

In thinking about the shift from the production of objects to the provision of services, we might look at a couple of transitional examples. Two works, both of which involve the production of objects from frozen water, signal this shift through the very ephemerality of their choice of material. Allan Kaprow's most frequently referenced happening, *Fluids*, enjoined participants to construct a "throw-away architecture" from blocks of ice, which then melted. Even though the piece featured manual labor, all that remained of the performance by the time it was completed were some documents and the experiences of the participants. While the goal might have seemed, at first, to involve the production of objects, such objects turn out to have been means, tools or props, for the production of an experience. The point, then, is that the shift to service work is not immaterialization at all (indeed, many services involve backbreaking labor: custodial work, for instance, or restaurant work) but a different arrangement of materiality, a liquefaction of materiality, one that aims at different results.[69] For Kaprow, experience is an objectless physicality; "an experience is thought which has been 'incorporated,' on a muscular, neural, even cellular level, into the body."[70] Frozen water also figures as an emblem of the transition from goods-oriented to service-oriented work in a later performance by David Hammons, *Bliz-aard Ball Sale*, in which the artist sold snowballs on the sidewalk in Harlem.[71] One bought in this case the experience of having bought a snowball, since the ball itself could not be preserved (unless one were particularly careful). One also bought the conceptual residue of the performance, which humorously counterposed black artist and white snowball.

We might also read the work of one of the most famous poets of this period, Frank O'Hara, as likewise entangled in the protocols and logics of contemporary service work. O'Hara's "I do this, I do that" poems are often read as examples of a postwar *flânerie*, detailing the poet's movements through the city during periods of freedom and leisure. But as I argue in Chapter 1, such leisures are usually, implicitly or explicitly, circumscribed by periods of work so that they take on a hurried or frenetic quality. This is especially true in *Lunch Poems*, the collection most widely available during his lifetime, where the conceit of the book is that many of the poems were written both during and about "lunch hour." Many of the most-celebrated poems in that collection seem, at first glance, a mere catalogue of what the poet saw, bought, and ate, as in the following well-worn stanzas from "The Day Lady Died":

> I walk up the muggy street beginning to sun
> and have a hamburger and a malted and buy
> an ugly NEW WORLD WRITING to see what the poets
> in Ghana are doing these days
>   I go on to the bank
> and Miss Stillwagon (first name Linda I once heard)
> doesn't even look up my balance for once in her life
> and in the Golden Griffin I get a little Verlaine
> for Patsy with drawings by Bonnard . . .[72]

As a record of the poet's interaction with various commodities—the poet as consumer—it is also a record of interactions with postwar New York's service workers: Linda Stillwagon, the bank clerk, the bookseller, and the waiter or waitress who serves him his hamburger and malted. But because "The Day Lady Died" is a poem rather than an actual lunchtime walk through the city, and because all of these commodities and sights and sounds are made available for us, the readers, as much as they are for the speaker of the poem, I think the consciousness at work in the poem should be identified as much with the position of the bank tellers and store clerks as the consuming "I." The moment of half-intimate recognition between Miss Stillwagon and O'Hara is particularly instructive. Balanced between personal acknowledgment and impersonal politeness—he almost knows her name; she recognizes him as a regular customer—the exchange mirrors our own relationship as readers to the flow of proper names in the text, which we experience as familiar simply because they are mediated by a consciousness that treats them as such.

O'Hara takes the vast, impersonal world of 1950s Manhattan and makes it familiar, provides an intimate and therefore less threatening view of it. This is, increasingly, the role that service workers are asked to play—providing a human face to abstract, alienating, and often overwhelming systems, personalizing them and making them sensible and coherent. This is something the store clerk does as much as the flight attendant, the waiter as much as the bank teller. Such workers are instructed to act "like a friend," to make the store or restaurant seem "like home," to compensate for otherwise disorienting social processes. O'Hara's charisma is the charisma of the salesperson. In the postwar period such affective performance will become more and more essential to the workplace. As the world of commodities that the consumer confronts becomes increasingly bewildering, and as the processes for getting them to the consumer submit to the same Taylorist pressures as all other industries, workers are asked to perform the kinds of personal recognitions that came with the neighborhood-based shops that the sites of mass consumption were displacing.

We might therefore begin to talk about a "front-office" and a "back-office" aesthetic, one based on the forced conviviality of service work and the other on the routinized cognitions of clerical and administrative work. The problem, however, is that things are not nearly so simple. In the course of the restructuring of office work, the new flexible, self-motivating white-collar workers are increasingly expected to display attitudes—sensitivity, charisma, lightheartedness—associated with in-person service work. This is part of a larger shift among firms to a focus on "corporate culture" and morale, which involves all kinds of "team-building" efforts designed to boost morale, foster affective links between workers (especially between workers and their managers), and establish forms of solidarity with the company.[73]

There are two things that we must note about these affective values and the activities that go with them. One is that these are attitudes associated with women, and with the kind of unpaid domestic work that women are asked to do as wives and mothers (work that women were contesting, with greater and greater intensity, during this period).[74] This transformation of the affective character of work is part of the overall "feminization of labor" during the period, where the term refers both to the entry of large numbers of women into the workplace and the transformation of occupational structures and tasks associated with them in such a way that work is "feminized." That is, even male workers are asked to display attitudes typically associated with women—sensitivity, tolerance, care—often resulting in hysterical attempts by feminized male workers to assert their masculinity, as both Sianne Ngai and Heather Hicks show in their readings of the art, film, and literature of feminized labor.[75]

The fact that workers are asked to bring to the workplace attitudes and affects associated with unpaid domestic work is part of a larger scrambling of the boundaries between the home and worksite, labor and leisure. As some work is recoded in the language of domesticity, so too is work made to seem, for some, a kind of leisure or hobby, especially as new technologies allow the worker to work from home and, therefore, remain on the clock continuously.[76] The importation of these values into the workplace therefore assists in the lengthening of the workweek—and with it the erosion of benefits and wages—that has occurred over the last few decades, such that Americans now work longer hours than their counterparts in other industrialized countries. Through a kind of cunning of reason and a reversal of the old Marxist thematic of the "transformation of quantity into quality," the qualitative critique of work passes into a quantitative worsening of work.

As we have seen, the challenges to postwar capitalism, as well as the actual restructuring that takes place, concern management as a concept, a set of practices, and an actual group of people within an enterprise. Because the managerial layers grow precipitously in the immediate postwar period, and because the challenges to capitalism from the lowest ranks concern deskilling, overmanagement, lack of autonomy, and routinization, this layer comes under attack beginning in the late 1960s, with firms attempting to institute forms of self-management, eliminate redundant managerial layers (particularly through the use of information technology), and introduce various forms of flexibility. At the same time as there is a compression or elimination of this managerial layer, there is also an extension of managerial protocols, attitudes, and processes across the entirety of the workforce: manufacturing work involves the supervision of automated processes; clerical jobs are reclassified as "administrative" inasmuch as they involve administering flows of data and, by extension, other people; and even in-person service jobs come to involve a great amount of administrative work.

Chapter 2, therefore, concerns itself with an investigation of this aesthetic of administration by way of the early poetry of John Ashbery. Despite its reputation as a poetry of cerebral and pastoral contemplation abstracted from everyday life, these early poems turn with surprising frequency to work and the workplace. Beginning with his early and frequently anthologized poem "The Instruction Manual," whose speaker is engaged in writing an instruction manual "about the uses of a new metal," Ashbery's poems investigate the class position and psychic entailments of the "new middle classes." These are people who exercise a "derived power," inasmuch as they are "links in chains of power and obedience, coordinating and supervising other occupational experiences, functions and skills," as Mills writes in his powerful early study.[77] Using Mills to understand the contradictory pressures on these workers, I focus in particular on the various images of work that appear in Ashbery's second book, *The Tennis Court Oath*. The multiple, fragmented voices in these poems, collaged together from found materials, inhabit a strange middle ground between autonomy and subjection. Through his subtle and inventive play with free indirect discourse and point of view, Ashbery treats these different voices as contributors to a vast production that he must organize, one that requires the "managerial" intervention of the arranging, supervising poetic voice or mind. The labor of the aesthetic itself and its constructive powers becomes identified, therefore, with management. But because Ashbery also sees himself as allied with a fundamentally pastoral poetry of refusal, the organizing structure of the book places him at odds with his own impulses. These contradictions result in frequent images of interpersonal (and interworker) antagonism in the book, antagonism that, I argue, picks up on the blue-collar blues and white-collar woes of the coming decade. In his later books, as I demonstrate, such antagonistics give way to a voice of ironic accommodation, an even-toned poetry of resignation that prefigures the plasticity and adaptation of workers in postindustrial workplaces.

Even though they remained hegemonic until the early 1970s, Taylorism and Fordism always had ideological rivals in the world of business management theory. Throughout the postwar period, in universities, government think tanks, and select firms, managers and researchers experimented with non-Taylorist protocols, ones that would become important to the construction of the new flexible structures of post-Fordist corporations. Among these heterodox theories, the discourse of cybernetics presents a particularly interesting example, since it provided inspiration not only to a generation of management theorists and economists but also to artists, intellectuals, and counterculture figures, establishing a strange elective affinity between the anticapitalist and pro-capitalist intelligentsia and providing, as a result, one of the obvious linkages that allowed for the recuperation of the artistic critique and its transformation into a mechanism of exploitation. Emerging out of the military industrial research programs of World War II, cybernetics was a would-be science of everything, purportedly capable of explaining the workings of a robot, an animal, a human being, and a multinational corporation alike, since each one of these entities operates, from a cybernetic framework, through processes of self-regulating "feedback." As an "applied social science"—in other words, a speculative attempt to reengineer corporations and other social forms—cybernetics presents an image of social self-regulation based on reciprocal, horizontal, and participatory relations rather than explicit hierarchies. This is appealing to firms looking not only for a way to cut administrative bloat and trim costs but to respond to the problems of worker disaffection and low morale as well. At the same time, the discourse appeals to artists and writers interested in developing a "participatory" practice, one that undoes the division of labor between reader and writer, spectator and art maker. Cybernetics promises a mode of collaboration and collectivity in line with ideas about the liberation of art from the narrow confines of artists. And because cybernetics treats "communication" and "action" as essentially equivalent terms, the cybernetic view of the world allows artists to inhabit that interzone between the world of embodied materiality and the world of disembodied signs where so much of the conceptual art and experimental poetry of the period resides. By bringing communication and action into alignment, for instance, cybernetics presents an image of a world in which every poem is, in fact, a performance, inasmuch as the signs from which it is made are never separate from the activities of human beings. In Chapter 3, I examine Hannah Weiner's *Code Poems* alongside Dan Graham's *Works for Magazine Pages*, both of which sit uneasily between the space of conceptual art (in the broadest sense) and experimental poetry. Both also put cybernetic discourse to work to model alternative social relations. I argue that in the case of both figures the real medium of their respective project is labor. And while both of them engage in an earnest attempt to model improved relations between people in acts of labor or communication, each of their respective projects turns unintentionally dark, as it becomes apparent that such participatory relations can quite easily turn into an indirect (and therefore efficient) method of social control.

The restructuring of work involves, as we have seen, the scrambling of previously steadfast oppositions: between work and leisure, and between the worksite and the home. At the same time as the art of the period submits itself to a zone of indistinction where it is impossible to distinguish it from any number of life practices or experiences that are not considered art, capitalist firms import values associated with leisure and the home to make work more tolerable. The confusion does not end there, however, since the protocols and routines of work begin to colonize the space of leisure as well. This crossing of spheres cannot be understood apart from the feminization of labor, since the entry of massive numbers of women into the workplace, women who are expected to bring with them the values associated with the home, effectively erodes the border between work and nonwork, especially once men, too, are expected to behave accordingly. Though there are many important artistic projects from the 1970s that investigate the place of unpaid "reproductive" or domestic labor, I structure Chapter 4 around Bernadette Mayer's multifarious project *Memory* (1972), which is, at one and the same time a performance, a conceptual work, an installation, and an epic poem. In attempting to document, down to the smallest detail, every aspect of her life for thirty days—using photographs, audio recordings, and written notation—Mayer effectively demonstrates the subsumption of the entirety of life by the protocols and routines of work. Though the project starts out with the intention to enlarge her experience of life, and her capacity for perception, through new technical means, the compulsion to document becomes very quickly tyrannical. In this sense, Mayer's elaboration of a "total" artwork that merges different technologies into one single apparatus prefigures the coming reorganization of office work around the personal computer, a technology that has probably done more than anything else to ensure that work and home life are unified by enabling white-collar workers to accomplish tasks from home and, in that sense, never leave work.

Chapter 5 skips forward several decades, to the 2000s, and looks at the legacy of these transformations, once the new relations and the new flexible, self-managing workers associated with them had become largely hegemonic. In particular, I examine the debates that followed the emergence of "Flarf" and "conceptual poetry," both movements that foregrounded their relationship to the conditions of contemporary office work in the age of social media. From conceptual poet Kenny Goldsmith describing his appropriation of information freely available on the Internet as the work of a "secretary" to Katie Degentesh performing absurdist disfigurations of the language of office memos, these new developments suggest that poetry has become a set of formal techniques for the management, indexing, and filtration of the unwieldy torrents of information we encounter each day. I focus in particular on the relationship between Flarf poetry, with its rebellious use of work time, work machinery, and work jargon to create intentionally "offensive" or "bad" poetry, and the increase in interworker aggression, which I attribute to the inability of workers to find meaningful outlets for resistance or even to locate the now-remote targets of conventional class struggle, given the horizontalization of work relations. I link this horizontalized aggression with the phenomenon of the "Internet troll," who responds to the emasculation and disempowerment that male workers feel as a consequence of the restructuring of labor, which by the 2000s had so thoroughly neutralized the aesthetic critique that it persisted only in various forms of minor rebellion, prankery, and acting out. How might these antagonisms be liberated from their domesticated, horizontalized, and internalized form? What happens to the aesthetic critique now that it has been subsumed by the restructured workplace? In the final pages of this chapter, I turn to the work of Sean Bonney, whose poetry manages to sidestep the recuperations of the new economy by locating antagonism and its pleasures beyond work and workplace.

An unemployed UK poet, Bonney addresses his epistolary poems to the conditions of the British welfare state as it is being dismantled under the austerity measures of the David Cameron regime. Bonney concerns himself with "unwork," with the worklike dominations of the British Jobcentre, where benefits recipients are sent to be warehoused and matched with the contingent employment on offer. In the Epilogue, I consider the future of the artistic critique and the possibilities for poetry in the coming decades, which seem very likely to be years of growing unemployment and precarity. Bonney's redirection of the aesthetic critique indicates some of these possibilities, but it also draws on a centuries-old connection between poetry and vagrancy, between poets and vagabonds, wanderers, beggars, and fugitives that poetry in the new age of wagelessness has already begun to reactivate. The Epilogue considers this long history, beginning with the Renaissance ballad and continuing through the Romantic poetry of vagrancy and the African American fugitive lyric. I conjoin this poetic history to a theoretical investigation of what Karl Marx calls "surplus population," those people who are either temporarily or permanently in excess of capital's employment needs. Described alternatively by contemporary thinkers in terms of bare life, precarity, wagelessness, informal economy, and migration, surplus populations are, by all accounts, growing worldwide and on track to continue growing. The long history of the poetics of wagelessness gives some indication of the aesthetic outlines of the coming era and, in closing my book, I look at two contemporary poets—Fred Moten and Wendy Trevino—who engage this long tradition and mobilize it to meet the specific conditions of twenty-first-century capitalism, giving some hints as to the shape of the poetry to come.

Rather than devote my conclusion to a discussion of methodology, as many scholarly works do, I thought it useful to try to look into the dim mists of the future and see where both poetry and the capitalist economy might be heading. Nonetheless, readers may benefit from some reflection on the way that I periodize, historicize, and establish linkages between postindustrial labor and postmodern culture, as well as the possibilities for applying these methods to other historical periods and other archives.

One of the reasons why so few cultural critics have paid adequate attention to the transformation of labor over the past decades is that the relationships between labor and its putative opposites—between labor and leisure, between home and worksite, between refusal of work and work itself—have been so scrambled as to render labor indistinguishable within the field of social activity. Thus, most accounts of the period with something to say about culture end up focusing less on the transformation of labor than on other elements of social and economic life, confusing it with mutations in the market, in the commodity form and consumption, changes to the built environment and its infrastructures, changes in technology (but not production technologies), or processes of globalization and financialization. Since so many of the new jobs created in the postwar world involve the circulation and sale of goods, the provision and distribution of credit, or the administration of people in new ways, it is easy to approach these new developments as if they were simply circulation or consumption or "culture," ignoring the work that makes such things possible: the production of circulation, the production of consumption, the production of culture, accomplished by truck drivers, supermarket clerks, accountants, editors, and gallery assistants.

When it comes to cultural artifacts, approaches from the side of consumption or the marketplace also foreground the reader, critic, or interpreter who encounters the cultural object as already complete, already constituted by mute, invisible labors that can be disclosed only through a post hoc hermeneutic. With the migration of manufacturing to industrializing or recently industrialized countries, this is a stance more and more residents in deindustrialized countries must take to the commodities they consume, produced as they are through globally distributed processes that remain necessarily opaque. But at the same time, millions upon millions of workers are constantly reorganizing this premade matter that arrives by plane or ship—transporting it, inventorying it, controlling its circulation, and selling it directly to the consumer. Attending to the moment of production within circulation means attending to the openness of the cultural object in its moment of facture, as it appeared to the makers in their own historical moment. Even if we understand cultural objects to be *symptomatic*, to reveal themselves as having been blind to what they really were, or what they really *could* be, we still must understand the desires and aspirations that formed them. Moving between the present and the past, or the past's future and the past's present, I understand the poetry and art of the 1960s and 1970s both as it was and as it would be. In both cases, labor and the labor process turn out to be key moments of mediation.

At a first pass, we can say that the social and technical conditions of labor in a given society delimit a "horizon of possibilities" for art. This is a loosely deterministic relationship, since it does not involve linear, one-to-one relationships between causes and effects. Rather, the technical means of labor present a boundary and a ground for artistic imagining, since art's technical capacities are, in large part, drawn from the technical and social means of production available in a society—its computers, typewriters, metalworking tools, chemical processes, organizational forms, grammars, vocabularies, spatial logics, and temporalities. Art, of course, establishes a critical relationship with these social and technical means, decomposing and rearranging them in new shapes or using them to model new relationships that might take place on the basis of those means. Art's autonomy does not lie in being separate from the world of labor but from being connected to it: it can select, reject, or negate certain technical processes, on the one hand, or push some to the point of failure, on the other, revealing their constitutive contradictions. This horizon-of-possibilities approach to the relationship between art and labor allows for a method of historicization and periodization that does not rely on simplistic notions of correspondence, homology, or reflection. Art does not simply reproduce what it finds in the world but reconstitutes and reconstellates it to form models of prospective futures. This speculative process makes art into a sort of social laboratory. The spheres of art and labor are therefore temporally disjoint: since the present conditions to which art responds are visible by virtue of being already in the past, art is an unfolding present that, in responding to the immediate past, models a potential and sometimes actual future.

The materials I work with in this book—experimental poetry and conceptual art—are particularly conducive to capturing the speculative, provisional, and exploratory aspects of art and writing. Some of these works were extremely marginal in terms of audience or the social position of the artists and writers. They were part of the leading edge of an unfolding cultural present rather than the elaboration of fully worked-out aesthetic programs. They are thus better objects to read against transformations that were, during the period under discussion, entirely tentative, marginal, incoherent, and undeveloped as well. Such works, because of their hazy, confused (and sometimes confusing) character, pick up on what Raymond Williams has described as the "preemergence" of new cultural values, attitudes, and perceptions. Writing about these preemergent phenomena, which he identifies as "structures of feeling," Williams puts his methodology into terms that offer an alternative to reading the past as already past, as already worked up and worked over, cautioning against the "regular slide towards a past tense" and the "regular conversion of experience into finished products" that make present-tense experience very difficult to register, as the following quote makes clear:

> If the social is always past, in the sense that it is always formed, we have indeed to find other terms for the undeniable experience of the present: not only the temporal present, the realization of this and this instant, but the specificity of present being, the inalienably physical, within which we may indeed discern and acknowledge institutions, formations, positions, but not always as fixed products, defining products. And then if the social is fixed and explicit—the known relationships, institutions, formations, positions—all that is present and moving, all that escapes, or seems to escape from the fixed and the explicit and the known, is grasped and defined as the personal: this, here, now, alive, active, "subjective."[78]

The horizon-of-possibilities approach I outline here, concerned with emergent and preemergent relationships between art and labor, should be applicable to literary and cultural investigation very broadly, from at least the beginning of capitalism to the present, and perhaps in some precapitalist formations as well. In capitalism, where labor manifests as a distinct social category, an activity distinguished from other activities (especially art) and as one of the defining features of human existence, the means and methods of labor cannot help determining the shape and character of art. They are a language that social activity speaks. In precapitalist formations, where art was one form of a broader set of social activities and not clearly distinguished from those activities we now assign to labor, the situation is both simpler and more complex. The bard at court was, for instance, not clearly distinguished from other court attendants, from chamberlains and falconers, playing poem-songs rather than attending to more mundane business. Thus, activities we now think of as belonging to the sphere of art no doubt soaked up all sorts of values, methods, and techniques from activities we would associate with labor proper. The reverse would also be true. It is difficult to speak of determination in these cases because the causal links are so strong that the distinctions have largely vanished.

Other aspects of my approach are less portable across periods. As discussed previously, the models that artists and poets developed in response to the hierarchies and routines of the postwar workplace eventually contributed to the restructuring of the labor process begun in the 1970s and 1980s. The artistic critique elaborated by the figures treated in this book provided a vocabulary for the dissatisfactions of 1960s and 1970s workers, deployed as a critique of unilateral decision making, a demand for more various and creative work activities, and a call for more autonomy. Faced with mounting resistance and loss of morale, employers met the call for self-management and increased autonomy by instituting forms of internalized, impersonal control that meant anxious self-harrying; they met the demand for community and cooperation with the organizational concept of "teamwork," in which employees drive each other to work harder, independent of managerial imperatives; they met the demand for variety in work by piling on new responsibilities; they met the challenge to the domination of work over life by shifting to part-time, contingent, and at-will work; and, finally, they met the demand for creativity and authenticity by incorporating elements of play, fun, de-repression, intimacy, and affective intensity into the workplace. This circular chain of cause and effect, in which an artistic response to the workplace eventually contributes to the restructuring of the workplace by way of numerous intermediating moments and institutions, was predicated on the prior separation of art and labor. The languages of art could provide a challenge to the workplace only because the workplace was defined as exclusive of art. Once the process described here has begun, the power of art both as medium of challenge and medium of recuperation wanes. The portability of this aspect of my account is therefore highly limited, though it is possible that further studies, dealing with different archives, might complicate the historical frame as I have constructed it here.

Some of the figures I describe in the following pages seem to have been particularly prescient about the fate of their challenges to the workplace, attempting to ward off recuperation by a restructured capitalism through a sort of preemptive sabotage. This provides the final layer of determination, as art foresees its inability to actually effect the futures it wishes and therefore must put itself into a state of vigilance against misuse or misinterpretation. No doubt, this explains some of the highly negative and inward forms of experimental art we see across the twentieth century, but in the case of the works discussed here such negativity is secreted within a more or less positive vision. The future these works offer, constituted by these different layers of determination, is therefore multiple rather than singular. My conclusion is devoted to an investigation of that future, knowing what we know about the fate of futures past.

Lyric and the Service Sector
Frank O'Hara at Work

Every story about the 1960s and its aftermath must begin, one way or another, in the 1950s. This is certainly true of any account we might give of Frank O'Hara's quintessential 1960s volume, *Lunch Poems*. Published in 1964, the book had been planned as early as 1959, when City Lights publisher Lawrence Ferlinghetti met O'Hara through Allen Ginsberg and asked him to collect the poems he had been writing on his lunch breaks from curatorial work at the Museum of Modern Art (MoMA). Later that year, O'Hara sent a postcard to Ferlinghetti promising that "lunch is on the stove," the beginning of five years of correspondence about the book, which would eventually include thirty-seven poems, some written as early as 1953 and others as late as 1964, dated and published in chronological order.[1] For a study of labor and poetry in the postwar period, the book is unavoidable, composed as it is of poems encircled by the workday. O'Hara was careful to highlight this lunch-hour setting in the blurb that he wrote for the back cover, a textual frame—a prose poem, really—that depicts the lunch-hour poet "strolling through the splintered glare of a Manhattan noon" and "paused at a sample Olivetti to type up thirty or forty lines or ruminations."[2] Number nineteen in City Lights's Pocket Poet series, the five-by-four book fits easily into a coat pocket, ready to be carried discretely to and from work. The poems in it are written, we are meant to imagine, by a worker on a lunch break for a worker on a lunch break, providing sustenance, as the conceit implies, for both parties. More than a mere frame for the composition of the poems, however, the lunch-hour setting is also continuously called forth and rendered vivid as poetic occasion by O'Hara's use of deictics and proper names, which take great pains to locate and date this lunchtime situation of utterance. The poems are written during lunch but also about lunch. The transformation of moment of composition into poetic *occasion* is, of course, a distinguishing mark of the lyric mode, and part of what the poem-blurb does is call to mind the lyric occasion and then mock it and himself slightly, describing its results as "computed misunderstandings of the eternal questions of life, coexistence, and depth."[3]

The carefulness of O'Hara's framing undoubtedly explains why his recent foray into popular cultural visibility, as leitmotif within season 2 of the acclaimed period drama *Mad Men*, begins in a bar during the lunch hour. Don Draper, creative director at a Madison Avenue advertising firm and the show's protagonist, first encounters O'Hara's poetry as the reading choice of the person on the bar stool next to him. The season takes place in 1962, before the publication of *Lunch Poems*, so the book featured is *Meditations in an Emergency*, published in 1957. Draper remarks without invitation that reading "makes you feel better about sitting at a bar at lunch, like you're getting something done."[4] His neighbor, wearing the corduroy coat and thick glasses that mark him as a member of the 1960s demimonde, responds condescendingly, "Yeah, it's all about getting things done." When Draper shakes off the implied insult and asks if the book is any good, the corduroyed O'Hara reader, having already sized Draper up, replies: "I don't think you'll like it." The title of the book resonates with the melodramatic trajectory of Draper's life; he has just been told that his blood pressure is high and that his predilection for working and drinking too hard will eventually kill him. The lunch-hour encounter therefore underscores the difference between the carefree, bohemian O'Hara reader and the stiff Draper, haunted by his traumatic past.

The opposition between O'Hara and Draper is mostly a bluff, however, or perhaps a moment of dialectic. The show very much wants us to identify the two figures, later using a voice-over of Draper reading the poem "Mayakovsky" to suggest that O'Hara's performative selfhood is a good match for Draper, whose entire identity is, as we learn, a construct.[5] I would argue, however, that this psychodramatic terrain distracts us from the real affinities between Draper and O'Hara. *Mad Men* is a show about work. Given O'Hara's insistent identification of poet and poem as islands within the workday, we might wonder what his labors share with Draper's. Despite the bohemian disdain of *Mad Men*'s imagined reader, the energetic poems collected in O'Hara's book *are* very much about "about getting things done" and thus might appeal to Draper. Many of his most famous compositions depict the poet hurrying through a list of tasks creative and banal; they hum with a frenetic intensity that is counterbalanced but not abnegated by their insistent *sprezzatura*. O'Hara's lunch-hour frame makes it seem as if the compression, urgency, and swift pleasure taking of the poems derived directly from the time constraints of the workday.

Consider these two famous examples:

> It is 12:10 in New York and I am wondering
> if I will finish this in time to meet Norman for Lunch
> ah lunch! I think I am going crazy
> what with my terrible hangover and the weekend coming up
>
> At excitement-prone Kenneth Koch's
> I wish I were staying in town and working on my poems
> for a new book by Grove Press
> which they will probably not print[6]

> It is 12:20 in New York a Friday
> three days after Bastille day, yes
> it is 1959 and I go get a shoeshine
> because I will get off the 4:19 in Easthampton
> at 7:15 and then go straight to dinner
> and I don't know the people who will feed me.[7]

O'Hara's lunch-hour pastorals are not so much opposed to the workday and its unfree time of getting things done as they are a space for an alternative kind of work—"working" on poems, the hurried accomplishment of shoeshines, gift buying, eating and drinking that fills his poems. Unlike many of his poetic contemporaries, who are infrequently treated to historicizing interpretation, O'Hara is often read as poet for an age of mass consumption, a writer of consumer odes and retail idylls, a lunch-hour *flâneur* in an urban landscape populated by commodities and celebrities. This follows a general scholarly tendency to approach questions of culture—especially in the late twentieth century—from the side of consumption, from the side of marketplace rather than workplace. But wherever there is consumption, there are specific acts of labor that mediate it. As an astute observer of the urban environment, O'Hara populates his poems with workers as well as with purchases: the service workers who shine his shoes, sell him liquor and books, and serve him lunch. My critical intervention therefore proposes that we see O'Hara as poet of service work as much as poet of consumption, reorienting ourselves to the presence of labor (his own and others') within the poems. By the light of this reading, the relationship between this lunch-hour timespace and the world of work is both temporal and spatial; work is before and after the poem but also right across the lunch counter, and that is what gives his poems their directed intensity.

Advertising work is also, like these face-to-face services, fundamentally oriented toward consumption, part of the production of consumption. This is one reason why O'Hara's poetry and *Mad Men* would seem poorly matched if Draper were an insurance executive (like Wallace Stevens) or a banker (like T. S. Eliot), and it is likewise hard to imagine the O'Hara reader instead holding a copy of *Harmonium* or *Prufrock and Other Observations* (and not just for reasons of anachronism). Advertising and poetry share a secret affinity, so much so that advertising is often held up as an example of what poetry becomes when rendered entirely mercenary. Ezra Pound, famously, in "A Few Don'ts by an Imagiste" exhorts his contemporaries to "consider the way of the scientists rather than the way of an advertising agent for a new soap."[8] His manifesto ran in one of the very first issues of Harriet Monroe's *Poetry*; thirty-three years later, the magazine published an article by semanticist S. I. Hayakawa, "Poetry and Advertising," that makes explicit Pound's aesthetic hierarchy. Hayakawa defines advertising as the "poeticizing of consumer goods" and is quick to note that, at a technical level, advertising and poetry are largely identical in the way that they use language.[9] The difference between the two obtains only at the level of intention. Implicitly drawing on Kant's distinction between a "free art . . . agreeable on its own account" and a "mercenary art . . . that attracts us only through its effect (e.g., pay) so that people can be coerced into it," Hayakawa defines literary poetry as "disinterested poetry" and advertising as "venal poetry."[10] In the age of advertising, he argues, venal poetry is omnipresent, "written by the highest paid writers in this country, organized into companies of poets, rhapsodists, sub-poets, and sub-rhapsodists." As a result, modern literary poets are forced to distinguish themselves through an abandonment of the poetic altogether: "In a world so filled with the clamor of venal writing . . . all poetry has come to sound suspicious, so that disinterested poets are practically compelled not to sound poetic."[11]

Though some of O'Hara's work does proceed according to the modernist disfiguration Hayakawa describes, rescuing the poetic through a resort to anti-poetry, he often takes a rather different path, following the lyric poem into its debasement as advertisement and trying to find moments of authentic poetry there nonetheless. While many of O'Hara's poems may be said to participate in "the poeticizing of consumer goods," they may mime the structures of the advertising world to run the Hayakawan process in reverse, finding in the language of consumer goods traces of a reified poetry that they can reconstitute.[12] The Hayakawan argument allows us to read a poem like "Having a Coke with You" not only as one of the great love poems of the twentieth century but also as, implicitly, a very fine advertisement for Coca-Cola (just as the frame poem on the back cover is a very fine advertisement for Olivetti). Like advertisement, the poem functions through an associational logic, usually comparative but sometimes metonymic, that imbues the referenced commodity with all sorts of desirable qualities. "Having a Coke with You," O'Hara begins,

> is even more fun than going to San Sebastian, Irún, Hendaye, Biarritz, Bayonne
> or being sick to my stomach on the Travesera de Gracia in Barcelona
> partly because in your orange shirt you look like a better happier St. Sebastian
> partly because of my love for you, partly because of your love for yoghurt.[13]

Certainly the poem is less about Coca-Cola as commodity than it is about the singular experience the cola facilitates. This makes the poem closest not to the advertisements of the 1960s but rather to the so-called postmodern advertisements that began to appear in the 1980s, whose development O'Hara seems to prefigure (and perhaps even contributes to, indirectly).[14]

Paradigmatic here are Wieden+Kennedy's memorable Nike advertisements, which eschewed all reference to particular qualities of the shoes and instead imbued them with various aspirational meanings, breaking with even the most "radical" advertising strategies of the 1960s and 1970s. In *The Conquest of Cool*, Thomas Frank advanced an important argument about how the touted "creative revolution" of 1960s advertising depended on an alliance between the 1960s counterculture and dissident fringes within the corporate world.[15] Agencies such as Doyle Dane Bernbach (DDB) broke with the established practice of distinguishing commodities according to what Rosser Reeves (advertising guru of the period) called Unique Selling Propositions, plying the consumer with qualitative claims that differentiated their product from those of their competitors. Instead, advertisements by DDB and its fellow travelers made fun of the grandiose claims of their competitors, turning to minimal and understated declarations. These so-called revolutionary ads still made reference to particular features of the products they were selling, however. The famous "Think small" advertisement for the Volkswagen Beetle emphasized, through its use of white space, the car's departure from the giant sedans of the time and the bloviating ad copy that sold them. But this modesty was associated with particular values: gas mileage, sturdiness, a distinctive look. Read as advertisement, O'Hara's poem makes only one mention of the product. The Coke enters only as part of the grammatical subject of the first few lines, separated from the poem proper by the title, but quickly displaced by the welter of comparative predicates it spawns, predicates that have nothing to do with the propositional qualities of Coca-Cola itself but pertain rather to the singular experience that the drink enables. Compare this to the advertisement that introduced the famous "Just Do It" slogan, still in existence almost thirty years later. It begins with an establishing shot of the Golden Gate Bridge, then an image of the elderly running-community icon Walt Stack jogging across it, who we learn, through intertitles and voice-over, is eighty years old and "keeps his teeth from rattling in the cold" by leaving them at home.[16] We find out that it's an advertisement from Nike only in the final shot, when the tagline appears. Other advertisements, such as the famous pair-up between Michael Jordan and Spike Lee, might highlight the shoes only to point out how little they have to do with true athletic (or human) achievement, with Lee asking Jordan repeatedly and ridiculously, the wide-angle lens exaggerating the physical difference between Lee's nerdy ungainliness and Jordan's muscled poise, "Is it the shoes? Is it the shoes?"[17]

The postmodern advertisements of Wieden+Kennedy and their imitators introduce a commodity-without-qualities, a commodity whose power to segment markets and differentiate itself from competitors is not a design feature but a rhetorical—or dare I say, poetic—one. They do this by following their antecedents in the 1960s and parodying the comparative structure of advertisement—as in the Lee/Jordan ad—but unlike those early ads they do not reintroduce comparison; comparisons are impossible, so the logic of the ads would imply, in light of the unique values that individuals bring to the items on display. Nikeism is a kind of Nietzscheanism for the rabble.

Drawing on the resources of the ode and the lyric poem of love, O'Hara's work with the structure of lyric comparative and superlative anticipates what happens in the Nike ads. By the light of this comparative logic (or perhaps illogic), "[h]aving a coke with you" is "more fun" than the predicates of the first two lines, but as we learn, the beloved is the real referent of the comparison, which does not turn on particular qualities of the Coke (or the moment of drinking it). This becomes obvious once, in lines 3 through 6, the poem begins justifying its comparative claims through anaphoric "partly because" clauses excerpted from what might seem a potentially endless series. Comparison not only provokes endless and partial explanations but seems fundamentally circular, as we note when the first clause unfolds a nested comparative, describing the beloved as a "better, happier St. Sebastian." Here, O'Hara steers himself straight into the middle of the most clichéd terrain for the lyric poem of love—that is, the use of poetic device to suggest that the beloved is "beyond compare." This is also, no doubt, where advertisements die the death of cliché as well. O'Hara succeeds where others would fail not only because of the quality of detail in the poem but because the superlative, incomparable quality of the beloved is given by the failure of poetic device rather than its transcendence: the "as" of comparison breaks down, so that "it is hard to believe when I'm with you that there can be anything as still / as solemn as unpleasantly definitive as statuary." Later, when simile is reintroduced, it is of a distinctly surreal variety that exists mostly to disclose its own improbable, incomprehensible character: "we are drifting back and forth between each other like a tree breathing through its spectacles." In this landscape, comparisons do not take; there are simply floating particulars that must be grasped in their utter singularity. As the argument of a love poem, there is in many respects nothing new in this claim: we love our lovers, as every lovesick schoolchild knows, because they elude definition and determination, resist objecthood, and therefore keep desire in circulation, as opposed to those delimited objects of attraction that are, according to the poem, "as still / as solemn as unpleasantly definitive as statuary." What is new, it seems to me, is O'Hara's placement of this shift from object to experience under the heading of advertisement, something that very much anticipates the rhetorical strategies of the postmodern ads and their dissolution of the object status of the commodity. In the poem as in the advertisement, the commodity-object itself is simply a placeholder, an empty form that facilitates experience but does little to shape it.

To be clear, O'Hara's aims were very different from Nike's (or Wieden+Kennedy's). O'Hara had little desire to reform the strategies of Madison Avenue or the fortunes of capitalism. Rather, he was eager to show how, through the poem, the commodity could be emptied of its content and made into a vessel for human interconnection, erotic or otherwise. As

José Muñoz asserts in his exemplary reading of the poem, treated as a signal instance of queer futurity, for O'Hara "the quotidian act of having a coke with somebody . . . signifies a vast lifeworld of queer relationality, an encrypted sociality, a utopian potentiality."[18] But this dereifying maneuver, dissolving commodities back into the human relationships whose place they have taken, is itself rather easily reified and, in the course of the last several decades, has become a highly effective technique for corporations, using human desire for meaningful engagement as a way to sell commodities, not as commodities per se but as relationships, as experience. The transformation of objects into experience has also helped firms avoid the problems caused by mass production of standardized goods, whose actual differences from the commodities of competitors are often negligible and whose generalization, standardization, and mass availability can run the risk of making the good in question seem prosaic, dull, and uninteresting. The jargon of experience allows the same commodity to be addressed to each person uniquely.

Whereas O'Hara imagined the Coke as placeholder for a queer "counterpublic," assimilating the universality of the consumed commodity with the "secrecy" of the lovers' smiles and certain queer icons such as St. Sebastian, for the advertisers that would follow in his wake, these gestures become a way to universalize the sense of special, encrypted, insider knowledge invoked by the poem, its aura of aesthetic and ethical knowingness. Michael Warner describes the space of consumption as offering, for queers and other "minoritized" groups, a version of the public sphere that affirms rather than negates social difference, unlike the bourgeois public sphere, which operates with a presumed indifference to the social actuality of interlocutors, under conditions in which "the validity of what you say in public bears a negative relation to your person." Against this "utopia of self-abstraction," the sphere of consumption offers a "counterutopia precisely in a balance between a collectivity of mass desires and an unminoritized rhetoric of difference in the field of choices among infinite goods." For this reason, "commodities were . . . used, especially by women, as a kind of access to publicness that would nevertheless link up with the specificity of difference."[19] O'Hara may offer an inversion of this relationship between embodiment and abstraction, particularity and universality. The Coke is a universal commodity rather than a differential one, not identified with a particular social group, but in the framing of the poem this universality is a screen that gives way to inimitably singular private experience, available anywhere. Under such conditions, the commodity becomes the one-of-a-kind object, the art object, in other words. And so it should come as no surprise, then, that the second half of O'Hara's poem consists of a number of comparisons of the beloved to art objects:

> and the portrait show seems to have no faces in it at all, just paint
> you suddenly wonder why in the world anyone ever did them
> > I look
> at you and I would rather look at you than all the portraits in the world
> except possibly for the Polish Rider occasionally and anyway it's in the Frick
> which thank heavens you haven't gone to yet so we can go together the first time
> and the fact that you move so beautifully more or less takes care of Futurism[20]

Arriving after the first stanza break, the couplet about the "portrait show" inaugurates a notable shift in the perspectival structure of poem: the beloved, the "you" addressed in its opening lines, becomes grammatical subject rather than grammatical object. We are "suddenly," to use the poem's own terms, confronted with what seems to be the beloved's indirect speech (a comment made by the beloved to the poet, while they look at the paintings, perhaps), although it is possible that the "wondering" happens mentally, as unvoiced thought to which O'Hara allows himself a narrator's access. The geometry of persons is also notable here, inasmuch as it works to reinforce the triumph of subjective experience over the object world in which it takes place: the beloved is looking at the portrait painting, and, in turn, the poet is looking at the beloved (though perhaps also looking at the painting). The parallelism stops there, however. While neither of them has any insight into the portraits, unable to locate any human faces therein, the poet does have access to the beloved's thoughts, whether vocalized or not. The unique, experience-transducing powers of painting have been suctioned away from the art object—now reduced to its own medium-specific materiality—and reinscribed on the verbal surface of the poem, as the failed site of reflection that is the portrait gives way to the poet's felicitous reflection on the beloved. All of this underscores the argument, in what follows, that the beloved (and implicitly, the poem in which their encounter occurs) is superior to all pictures save one.

But even that painting is valued only as the site of a future experience poet and beloved might share. Experience trumps all.

Despite his protests here, O'Hara remained a champion of painting and painted objects until the end of his life, particularly the figurative expressionism and second-generation abstract expressionism that many of his contemporaries began to view as recherché by the mid-1960s. He exhibited little interest in the new, experiential modes of art making that were gaining traction during the 1960s, although he died before a verdict on these developments would have been unavoidable. Nevertheless, his emphasis on experience over objects in this poem is unmistakably of a piece with the anti-objective turn to process, performance, and phenomenology in the art of the period. This seems clear in the final lines of the poem: Leonardo Da Vinci, Michelangelo, and Marino Marini and other master artists "were all cheated of some marvelous experience," the poet tells us, "which is not going to go wasted on me which is why I'm telling you about it." In other words: *just do it.*

Here I must admit, yet again, the utter unoriginality of the concluding sentiment, however charmingly and complexly expressed. Dressed down as paraphrase, the lines are indistinguishable from the carpe diem admonitions that poets have been writing since the time of Horace and probably earlier. The uniqueness of the sentiment comes from its placement in the world of commodities and the implication that the specialness of this experience is available to all, free with purchase. In my reading, O'Hara's poem is a critical engagement with the long history of the lyric poem as received in the twentieth century—lyric as technics of individual utterance occasioned by singular experience—and an anticipation of the new social uses to which this technology might be applied.

Lyric Service

Advertising is only one among many of these new social uses. The experiential turn within advertising described previously is one facet of a more general transformation of capitalism in the United States and other early-industrializing countries during the second half of the twentieth century. In particular, the shift from object to experience reflects the reorganization of the occupational structure of capitalism in the postwar period. As manufacturing and other industries became more highly productive, requiring fewer people per unit of output, workers in early-industrializing countries like the

United States instead sought out employment in the fast-growing service sector, in occupations whose aim was not the production of goods but the facilitation of the movement of goods through space; the management, training, and caretaking of bodies; and the production of vendible experiences. By the time *Lunch Poems* was published, white-collar workers already outnumbered their blue-collar counterparts. Particularly important for understanding the relevance and applicability of O'Hara's poetry is the rapid growth in what Linda McDowell calls "interactive service employment," jobs "where the worker and consumer are present and, in the main, where the service provided is used up at the time of the exchange."[21] Work defined by "co-presence" is often, as McDowell notes, dependent on "embodied" and in many cases feminized interactions, either because "the personal embodied attributes of workers enter into the exchange process in a direct way" or because these jobs involve "servicing the bodies of consumers, clients, and patients."[22] These services are experiential, in other words; even where a durable or perishable good is exchanged, as in retail service, the quality of the encounter is an important part of the transaction, sometimes the most important part, and consumers will rate the overall experience based on their encounter with the worker as much as on the quality of the good or service purchased.

The result is that an entire managerial corpus has been built up around analyzing and rationalizing the experiential aspect of in-person service encounters and the values that might make a customer choose one firm over its competitors: values such as "familiarity, care, friendship, rapport, and trust."[23] This is all the more important in the atomized societies of the late twentieth century where people are far less likely to develop the kinds of long-term relationships with petty proprietors—butchers, tailors, bakers, cobblers—that characterized life in town and city in ages past. These relationships must instead be conjured into being through managerial wizardry. The key term here is "rapport," and indeed there is a vast business management literature theorizing, dissecting, quantifying, and otherwise instrumentalizing rapport. As the authors of one survey of the rapport literature note, these feelings are particularly amenable to managerial manipulation, unlike trust or care. Rapport depends either on "enjoyable interaction" or "personal connection" or, under ideal conditions, both. And while the latter quality "may require a more extensive interaction (or series of interactions) in order to develop," through enjoyable interaction rapport can be "established in a single service encounter between a customer and an employee who previously have never interacted."[24] It is no exaggeration to say that, in the world of in-person service, it is the customer-employee relationship that is commodified and customers go to market to experience the kind of authentic interaction that they once might have sought outside or beyond it. The needs of workers in this nexus are complex: many of them, no doubt, might enjoy developing rapport with the customers and find the human interaction a relief from the tedium of work; at the same, as Arlie Hochschild has shown in her seminal work on flight attendants, performing emotional availability for the length of a work shift can be enormously alienating. Interactive service workers might, as some studies show, welcome any scripting or routinizing of these encounters that can insulate them from unreasonable emotional demands.[25]

O'Hara's poems continuously thematize and model moments of intersubjective rapport, often across the space of commodity exchange. The casual informality of O'Hara's poetry has been described by numerous readers (Lytle Shaw, in particular) as a poetics of intimate intersubjective connection, and rapport appears to have been an important element in O'Hara's work life as well.[26] O'Hara worked in both an in-person and back-office capacity during his lifetime, starting off at the front desk at MoMA, where he sold tickets, postcards, and publications, socializing with his artist and writer friends as they came to see exhibitions. After a hiatus, he returned to the MoMA and took a position as assistant to Porter McCray, director of the International Program, helping with and eventually curating the MoMA's overseas exhibitions.[27] This latter work was largely done in the back office, yet it was fundamentally based on his personal relationships with artists and oriented directly toward interface with the public, toward curating and, in a manner of speaking, selling an image of the United States and US artists. By all accounts, O'Hara succeeded not only because he was smart and had a good eye but also because he was adept at navigating complex and ego-fraught social interactions with artists and museum staff.

Thematizations of rapport are perhaps clearest in the anthologized "I do this, I do that" lyrics he included in *Lunch Poems*: for example, "The Day Lady Died," a poem that marks the singularity of the day of Billie Holiday's death by reference to a time- and place-specific constellation of items and services purchased: a shoeshine, a train ride, a hamburger and malted, and famously, the "ugly NEW WORLD WRITING." His lunchtime poems often feature

Lyric and the Service Sector   49

encounters with various workers—cab drivers, construction workers, store clerks of all sorts—although the person on the other side of his purchases is unnamed as often as not. Note, for instance, the difference between bank teller and bookseller in the following stanza:

> I go on to the bank
> and Miss Stillwagon (first name Linda I once heard)
> doesn't even look up my balance for once in her life
> and in the GOLDEN GRIFFIN I get a little Verlaine
> for Patsy with drawings by Bonnard although I do
> think of Hesiod, trans. Richard Lattimore or
> Brendan Behan's new play or *Le Balcon* or *Les Nègres*
> of Genet, but I don't, I stick with Verlaine
> after practically going to sleep with quandariness[28]

This brief moment of rapport between the poet and Miss Stillwagon provides an affective image of interpersonal intimacy around which the rest of the poem will revolve. Miss Stillwagon's surprising familiarity with the poet humanizes her and calls to mind, in return, her first name; as a result, this moment of reciprocated intimacy extends through the rest of the poem, with its first-name reference to a gift recipient, Patsy, whose singular specificity appears here as the quandary the poet confronts in literary commodities. The effect of all this is to draw the reader into the informal, intimate relations that constitute O'Hara's world. By "[f]amiliarly presenting unfamiliar people, events, and attitudes," by acting as if the reader knows exactly who Patsy is, in the same way that poet and the bank teller know each other, the poem might temporarily seduce us into believing that we really do.[29] In fact, we might conclude that one of the reasons the bookseller is not present here is that O'Hara has assumed this role for us, his readers, facilitating our own career through the literary choices, performing the role of salesclerk who makes recommendations for a customer. Many parts of the poem seem to be about recommending and modeling for the reader a nonchalant, easy attitude toward the world of purchases: he "stroll[s] into the PARK LANE / Liquor Store and ask[s] for a bottle of Strega"; at the Ziegfeld Theater, he "casually ask[s] for a carton of Gauloises" in the same way that, in the collection's frame poem, he casually sits down at a sample Olivetti.[30] This kind of gestural intimacy at the point of purchase is explicitly connected to the performance of Billie Holiday, whose relation to the poet is mediated by a purchased commodity, the *New York Post*, but nonetheless remains direct, intense, and bodily:

> and I am sweating a lot by now and thinking of
> leaning on the John door in the 5 spot
> while she whispered a song along the keyboard
> to Mal Waldron and everyone and I stopped breathing[31]

Holiday's intimately "whispered" vocal phrasing has both a particular and a general addressee: "Mal Waldron" *and* "everyone." But the power and surprise of the last line derive from the manner in which O'Hara's panting syntax forces the grammatical object of the final sentence to double as subject, so that the prepositional object of Holiday's whispering, "Mal Waldron and everyone," slides into "everyone and I," the grammatical subject of "stopped breathing," a transformation that manages to preserve the union of a particular person with "everyone." This union of particular and universal addressee is echoed by the naming convention for Billie Holiday: the public refers to Holiday familiarly by a nickname, Lady Day, originally given to her by an intimate, Lester Young.

O'Hara's reflection on the singer is therefore a reflection on his own lyric powers and the kind of public intimacy, directed at both a universal and particular auditor, that his poems strive to create. Terrell Scott Herring describes this as an "impersonal intimacy," a strange sublation of modernist impersonality that substitutes for it something "personal in form but impersonal in content." From the standpoint of his "poetically open closet," O'Hara and his readers are "collective and individual, abstract and particular, private and public."[32] Placed back into the context of the exchanges between service workers and customers, where O'Hara's meditations on intimacy begin, we can begin to see the social usefulness of his engagement with the technology of the lyric poem, specifically its modes of address. Though developed to solve the specific problems of queer counterpublics and, more broadly, to challenge the opposition of public and private, O'Hara's impersonal intimacy anticipates quite well the affective rhetorics that advertisers and retailers will use to lubricate the flow of commodities, generating rapport in the absence of familiarity.

Paramount here is the idea of lyric as indirect address, as a fundamentally "overheard" form of speech and writing, according to the articulation of J. S. Mill and later Northrop Frye. In this view, "impersonal intimacy" emerges from the lyric as a function of its mode of address: the speech of a familiar directed to no one in particular, or perhaps to everyone. For these writers, lyric is the direct presentation of voice or mind, where "this poet"—to use the language of O'Hara's frame poem—speaks *in propria persona* and, abstracted or turned away from the world, addresses himself directly to what O'Hara calls, in his burlesque of lyric selfhood, "the eternal questions of life, coexistence, and depth." For Northrop Frye, the lyric is defined by the concealment of poet from audience, making only indirect address possible. As a result, the lyric comes to imply private and asocial experience. But in O'Hara's frame poem, this act of concealment involves retreat into already social spaces, the "darkened ware—or firehouse," where whatever meditative understanding that might occur is "computed" rather than authentically evoked. O'Hara's satiric recasting of the lyric situation sheds an interesting light on the current debate within so-called lyric theory over the historical status of the genre. Lyric pessimists such as Virginia Jackson argue that the genre is largely a post-Enlightenment invention, a mode of reading popularized by New Criticism and applied after the fact to literary history, while lyric optimists such as Jonathan Culler argue for a long-standing tradition of lyric reading and writing that connects twentieth-century practitioners to Roman and Greek predecessors.[33] Though Jackson is persuasive about the absence of any clear, pre-Romantic concept of what would eventually come to be called the lyric, and convincing also in her treatment of the ex post facto reconstruction of this concept by New Criticism and its fellow travelers, her reception-centric approach misses the ways in which anti-lyric and a-lyric poetry developed and thrived in Anglo-American modernism and its postwar successors such as O'Hara. She also ignores the question of how "lyric reading" affected writing practices, giving birth not only to an interpretive framework but a real genre, albeit one with a fictive genealogy. O'Hara's positioning of his poetry in the *Lunch Poems* blurb and in the poems themselves suggests a savvy, playful, and critical engagement with lyric practice, no longer the insuperable hegemon it appears to be in Jackson's account. His comedic location of the technology of the lyric in the open space of commodity exchange rather than behind the screens of self-reflexive feeling indicates that the lyric model developed by New Criticism was far from total in its uptake. If we want to historicize not just the reception of poems but their production as well, we must attend to the way writers understand lyric technology in relation to their historical moment. If lyric is fundamentally about address, and if address means, in the end, relations between persons, then historical inquiry into the modern lyric and modern forms of lyric address implies inquiry into the changing status of social relations in societies where capitalist relations—between buyers and sellers, employers and employees—predominate.

Most treatments of O'Hara's famous but famously difficult mock manifesto, "Personism," have missed the extent to which it engages questions not only of social relation but also mode of address, reading it simply as a rejection of modernist impersonality (which it most certainly is) and a call for a new directness in poetry (which it also is, but in a more complicated way). As Oren Izenberg notes, many have read the manifesto "as though it advocated for poetry as a form of interpersonal conversation," focusing on O'Hara's remarkable claim that he "could use the telephone instead of writing the poem."[34] They ignore that O'Hara imagines a form of communication that is both direct *and* deflected. His reaction against the modernist impersonality that would replace "nostalgia for the infinite" with the depersonalized "nostalgia of the infinite" is paradoxical. "Personism," O'Hara writes, "is so totally opposed to this kind of abstract removal that it is verging on a true abstraction for the first time, really, in the history of poetry." While Personism puts "the poem squarely between the poet and person, Lucky Pierre style," the result is not directness of communication but rather that "the *poem* is correspondingly gratified."[35] The abstraction that O'Hara imagines here is an *interception* of the directed energies of intimate address by the poetic apparatus: "[O]ne of its minimal aspects is to address itself to one person . . . sustaining the poet's feelings toward the poem while preventing love from distracting him into feeling about the person."[36]

What happens when the surface of the poem intercepts these otherwise directed feelings? In general, O'Hara's remarkable poetry, of course; but one specific result is the frequent turn to exclamation and the exclamatory mood. Exclamation occurs, I would argue, at the precise site of this interception and deflection. Exclamations are, for O'Hara, affects that might have been directed or addressed to a particular individual but have instead become open-ended, undirected, and available as models for the reader. Eight out of the thirty-eight poems in *Lunch Poems* begin with exclamation, and just as many poems feature this modal shift at one point or another, while "Ave Maria" features an imperative apostrophe with an exclamation mark:

> Quick! a last poem before I go

off my rocker. Oh Rachmaninoff!
> "On Rachmaninoff's Birthday"[37]

So many things in the air! soot,
elephant balls, a Chinese cloud . . .
> "Three Airs"[38]

Khrushchev is coming on the right day!
                                   the cool graced light
is pushed off the enormous glass piers by hard wind
and everything is tossing, hurrying on up
> "Poem"[39]

Ah Jean Dubuffet
when you think of him
doing his military service in the Eiffel Tower
> "Naphtha"[40]

How exciting it is
               not to be at Port Lligat
or learning Portuguese in Bilbao so you can go to Brazil
> "Hôtel Particulier"[41]

Mothers of America
               let your children go the movies!
> "Ave Maria"[42]

Shade of Fanny Elssler! I dreamt that you passed over me last
                                       night in sleep
was it you who was asleep or was it me?
> "At Kamin's Dance Bookshop"[43]

How funny you are today New York
like Ginger Rogers in *Swingtime*
and St. Bridget's steeple leaning a little to the left[44]
> "Steps"

Lana Turner has collapsed![45]
> "Poem"

The pattern should be apparent. Exclamation for O'Hara bears a particular relationship to proper name; it is a mood occasioned by an emotional reaction to people and places, though this reaction is often enough directed toward properly named objects (Coca-Cola, the sample Olivetti, Alka-Seltzer). Exclamation in O'Hara performs a relationship to proper names, to celebrity and location, that accommodates and seems available to us as mode and mood and model because it is not clearly addressed toward anyone or anything in particular.

Though O'Hara's exclamations are not often apostrophic (only the first line of "Steps" is a clear apostrophe, joining the imperative beginning of "Ave Maria"), they share something with the apostrophe's odd form of address, which Jonathan Culler famously describes as a "scandal." Sentence mood pertains to the function of sentences, but questions of linguistic function—describing, commanding, questioning—are entangled, it would seem, with address. Culler proposes that we take "apostrophe as the figure of all that is most radical, embarrassing, pretentious, and mystificatory in the lyric," arguing that we would be justified in "seeking to identify apostrophe with lyric itself."[46] For Culler, apostrophe lays bare the lie of signification. By addressing inanimate objects, abstractions, or the dead, the apostrophic poem admits that its addressees, and by extension everything else, have no life except in and through the poem. Apostrophe is therefore another name for the power that separates the lyric literary mode from its opposite in Culler's schema, narrative. In lyric, the elements of a poem have no being except inasmuch as they are brought together by the poet's mind; in narrative, the elements inhabit a sequential relation that exists independently of its telling. Lyric creates, in this regard, "a special temporality which is the set of all moments at which writing can say 'now' . . . a time of discourse rather than story."[47] Since apostrophe only pretends to address someone or something, and in reality performs an attitude toward objects for the benefit of an audience, this expanded definition of lyric apostrophe fits the cases of exclamation that are not grammatically apostrophic, where the exclamatory mood gestures and points to the things in the poem without exactly calling out to them or addressing them: Jean Dubuffet! Lana Turner! Khrushchev! Things in the air! The effect of this exclamation is not to describe but to invest the objects of apostrophe with affective energy; their value comes from being an element of the poet's universe. They become valuable not for an objective character they have but as placeholders for the kinds of affects and values O'Hara brings to them. Exclamation is, in this sense, part of O'Hara's general practice of making evaluative claims, making distinctions, and stating aesthetic preferences—for Duke Ellington, or Donald Allen, or the music of Adolph Deutsch—without needing to offer any argument for his preferences. The exclamation mark does that work for him.

O'Hara's use of exclamation and apostrophe, performing an attitude toward proper names, toward celebrity and brand, anticipates particularly well the new affective grammars and styles of interactive service work as they have developed in the half century since the publication of *Lunch Poems*. O'Hara immerses himself in the space of exchange, modeling a pure enthusiasm, an enthusiasm of entirely nominal rather than descriptive contents that offers a particularly salient prefiguration of the affective labors we encounter in today's service workers, who must at every turn simulate the intimacy, familiarity, and warmth that have fled the icy calculations of the cash nexus, a rapport in the absence of true relation. For O'Hara, this immersion in exchange is, in part, a critique of the lyric concept as it operated at the time and of attitudes that assumed, like Hayakawa, that the poem's authenticity was vouchsafed by being held apart from the space of mercenary activity. O'Hara would no doubt have seen his poetry as strongly opposed to Adorno's account of the lyric as "a sphere of expression whose very essence exists in either not acknowledging the power of socialization or overcoming it through the pathos of detachment."[48] In Adorno's dialectical account, these forms of overcoming or nonrecognition are social in nature, indirectly social, inasmuch as they "impl[y] a protest against a social situation that every individual experiences as hostile, cold, oppressive." The lyric is an image in reverse of these social forces: "the more heavily the situation weighs upon it, the more firmly the work resists it by refusing to submit to anything heteronomous and constituting itself solely in accordance with its own laws."[49] O'Hara's entire project might be characterized as an attempt to invert the Adornian inversions of the lyric modality. For instance, in his prose poem "Meditations in an Emergency," after submitting various lyric gestures and attitudes to his bathetic reconstructions, he characterizes the lyric poet's conventional retreat from the social as follows:

> However I have never clogged myself with the praises of pastoral life, nor with nostalgia for an innocent past of perverted acts in pastures. No. One need never leave the confines of New York for all the greenery one wishes—I can't even enjoy a blade of grass unless I know that there's a subway handy, or a record store or some other sign that people do not totally *regret* life.[50]

In submerging himself affirmatively within the space of social experience—described here as commercial experience (record stores)—O'Hara demonstrates quite well how easily the lyric can be put to work within the space of exchange. Indeed, if interactive service work is by definition that which produces a commodity "used up at the time of exchange," perhaps its elective affinity with the lyric poem, which has always emphasized its own evanescence alongside its reproducibility, is not so surprising. And if the essence of the new service economy is its insistence on "customer experience," what better model than the lyric poem, which has for the last two centuries been considered the ideal medium for the communication of experience at its deepest level? O'Hara had, it should be clear, other plans for his adaptations of lyric technique to the service environment. He wanted to show how the lyric modalities that were presumed to require exit (or at least critical distance) from the mercenary exchanges and exacting labors of the workaday world could instead take place among and through them, allowing for meaningful human interaction, erotic or otherwise. The fact that the poem can only be overheard, however, means it can also very easily be *misheard*.

O'Hara and the World

O'Hara's ascension from front desk to back office, and from in-person service to administrative service, provides some insight into the possible connections between these different forms of labor. Though advertising is a business service, a service provided to corporation rather than consumer, its ultimate target is the consumer. It aims to intervene directly in the exchange relation, to shape, craft, and facilitate it. We might think of it as an "out-of-person" service, a way of interacting with the consumer or customer at a distance. Increasingly, advertising is one part of an "integrated" marketing and public relations strategy that superintends not only communication with the customer via old and new media but also takes charge of the scripting and instrumentalization of "personal selling" and "point of purchase" advertising.[51] In this sense, the attitudes and values that we see in O'Hara's poems and in the previous postmodern advertisements, the vocabularies of rapport we have been exploring throughout this chapter, are now part of a general ethos that stretches from upper-middle-class executives to fully proletarian waitresses, shop clerks, direct marketers, and call center workers. As we will see, the restructuring of labor and the cultivation of new values in the workplace often begin with more privileged strata, before working their way down to the lowest levels of the workforce.

Curatorial work is similar, in this regard, if less hypermanaged than work in the corporate sector. The curator does not interact with the museum-goer directly but does craft and refine that person's experience. The curator produces an abstract docentship, directing experience from the back office. In other words, O'Hara's interest in the kind of work that takes place at point of service or point of purchase has to do with the fact that his work concerned these sorts of interactions, at a distance. The shows that O'Hara curated are especially notable in this regard, since they concerned not museum-goers in general but a particular "international" audience whose perspective MoMA hoped to shape. MoMA's International Program was begun at the behest of its president at the time, Nelson Rockefeller, whose private foundation donated the initial grant for the program. The MoMA was a family institution (started by Rockefeller's mother) but also connected to the political class and the agendas of the US state through the future governor and presidential candidate. Both the director of the museum, René d'Harnoncourt, and O'Hara's boss, Porter McCray, had worked for the wartime government agency run by Rockefeller, the Office of the Coordinator of Inter-American Affairs, which organized exhibitions of American painting in Latin America.[52] As detailed in numerous historical treatments, beginning with Eve Cockcroft's seminal article, "Abstract Expressionism: Weapon of the Cold War," the International Program of the MoMA served as a proxy Ministry of Culture for the United States, overseeing tasks such as the selection of artists for the American Pavilion at the Venice Biennale that were handled directly by the state in other countries.[53] While many policy elites in the United States were of the opinion, like Rockefeller, that the homegrown avant-garde of abstract expressionism could be used to counter the images of the United States disseminated by Moscow and its supporters in Europe and elsewhere, other less enlightened anticommunists saw these painters as crypto-communists, declaring that "all modern art is Communistic," and scuttling attempts by the US state to organize exhibitions directly. As a result, the MoMA, already connected to policy elites through its board of directors, took up the job.

The most scandalous part of this story is the unfolding and successive revelations about the role of the Central Intelligence Agency (CIA) in this "cultural Cold War" strategy, through the agencies of its proxy committee, the Congress of Cultural Freedom (CCF), and the CIA's dummy nonprofit group, the Farfield Foundation. The International Program at MoMA collaborated with the CCF on a number of shows and received funding from the Farfield Foundation as well. O'Hara was not a part of those exhibitions, but searching for direct CIA collusion, however, misses the point, since the MoMA's explicit sense of its vocation was essentially identical with the uses to which the CIA and its counterparts in the State Department would put it. The CIA strategy centered on cultivating anticommunism among the noncommunist left, especially among former fellow travelers. MoMA was committed to advancing the idea that the United States had generated a nonconformist and yet apolitical avant-garde, freeing itself from formal constraints on pure self-expression. While these artists might, in the words of MoMA president Alfred H. Barr Jr., "defiantly reject the conventional values of the society that surrounds them, they are not political engagés even though their paintings have been praised and condemned as demonstrations of freedom in a world in which freedom connotes a political attitude."[54] As Serge Guilbaut argues persuasively, regardless of the scope of the conspiracy, there was no need for the US state or the CIA to distort or falsely represent this art, since the abstract expressionists and their critical epigones such as Clement Greenberg emerged precisely as a reaction to the political and aesthetic failures of Stalinism and its fellow travelers in the wake of the Moscow Trials, the Molotov-Ribbentrop Pact, and the Soviet invasion of Finland, as well as the strictures of *Kulturbolschewismus*, when a distinct subset of the artists of the 1930s embraced the forbidden formalism and abstraction of modernist painting and rejected explicit political content in favor of uninflected aesthetic innovation. The messages that the United States wanted to send the world did not need to be affixed to these paintings; they spoke quite eloquently on their own about "the political choice of giving up politics," as their champion Harold Rosenberg put it.[55] Their refusal of political content and the propagandistic aims of social realism made them the perfect propaganda.

This politics of no politics is echoed in O'Hara's "Fantasy," which concludes *Lunch Poems*. The end of this poem, a dialogue of sorts, has his politically radical friend Allen Ginsberg uttering the uncharacteristic lines "I'm glad Canada will remain free. / Just free, that's all, never argue with movies."[56] This was part of a suite of O'Hara poems, written in the last years of his life, that adopted the language of hard-boiled fiction and spy thrillers. Here, his preference for film-music composer Adolph Deutsch gives way to an espionage narrative that this music evokes, placing this "mere freedom" in a decidedly Cold War context and notably recruiting a noncommunist radical like Ginsberg to the cause of liberty. O'Hara was only a subordinate of the people who worked with actual spies and had direct contact with the CIA, but he was still responsible for organizing touring exhibitions in line with these values, and his participation in the "cultural Cold War" sheds some interesting light on the "worldly" character of his poems and his tendency to address himself to and position himself in front of vast, international cultural audiences. Whether or not this poem, and the others like it, reflect his awareness of his proximity to actual spies and his involvement in cultural espionage, we cannot know. But it does allow us to think about how many of his poems situate themselves among a chain of international signifiers that point back to the United States and often do the important cultural work of superimposing New York on European cultural centers such as Paris. We might think of the poem "Naphtha," which begins by invoking, in an exclamative, Jean Dubuffet and the Eiffel Tower but then transmutes these cultural icons to Duke Ellington and Manhattan skyscrapers.[57] If the exclamation in O'Hara is connected to in-person services of exchange, here the transactional space is an international one; O'Hara's out-of-person service provides an image of US cultural dominance, of US celebrity and cultural curation, for the reader or viewer.

This line of inquiry illuminates his offhand remark in "The Day Lady Died" about his purchase of "an ugly NEW WORLD WRITING to see what the poets / in Ghana are doing these days."[58] His purchase records a veritable business expense, since these were precisely the cultural audiences the MoMA expected O'Hara to cultivate. We might think, likewise, about his poem "Image of the Buddha Preaching," a dramatic monologue in the voice of the Indian ambassador to Germany, commemorating an exhibition of Indian art at a German cultural institution (the Villa Hügel). This Indian-German cultural cooperation is secured against a number of Cold War and Marshall Plan objectives, with the speaker declaring:

> Anglo-German trade will prosper by Swansea-Mannheim
>   friendship
> waning now the West Wall by virtue of two rolls per capita
> and the flagship berlin is joining its "white fleet" on the Rhine
> though better schools and model cars are wanting, still still oh
>   Essen[59]

Cultural superiority (given by Indian-German collaboration in the field of art) leads to economic superiority, to more toilet paper per person and, eventually, better schools and cars. As with exclamation and apostrophe, dramatic monologue here cultivates rapport precisely by demonstrating a unique personalized relationship to his audience and their concerns, chiefly German Indology.

Other poems concern themselves quite directly with O'Hara's labors at MoMA, cultivating an image of the worldly cultural space of New York for an equally worldly, international audience in the discursive context of the Cold War. This is most certainly the case with a poem like "Poem (Khrushchev is coming on the right day!)," which imagines Soviet-American rapprochement in fundamentally cultural and aesthetic terms, placing the Soviet leader in the aesthetically superior space of Manhattan, where "the cool graced light / is pushed off the enormous glass piers" of its international-style buildings. O'Hara's New York is, of course, a condensation of vast international spaces, a "logarithm of other cities" as his friend Ashbery will later note.[60] It has "everything but *politesse*" and brings together Puerto Rican cab drivers and Ionesco and Beckett, travel to Sweden, Spanish painters, and François Villon, placing them in a "light [that] seems to be eternal."[61]

Perhaps the finest example of O'Hara's curatorial arrangement of New York as cultural commodity is "Steps." Here, the overriding metaphor for such curation is choreography: "How funny you are today New York / like Ginger Rogers in *Swingtime*." The apostrophic, exclamative address allows O'Hara not only to personalize New York but to contain it within the space of cultural performance, and this kinetic performance continues throughout the poem: the speaker jumps "out of a bed full of V-days"; people rub up against each and their "surgical appliances lock"; there is a vast disrobing as "everyone's taking their coat off / so they can show a rib-cage to the rib-watchers," while simultaneously "the park's full of dancers and their tights and shoes / in little bags." This is a New York convoked, it seems, around a memorial moment of American triumph, a V-day reenacted in various celebratory choreographies that have as their basis an existential truism: "the Pittsburgh Pirates shout because they won / and in a sense we're all winning / we're alive." Most important, though, US dominance here is secured through a cultural excellence divorced (seemingly) from the political sphere: when O'Hara expresses his happiness that "those liars have left the UN / the Seagram Building's no longer rivalled in interest," he is comparing two famous examples of international-style architecture and declaring his preference for the version that is at least superficially separated from political objectives.[62]

"Steps" discloses the peculiarities of O'Hara's "Personism," which allows intimate address to become universalized without becoming public speech, allows him to cultivate rapport despite the fact that his addressees are vast and dispersed. This is something different from the "salut au monde" one finds in Walt Whitman, which still preserves something of the oratory tradition of public address and its formalities, despite his infusion of these encounters with erotic overtones and intimate knowledge. As we have seen, this technology of address anticipates changes in the nature of in-person service work, but the international, Cold War thematic also points to the increasingly globalized character of postwar capitalism. As multinational firms conquer the world market and develop universal brands like Coca-Cola, they come to embody values of universality and worldliness, which explains, in part, why "having a coke with you" can be, for O'Hara, *better* than traveling to a number of overseas destinations. Workers, too, might value multinational firms for the supposed opportunities for advancement, travel, and personal transformation they allow. These opportunities are counterbalanced, however, by the sense that the larger the firm becomes, the more bureaucratized, rule bound, stifling, deadening, and uncreative it becomes. As we will see, capitalist firms learn, in part, how to counter the sclerotic effects of growth from poets and poetry and art more broadly, through a corporate subsumption of the vocabularies, concepts, and techniques of literature and art and their adjacent countercultural zones.

The television series with which I began, *Mad Men*, functions throughout as an investigation of the dialectic of corporate culture and counterculture, not only because the offices of the firm where the show takes place reflect the collections of the MoMA and its peers, such that one can read off its backgrounds the progressive, decade-long canonization and institutionalization of various art movements, from abstract expressionism to post-painterly abstraction, pop art, and op art. (The show begins in 1960 and ends in 1970.) Draper's iconoclastic creativity, the show wants to tell us, derives not only from the prodigious amounts of alcohol he consumes but from two other sources: his authentic experience of poverty and suffering in the Great Depression; and his proximity to liberated, bohemian spaces. In the final season of the show, the creativity and authenticity of Draper's small firm, Sterling Cooper & Partner

(SC&P), is threatened when it merges with its behemoth competitor McCann Erickson, though the cultural difference between the two firms is reproduced internally in the split between "creatives" and "account men," between Draper and his nemesis, account executive Jim Cutler.

Throughout this season, the dangers of McCann Erickson and its gray flannel conformity are emblematized by the new mainframe computer that SC&P has purchased, auguring an era of depersonalized, uncreative, and purely instrumental advertising based on numerical calculation and market research. At the same time, McCann Erickson's immense size and power mean that it has premier brands, including Coca-Cola, which the head of McCann Erickson dangles in front of Don Draper, indicating it could be his account if he complies with his new bosses. Predictably, Draper rejects the firm, walking off the job and setting out on a cross-country journey of self-discovery that he likens to Jack Kerouac's *On the Road* and that also involves a reckoning with the rural America of his birth. Coca-Cola hounds him throughout this journey, such that his engagement with his own past and the American past involves fixing up an old Coca-Cola machine in a small-town motel. Finally, his time on the road spits him out in California, in the New Age community of Esalen, which offers up, in the form of its therapeutic encounter groups, the antidote to the cold, computerized rationality of McCann Erickson.[63] At the end of the final episode, we find Draper meditating on a hilltop, in front of the Pacific Ocean; a smile comes across his face, and the show cuts to Coca-Cola's 1971 "Hilltop" commercial (implying that he returns to McCann Erickson and comes up with the advertisement). The advertisement features a multiracial and multinational group, whose diversity of dress we must assume indexes a range of attitudes to the transformations of the 1960s, standing on a hilltop very similar to the Big Sur cliffs, singing:

> I'd like to teach the world to sing
> In perfect harmony
> I'd like to buy the world a Coke
> And keep it company
> That's the real thing

Though the "Hilltop" ditty is clearly not up to O'Hara's poetic standards, it does manage to combine the values of worldliness and personalization discussed earlier. *To buy the world a Coke* is a particular kind of gesture, both universal and particular, that seems to indicate that for Draper, for McCann Erickson, and for Coca-Cola, the synthesis of counterculture and corporate culture was well on its way to being achieved. The means of this synthesis were, in this case, poetic in nature, effected in part through transformations of the inheritance of the lyric poem and its technologies of address by poets such as O'Hara, producing a lyric mode both worldly and intimate at once. This allowed for highly flexible modes of interaction that could be scaled up and scaled down, extended and expanded without being, at the same time, depersonalized. "Having a Coke with You," as *Mad Men* seems to recognize, is the parent of the "Hilltop" ad and much more besides.

 # John Ashbery's Free Indirect Labor

John Ashbery's "The Instruction Manual" is arguably one of the most memorable poems about office work in English. Nonetheless, Ashbery's poetry may seem an odd choice for a book about labor, just as "The Instruction Manual" will seem an odd place for any account of his poetry to begin, because, as Marjorie Perloff notes, the transparency and directness of the poem is not exemplary of anything else in *Some Trees* (1956) or the later books. It is an anomaly in a book of anomalies, a book that, compared with the more thematically unified later volumes, seems a mere miscellany, a "collection" of experiments, pastiches, and sketches for a variety of germinal styles that never came to fruition. Yet the fact that Ashbery almost never again wrote anything so flat and transparent might make it a *more* appropriate place for an investigation of Ashbery's early work to begin, as if he had disclosed something in that poem that needed to be covered up again just as quickly. If "The Instruction Manual" is a set of instructions, an *ars poetica*—and Ashbery wrote many of these—it is one for a poet that never emerged, a how-to that Ashbery never took up. It is a set of instructions made to be disobeyed, perhaps because it makes his poetry all too simple and diagrammatic, contains its sleight of hand and casual mastery within a petty frame about alienated life and work.

> As I sit looking out of a window of the building
> I wish I did not have to write the instruction manual on the uses of a new metal.[1]

There is no better figure for the subsumption of the writer and writing by capital and its compulsion to work than the technical writer, the writer of manuals, whose every sentence is both subject and object of the managerial hierarchies of postwar society. By the middle of the 1950s, white-collar workers like the one pictured in "The Instruction Manual" had begun to outnumber their blue-collar complement, and a series of defining and popular books—from C. Wright Mills's *White Collar* (1951) to William Whyte's *The Organization Man* (1956)—singled out this group as a crucial and contradictory feature of the new society, ambiguously situated between the two poles of capital and labor.[2] Because wartime and postwar automation in the manufacturing sector aimed not only to reduce the number of laborers needed to produce everyday items but also, in the view of David Noble, to wrest control over the speed and quality of labor from their hands and place it in the care of a vast technical, clerical, and managerial superstructure, the white-collar workforce multiplied even while US dominance in manufacturing was still reaching its peak.[3] As manufacturers learned to exploit the "uses of . . . new metal[s]," they required more and more white-collar workers to supervise and design work processes or write about them in instruction manuals. Still, these white-collar workers were not the simple beneficiaries of Henry Ford's assembly line and Frederick Taylor's "scientific management," which attempted to reduce mental and physical activities to easily reproduced and fragmented routines. As Harry Braverman makes clear in his influential study of automation, *Labor and Monopoly Capitalism*, they were also, in turn, submitted to the same processes of automation, routinization, and deskilling.[4] When the speaker of Allen Ginsberg's "America," published the same year as "The Instruction Manual," declares that "I will continue like Henry Ford my strophes are as individual as his automobiles more so they're all different sexes," he is reflecting less on the dehumanizing and deindividualizing character of Fordist industrial work than the application of these processes to mental labor, and writing in particular.[5]

Such workers are in a curious position. They are not owners—in other words, they are not entitled to the profits from the firm—but they are proxies, often, for the will of the owners. Indeed, a technical writer seems a perfect example of the double-edged nature of Taylorization for white-collar workers. The instructions that the speaker writes *are* the routines that other workers follow. Yet their production is itself scripted and routinized. With the development of the corporate form, the functional aspect of capital (command, organization, management) gets hived off to employees, and the single unifying consciousness that might have existed in the small firm, supervising every aspect of a production process, shatters into scores of small tasks and positions, each one correlated with some aspect of a process that can no longer be visualized in entirety. While the writer of the instruction manual might well grasp the totality of the work process, this overview is paradoxically inscribed within a singular, monotonous task. Hence, as Andrew Hoberek notes in his study of the white-collar middle class in postwar American fiction, workers like the speaker of "The Instruction Manual" tend to experience "mental labor [as] the site of both transcendence and disempowerment," the former indexing a past life of petit-bourgeois entrepreneurialism and the latter a future life of thoroughly proletarianized drudge work.[6] But whereas Hoberek wants to demystify white-collar pretensions to universality, I argue that such claims derive from real features of white-collar work, since these workers were, in fact, often both bosses and employees, as well as mediators between executives and simple subordinates. This does not make their experience universal, but it does give such workers a uniquely privileged viewpoint, however full of contradictions.

Written during Ashbery's time working for a textbook company, "The Instruction Manual" dramatizes the doubleness of white-collar work by making the speaker both the commander and executor of commands, both the one who imagines an excursion away from the banality of the working day and into the streets of an idealized Guadalajara and the one who actually carries it out. And therefore when the dual subject of the poem (both "I" and "you") encounters an old woman whose son is absent because he has a job at a bank in Mexico City, he is reminded of his own similar absence and the job from which he strives to escape. He is thrust back into the spectatorial or touristic mode. This is the point of the dual subject: the "I" commands a "you" to submit to an experience but reserves himself and stands apart from the experience. The circularity of the poem, descending from its office window into the city and then rising to a church-top vista at the end, the whole of the city spread below, underscores the uncrossed distance between the "I" in his office and the doppelganger "you" he addresses. This kind of play with point of view is a constant in Ashbery's poetry and, in later books, remains connected to the theme of white-collar work because, like literary point of view, such work involves administering relations between people.

Inspired by Raymond Roussel's *La Vue*—an elaborate fifty-page meditation on a beach scene suspended inside a penholder—"The Instruction Manual" was one of the last works Ashbery wrote for *Some Trees*, after the book had already been accepted by W. H. Auden for the Yale Younger Poets award. At the time, Ashbery worked at "various menial jobs in publishing," including a job in the college advertising department at McGraw-Hill.[7] Soon after, he left for Paris and stayed there for ten years, writing the poems in *The Tennis Court Oath* (1962), to which I will later turn. The flight from work and into the scenery of Guadalajara in the poem therefore anticipates, in a sense, his flight from the United States and his jobs there. The later poems are written in "a state of restless experimenting," as Ashbery notes, cobbled together from cheap English-language paperbacks bought on the Paris quais, magazines like *Esquire*, and other material found in the American library.[8] Going forth, in this sense, also involves looking back. The flight from the United States into the experimental climes of France required a recourse to the conversational, demotic language he had left behind, as well as images of the alienated labor and office work that the United States now signified. His later remarks on Gertrude Stein's self-imposed exile could also be said of himself during this period: "[Her] distance from America afforded the proper focus and even the occasion for a monumental study of the making of Americans; the foreign language that surrounded her was probably also a necessary insulation for the immense effort of concentration that this book required."[9]

From the Poetry of Production to the Poetry of Circulation

As a poem about work, "The Instruction Manual" brings us a great distance from the ethos of craft one finds in the modernism of Pound and Williams, Oppen and Zukofsky. For these poets the representation of contact with elemental materials (wood, stone, metal) vouchsafed an artisanal dignity, where the made thing bore witness to the distinct hand of its maker. Oppen: "Native now / Are the welder and the welder's arc / In the subway's circuit." As elsewhere, Oppen's central figure is that of human activity hardening into an inert form that, while still testifying to the dignity of human action, is also and always a block for us, a form of maiming.

> The crippled girl hobbles
> Painfully in the new depths
> Of the subway, and painfully
> We shift our eyes. The bare rails
> And black walls contain
> Labor before her birth, her twisted
> Precarious birth and the men
> Laborious, burly . . .[10]

For Oppen, poetry is a language of craft and things, capable of restoring, and making visible, the work contained in the reified world around us; it proposes, against the mercenary and technocratic barbarization of matter and bodies, an artisanal grammar of tool, matter, environment, a grammar of the dignity of materials and makers, and a potential reciprocity between bodies and objects not possible in fully industrialized capitalism. Oppen's late books often mourn this lost relationship to the world. They are a sad, Heideggerian dirge for the lost fight against the infernal, practico-inert materiality that modernity and industrialization had become.[11]

Though Ashbery and Oppen were writing at the same time, none of this elemental or vital contact with materials is available for Ashbery—there is no primary relationship to matter, no craft really. His matters are verbal, prefabricated, demotic; they are made elsewhere and by others, and what they offer to the intending consciousness is arrangement, not making. The sentimental, clichéd phrases and images that flash up in Ashbery's poems are not merely objects of ironic ridicule, though they are ironic. They are literally *what there is to say*: they are the life we live, the general form of experience that we must fill out. Ashbery's attitude toward these languages is a mostly loving one—no one has ever had a clearer sense of how a cliché can dawn like a revelation. His goal is to make this debased language come alive, not to replace it with a new language more erudite or more able to absorb the weight of past history, as with Pound or Eliot. As he says in an essay on the New Realists—artists such as Yves Klein, Jean Tinguely, and Raymond Hains—their attempt to "come to grips with the emptiness of industrialized modern life" requires them "to accord it its due."[12] The products of the age of mass production and consumption from which they construct their art "are a common ground, a neutral language understood by everybody, and therefore the ideal material with which to create experiences that transcend these objects."[13] What does it mean to treat mass-produced objects as a given? For one, it means the impossibility of imagining them as objects one might make. Such objects simply appear, prefabricated. If one has a responsibility toward them, it is only to move them around, administer and rearrange them, sort and inventory them. In other words, the attitude that Ashbery approvingly attributes to the New Realists belongs to those white-collar and service-sector workers who, rather than produce commodities, ensure that they arrive at their destination.

"Chains of Power and Obedience"

These themes are developed in *The Tennis Court Oath*, a book that has remained something of a shibboleth, polarizing Ashbery's admirers, who treat it alternately as his most interesting or his most unsuccessful work. As described previously, the poems keep looking over their shoulder at the America from which Ashbery has fled, in the same way that the speaker of "The Instruction Manual" is forced to return to the "emptiness of industrialized modern life" after his imaginary jaunts. Andrew Ross reads the book as a poetic homologue to pop art, linking its deployment of "demotic elements" to a new "consumer imagination," and while his early essay is commendable for articulating the relationship of *The Tennis Court Oath* to an evolving capitalism, I argue that the book approaches the new products and processes of industrialized life not as consumer but as worker.[14] In *The Tennis Court Oath*, the emptiness of industrialized modern life is the emptiness of work life:

> The Division was unsuitable
> He thought. He was tempted not to fulfilling order written down
> To him. The award on the wall
> Believing it belonged to him.
> Working and dreaming, getting the sun always right.
> In the end, he had supplanted the technician
> With the bandage. Invented a new cradle.
> The factory yard resounded
> Filling up the air.[15]

The start of this poem is a near match for that of "The Instruction Manual," except here the rebelliousness is a bit more explicit: "He was tempted not to fulfilling" is one shade away from Bartleby's "I prefer not to." While the earlier poem is limpid, here a slippery, disorderly grammar is part of his insubordination. Is he not at all tempted to fulfill the order, or is he merely tempted to not fulfill the order? This is a written "order"—both a message and organization—dependent on a "division" of labor between command and execution that is grammatical and social at once. Language and social hierarchy intertwine so that orders are "written down" in the double sense of being committed to paper and sent down the command chain to subordinates. However, this hierarchy is not maintained by direct relations between people but relations between people and things, as Marx's account of the commodity fetish implies. The position the speaker inhabits is reinforced by "an award on the wall / Believing it belonged to him."

The reification of the subject (as grammatical and social object of orders) finds its complement in the personification of the object. The problem that the book confronts, however, is a situation where the person who resists commands, or is tempted to resist them, is also someone who gives commands, a "link in chains of power and obedience," as C. Wright Mills describes such workers.[16] Although the speaker is object of an invisible superior whose orders are conveyed by way of impersonal things, his own powers are transferred to other workers, and likewise effected by things, such that "he supplant[s] the technician with the bandage."

While labor is clearly only one of several important leitmotifs in *The Tennis Court Oath*, scenes of employment, images of the "factory," and characters named not by proper name but by employment—teacher, janitor, secretary, pilot, soldier, policeman—merit extended attention, probably because Ashbery seems the last person to treat labor as a central category. Labor is perhaps best understood as the hidden and necessary correlate of what the book presents as its central theme, political representation, or representation in general. Factory yard and tennis court, workplace and political assembly, are thus parallel sites where "representatives" and "managers" speak on behalf of their constituents or subordinates. Despite the allusion to the French Revolution in the book title, for the most part, the theme of political representation hangs under the sign of America, and the poem "America" is one of the clearest expositions of the themes and devices at work. With its collection of subjects without predicates and predicates without subjects, the fragmented grammar of "America" allegorizes the problem of representative democracy: "Millions of us / The accident was terrible." The poem presents "a the stars," where the question of the relationship between individual "stars" or citizen-fragments to their total coherence as nation is radically indeterminate, carrying both a definite and indefinite article. Ultimately, the poem attempts to imagine, with its confected syntax, new relations between the stars:

> And I am proud
> of these stars in our flag we don't want
> the flag of film
> waving over the sky
> toward us—citizens of some future state.[17]

The poet rejects the flag as ground and containment, as the grammar of belonging for the particle-stars, just as he rejects conventional relationships between phrase and sentence in anticipation of some new mode of interrelationship, some "future state." The flag is a principle of collection and assembly. In the logic of the poem, it becomes a "chain," an "order," and a "border." But it is also a made thing, a product of labor and its technical means, the "lathes around / the stars with privilege jerks." Three times in the poem, a janitor appears, threatening class violence like the "cold anarchist standing / in his hat" at the start of the poem. In his second appearance, he stands opposed to the "conductor" and, consequently, the principles of arrangement and ordering of the flag: "Person / blocking the conductor / Is the janitor with the red cape . . . His face hidden by the shelf / thought intangible."[18] As character, the janitor opposes at a thematic and formal level the ordering syntax of the flag: his custodial labor dwells contentedly among waste and disorder.

The conductor in this poem resembles the director of the opera, who might also be a conductor, in the sestina "Faust." In that poem, which describes a production of *The Phantom of the Opera*, the musicians and the "phantom / scene painters" threaten a strike whose point, we might say, is to disrupt the repetitive, serialized form of labor inscribed within the compulsions of the sestina form.[19] Like the janitor, the scene painters are opposed to the "director." And like "America," "Faust" presents a vision of the backstage labor that goes into any cultural production, the phantom of labor that, having constructed the opera house, still remains hidden within it as a tormenting demon. It is no wonder, then, that when the janitor appears for the third time in "America," he returns with a "wrench with which he'll kill the intruder."

In *The Tennis Court Oath*, the aesthetic shares elements with both political and economic modes of management: political because it determines who speaks and how, and economic because it likewise determines who works and for whom. The poet identifies uneasily with the figure of the conductor or director, whose technical-managerial labor, creative, colored by art and the aesthetic, confronts a deskilled and purely subservient labor. Consider, for example, the opening of "A Life Drama," later in the book:

> Yellow curtains
> Are in fashion,
> Murk plectrum,
> Fatigue and smoke of nights
> And recording of piano in factory.[20]

Here again, terms of art are superposed on terms of work, and the two become difficult to disentangle. At a certain level, these lines seem to say, making music is little different from the use of machines one might find in a factory, involving here the striking of a dull pick—"Murk plectrum"—on strings. But at another level, perhaps, music is compensation or illusion, laid atop the brute materiality of labor, "[t]he factory to be screwed onto palace / The workers—happy." The production of the music itself, at a certain level, is simply the movement of labor—"[t]he tears a fifth time of the workers pulling down the board through the trees / Plectrum."

Free Indirect Labor

The preceding discussion has been largely oriented toward the content of the poems. But Ashbery's thematic elaboration of the different types or moments of labor is complemented by a formal exposition. We cannot fully understand what he is saying about intersubjective relations in and as labor without taking account of the overlapping points of view, frequent pronominal shifts, and species of direct, indirect, and free indirect discourse he employs. Experimentation with point of view is one of the primary means through which the poems explore the complicated and sometimes contradictory social relations of the postwar workplace. Although Ashbery's poems almost never feature narrative beyond the level of the anecdote, they are nonetheless highly novelistic—frequently resorting to pastiche of nineteenth-century melodrama and to the technical machinery of point of view and free indirect discourse used in the realist novel. Many of his poems—especially those in *The Tennis Court Oath*—read as if someone had deconstructed a novel by Henry James, removing all of the contextual material so that what remains are epiphanic fragments, snippets of dialogue, and incomplete descriptions.[21]

The longest poem, "Europe," draws much of its language from a British young adult novel, *Beryl of the Biplane*. It begins in the register of "employment" and "construction":

> To employ her
> construction ball
> Morning fed on the
> light blue wood
> of the mouth
>   cannot understand
> feels deeply)[22]

Curiously, though, at some level this construction connotes destruction, since, as David Herd notes, "construction ball" is a particularly paradoxical adaptation of wrecking ball and invokes the necessary disarticulation of fragments of speech and writing out of which the new constructivism of the poem might emerge.[23] The objects of this construction are as much subjects and subjectivities as they are materials. Like "America," its cross-Atlantic complement "Europe" pictures a play of partial subjects unmoored from any containing frame. Here as elsewhere, Ashbery establishes an indeterminacy between subjects and predicates, exemplified in this instance by the uncertain relationship between the "mouth" (metonym for speaker or speech) and the final two phrases that seem to float free from it. The indeterminacy about who is speaking models the indeterminate class position just described, the white-collar worker who is both commander and commanded, the speaking mouth and its object. Exploring this position, the poems in the collection take on a curious mixture of obedience, insubordination, and authority. These are contradictory personalities, or contradictory combinations of personalities, about whom Ashbery can write: "You had no permission, to carry anything out, working to carry out the insane orders given you to raze / the box."[24]

Many Ashbery critics have written about this hallmark indeterminacy of point of view, most of them helped along by his provocative remarks about how the movement in his poems "from one person in the sense of a pronoun to another . . . helps to produce a kind of polyphony."[25] But for the most part these studies, by Bonnie Costello or, more recently, John Emil Vincent, have focused on Ashbery's complex deployment of the second-person pronoun (which can function as both pronoun of direct address and impersonal pronoun). Though important, singular attention to the "supremely elastic" character of the second-person pronoun and its ability to allow for "a polyphony of writer and reader" distracts from an examination of polyphony in his work more generally, with its cascade of characters and subjects, pronouns and points of view.[26] Ashbery's remark that "we are somehow all aspects of a consciousness giving rise to the poem" seems just as much a reference to the wider social field from which the poems emerge—involving not just an "I," a "you," and a "we" but also "he," "she," and "they"—as an attempt to trouble or reconstitute the relationship between writer and reader, especially in light of passages like the following:

106

she was trying to make sense of
what was quick laugh
hotel—cheap for them
caverns the bed
    box of cereal

Ere long a flare was lit
I don't understand wreckage

107

        blue smoke?   The steel bolts
           It was as though   having been replaced
               She had   by a painting of
the river   one of wood!
           above the water   Ronnie, thoughtfully

                                      of the silencer

           plot to kill both of us, dear.

    oh
        it that she was there [27]

Here, in a mere dozen lines, Ashbery decocts a welter of points of view and modes of address, involving five different pronouns and characters. Fragments of reported speech, reported thought, and free indirect discourse crystallize around the different perspectival centers. But Ashbery's technique is syntactical as well as grammatical: the multiple perspectives of the passage find their complement in the different reading pathways the poem allows. In the first lines of section 107, for instance, one must equally choose a path through the jumble of fragments and a subject to whom one attaches the various fragments. The muddle of viewpoint and standpoint finds its complement in the various states of matter and different textures that flash up in the poem—*smoke, water, wood, metal*—as if the problem for the poet were the correlation of different subjectivities or points of view with different states of matter. But as with almost all of Ashbery's poems, synthesis is merely hinted at, and what remains is a bland, impersonal pronoun, an "it."

Poetry criticism is mostly ill equipped to account for what Ashbery is up to in these kinds of passages, at least at a technical level, inasmuch as his experiments with point of view and narrative style are the sort of thing expected in a modernist novel. But the poems are not narrative, and much of the pleasure of the novel and its special resources with regard to point of view has to do with the particular continuities that narrative creates, even in writers like Virginia Woolf or Samuel Beckett or Jean Genet. Fragmented poetry of the sort that Ashbery writes offers no such continuities, either of character or point of view, even if point of view is still one of the chief points of interest in these poems, part of their exposition of a complex collectivity. What we have, instead, are "cameos" emerging out of a social field—brief magnetizations of predicates to different grammatical subjects, often pronouns, such that personalities take shape out of the welter of language:

> More upset, wholly meaningless, the willing sheath
> glide into fall . . .   mercury   to passing
> the war you said won—milling around the picket fence, and noise of
>   the engine from the sky
> and flowers—here is a bunch
> the war won out of cameos.
> And somehow the perfect warrior is falling.[28]

In this exemplary passage, it becomes more than difficult to attach predicates to subjects or determine the register of the various phrases. Is "the war you said won" the indirect speech of the "you"? The free indirect speech or thought of someone describing the "you"? Is the pronoun meant as self-description (or self-dialogue), as in so-called second-person point of view—that is, the "you" of a speaker describing himself or herself in free indirect discourse? The fragmentation and rapid passage from one phrasal unit to another makes such questions undecidable, and that is indeed the point of these experiments.

There are several accounts of free indirect discourse and its functioning, most of them highly technical and, in the last few decades, many theorists (Ann Banfield, in particular) have advanced substantive critiques of the way that earlier theories, especially by Mikhail Bakhtin and others in the Bakhtin circle, such as Valentin Volosinov, treated free indirect discourse as a kind of double-voice, blending together author and character.[29] But whether or not the Bakhtinian view is correct might matter less, in the end, than Ashbery's own ideas about language. In terms of a philosophy of free indirect discourse, we might find a better match for Ashbery in the post-Bakhtinian tradition, especially those expansive definitions one encounters in Gilles Deleuze's work on cinema and in *A Thousand Plateaus*, with Felix Guattari, as well as in the thinkers he draws on: Volosinov and Pier Paolo Pasolini. For Deleuze and Guattari, who explode the Bakhtinian model, free indirect discourse subtends all language; a swarm of unattributable voices, ideas, and expressions precedes any individuation of language into direct discourse, into the saying or writing of an "I," a "He," or a "She." It precedes any tagging of one piece of language to a particular body: "Language in its entirety is indirect discourse. Indirect discourse in no way supposes direct discourse; rather, the latter is extracted from the former. . . . My direct discourse is still the free indirect discourse running through me, coming from other worlds or planets."[30] This seems an apt characterization of the basic philosophy of language at work in "Europe" and elsewhere, with Ashbery's poems "receiving / dreams and inspirations on an unassigned / frequency," as he writes in "Self-Portrait in a Convex Mirror."[31]

But the concept of "free indirect discourse" offered up by Deleuze and Guattari, as germane as it is to Ashbery's sensibility, will not get us to the properly historical character of the technique in *The Tennis Court Oath*. Ashbery's stance as receiver, assembler, and distributor of social voices has to do with the changed character of the capital-labor relationship in the 1960s. As with "The Instruction Manual," the ambiguous attribution of the phrasal units in the poems of *The Tennis Court Oath* reflects the administrative language coursing through capitalist firms, a social ventriloquism through which white-collar workers simultaneously speak and are spoken for. If early modernist experiments, under the ethos of industrialization, could imagine the artist as maker, as fabricator and artisan of social forms—as the creator of a new language, sui generis—deskilling and, later, deindustrialization remove this contact with primary materials and reposition the artist as administrator of prefabricated forms, received from elsewhere, made by unknown characters. In the same way, Ashbery received the fragments of an American vernacular in France, attempting to remove the "stars" from "the flag we don't want," and to understand forms of American English as implicated within questions of political representation, alienation, and exploitation. The free-floating discursive fragments received hearken both to the political self-representation of the multitude of voices and their exploitation or manipulation by the receiving subject. Free indirect discourse, in this way, is a product of struggle between represented and representing voices.[32] The swarm of indirect discourse that forms the preindividual "plane of consistency" is not originary, as Deleuze and Guattari sometimes indicate, but the product of the abstractive, "deterritorializing" machine of history and its production of new subjects and new class relations in capitalism.

At the base of this social relation is nothing less than the building block of capitalism, the commodity and its attendant social relations, which Marx likens to the biological cell in its relationship to life. Marx's treatment of the commodity form involves a number of rhetorical techniques, prosopopoeia (personification) chief among them. The transformation of a simple useful object into a commodity effectively personifies it, so although "the table continues to be wood, an ordinary, sensuous thing . . . as soon as it emerges as a commodity, it changes into a thing which transcends sensuousness. It not only stands with its feet on the ground, but, in relation to all other commodities, it stands on its head, and evolves out of its wooden brain grotesque ideas."[33] The commodity is a thing that speaks to others for us, and speaks for others to us. When I buy shoes with my wages, I am trading some portion of my own time and the goods or service it might create for a related portion of time that the shoe factory's workers devoted to making my shoes. While the presence of profit-seeking owners makes these exchanges unequal in terms of actual hours worked, not to mention conditions of work, the important point is that the act of exchange brings my own activity into relation with other people who are unseen and whose contributions I might easily overlook. Because the act of exchange is mediated by money, it occurs indirectly, separated into two acts whose connection is not always obvious: an act of selling my time and an act of buying the product of some other person's or persons' time. Money and commodities stand in for (and act on behalf of) other people in this scenario, such that we never actually meet or see those with whom we are brought into relation by the market. There is thus, in capitalism, a constant alternation between what Marx calls "personification of the thing and a reification of the person" as commodities come to act as stand-ins for us.[34]

Such transactions are not only indirect, however. They are also free in the sense that the things we make or do are stripped from us, freed from us, and appropriated by others. Furthermore, since most production is collaborative and social in character, performed by groups of people rather than individuals, collectively produced goods get appropriated by individuals, just as is the case with the transindividual flows of language in Deleuze and Guattari's schema. The legal conventions of private property, which attach to the various forms of fixed and circulating capital, exist in opposition to the social and collaborative character of production. In capitalism, however, production is undertaken not only with others but for another. We do not work to produce objects or services for our own consumption but so that our employers can sell our products or services for profit. In this sense, labor is both indirect (undertaken on behalf of others) and free (capable of being stripped from its producers and appropriated by someone else). We might say, therefore, that labor in capitalism is a form of *free indirect activity*, in which others act through us or we act on behalf of others. This should explain the relationship between the indeterminacy of point of view in *The Tennis Court Oath* and the frequent images of labor.

The Tennis Court Oath describes a particular variant form of this labor and a particular moment in the historical transformation of labor, when the relationship between commander and commanded in free indirect activity becomes entirely reversible and increasingly complex. As corporations increase in size and scope, requiring more elaborate systems of administration, control, and accounting, management becomes more difficult to locate in a particular person, and the source of particular commands becomes more difficult to trace. Here is how Mills describes the confusion:

> Seen from below, the management is not a Who but a series of Theys and even Its. Management is something one reports to in some office, maybe in all offices including that of the union; it is a printed instruction and a sign on a bulletin board; it is the voice coming through the loudspeakers; it is the name in the newspaper; it is the signature you can never make out, except it is printed underneath; it is a system that issues orders superior to anybody you know close-up; its blueprints, specifying in detail your work-life and the boss-life of your foreman. Management is the centralized say-so.
>
> Seen from the middle ranks, management is one-part people who give you the nod, one-part system, one-part yourself. . . . Your authority is confined strictly within a prescribed orbit of occupational actions, and such power as you wield is a borrowed thing. . . . You are closer to management than the wage-workers are, but yours is seldom the last decision.[35]

This passage is a remarkable treatment of point of view as seen from different points of view within the contemporary organization. It demonstrates that the "centralized say-so" is not attributable to any particular person but exists in a strange interspace similar to the difficult-to-attribute predicates of Ashbery's poems.

Many commentators on the class politics surrounding free indirect discourse suggest that the indeterminacy of consciousness in such texts produces what Pasolini calls "an irrational interclassism" where "the bourgeois class itself, even in sum, in cinema, identifies itself, again with all of humanity."[36] For Pasolini, who follows earlier commentary by Volosinov, the breakdown of the dividing line between character and author marks the inability of literature (or film, which is his object) to encounter proletarian life as such. All of these writers argue, in one way or another, that such techniques produce an abstract and average middle voice that negates the particularity of any specific life. While this is no doubt one possible result of these literary techniques, in Ashbery these devices do not reconcile the various voices but instead stage their antagonism to each other. The particularly experimental character of Ashbery's use of free indirect discourse seems designed to make us experience the incompatibility of each voice or moment, their refusal to fit together into the presentation of a single, stylized spread. The reason is that, as much as Ashbery must identify the work of producing these poems and joining together the various found voices (the "papers" that bear "somebody else's marks") with the arranging, directing consciousness of the "conductor" and the "centralized say-so" of management, he also identifies with the insubordination such a system incites.

Among the poems in *The Tennis Court Oath*, "Landscape" best reflects the contradictory stances described previously. The poem is notable because the first half features an impersonal third-person description, hence "landscape"—concerned with various dysfunctional features of the life of a "village," which then gives way to first-person and second-person address attributable to the original speaker. The unitary speaker acts as a counterpoint to the persistent images of breakdown proffered throughout:

> The pest asked us to re-examine the screws he held.
> Just then the barman squirted juice over the lumps.
> It decided to vote for ink (the village)
> There was surprise at the frozen ink
> That was brought in and possibly rotten.[37]

One is in a bad place when "a pest"—an agent of corruption—is responsible for various interconnecting ligature or "screws." And just as we should expect from a reading of previous poems, problems with interconnection are also problems with representation—in other words, with the ink. Likewise, "the rapid extension meter" and whatever measurements it might provide is "thrown out of court." Such problems continue in the second stanza:

> The charcoal mines were doing well
> At 9½ per cent. A downy hill
> Announced critical boredom for the bottler
> Of labor tonic. It seemed there was no more
> Steering-wheel oil or something—you had better
> Call them about it—I don't know,
> I predisposed the pests toward blue rock.
> The barometer slides slowly down the wall
> It has finished registering data.

Despite a certain prosperity—measured at "9½ per cent" of something—the alienation of work ("critical boredom") has begun to afflict the bottlers of "labor tonic," where the latter refers to something sold to induce labor in pregnant women that, in this context, might instead refer to a tonic used to assuage resistant laborers: a managerial tonic, akin to "steering-wheel oil" in its ability to reduce the problems associated with directing the activity of others. The workers are reduced to (or spoken for by) a mere thing—"a downy hill"—just as their village has become an "it." The stance of the speaker here is supervisory, moving from observations about the global state of things to recommendations for actions to improve them. In "Landscape," subordinate characters are figured as objects and the effaced agents of passive-voice constructions by the speaker in the guise of manager: "[t]here was surprise," "ink / . . . was brought in," [i]t seemed there was no more," "the paper lining had gotten / unpinned, or unstuck." Indeed, only inanimate objects take on active verbs: "the bathers' tree explained," "the barometer slides," "the glass sanctuary repeated . . ." These objects mediate and transmit the effaced activity of the subordinates and workers in this poem. The barometer, then, is a metonym for some kind of associated and displaced refusal, just as the coming apart of the square doctrines and paper lining is most likely the unattributed work of "pests" and saboteurs. Though Ashbery does not flesh out these antagonisms through the technical means of free indirect discourse, the relationship established between speaking subject and spoken object (here, personified in various inanimate agents) is largely the same. The mediating (in this case, managerial) voice fails to speak for another. The final line of the poem suggests that the breakdown in hierarchy is terminal: "The ladder failed."

The Tone of Flexibility

The white-collar middle class of the immediate postwar period, as described by Mills, Riesman, Whyte, and others, was a class in transition, its already-circumscribed powers quickly evaporating through the very processes of routinization and deskilling that conjured it into being. Perhaps more accurately, a certain portion of the postwar white-collar middle class—clerical workers and certain lower-rank managers and technicians—had its autonomy and privilege eroded, while another portion, comprising executives, directors, and professionals, continued to enjoy a fair amount of power. The transformation of the white-collar middle class might be better described, then, as a polarization rather than a deterioration, such that certain white-collar workers come to resemble their blue-collar counterparts, experiencing with them a shared condition of "critical boredom," to use the idiom of Ashbery's poem. These white-collar workers saw their own "derived power" as, ultimately, the power of another and participated in a broad-based revolt against the alienation of modern work, especially its dull, hierarchical, and authoritarian character. Toward the end of the 1960s, this revolt meant a marked uptick in strikes, absenteeism, sabotage, low productivity, and a general loss of morale. Broadly understood as emerging from a newly dominant qualitative critique of work that focused on domination and disempowerment rather than exploitation, the new struggles made management as such their explicit object, taking aim at the "right to manage" that many firms had reserved in exchange for wage increases. Examined in light of the struggles of the coming years, "Landscape" seems a portrait of this breakdown of management and the polarization it produced among white-collar workers.

This convergence of "white-collar woes" and "blue-collar blues" led capitalist firms to propose a large-scale transformation of organizational structure, designed not only to neutralize the antagonism described in this poem but to cut down on labor costs. Part of this meant generalizing the standpoint of white-collar workers, by forcing all workers, even those at the lowest ranks, to perform routine administrative and bureaucratic tasks. Many firms organized low-level workers into partially self-directed teams engaged in a variety of rotating tasks and eliminated as many middle managers as possible. In a sense, such attempts to improve corporate culture and encourage teamwork aimed to produce the kind of "irrational interclassism" described by Pasolini in his critique of free indirect discourse. They aimed, in other words, to produce a universalized solidarity with management, where management means, as Mills makes clear, a pervasive structure of intentionality more than a set of persons.

The problem for Ashbery in the poems discussed here is that he cannot imagine any form of collective life outside the administration of white-collar work: his experimental rearrangement of varied social materials through collage no longer seems an act of avant-garde negation but part and parcel of capitalist logic. At the same time, he identifies with a pastoral poetry of leisure, refusal, and distancing, through which he attempts to turn his back on modernity and its urgencies.[38] This contradiction is never resolved in *The Tennis Court Oath*, and it is one of the reasons why his later books depart so strongly from its modes and methods. Indeed, these later books resolve the antagonistic play of voices and points of view in *The Tennis Court Oath* by adopting a much more amicable alternation of pronouns and viewpoints—usually "I," "We," and "You"—which seem essentially fungible perspectives on a central experience rather than irreconcilable singularities. They orient their play with point of view toward a new humanism or, in Pasolini's less-than-charitable terms, "a pseudohumanistic function."[39] When work appears in these later books, it is drained of all antagonism. Even violence is strangely muted. This is a world in which "quelled / The rioters turned out of sleep in the peace of prisons / Singing on marble factory walls."[40] In place of the antagonism of the earlier poems here there is an affective compromise with management:

> . . . keeping the door open to a tongue-and-cheek attitude on
>   the part of the perpetrators,
> The men who sit down to their vast desks on Monday to begin planning the
>   week's notations, jotting memoranda that take
> Invisible form in the air, like flocks of sparrows
> Above the city pavements, turning and wheeling aimlessly
> But on the average directed by discernible motives.[41]

While "The Instruction Manual" opposed daydreaming to work, here the aimless flight of the sparrows converts seamlessly to notations and memoranda. The change is consistent with the restructuring of labor that occurred from the 1970s onward. To make work tolerable and reconcile workers to management, firms imbued the workplace with values associated with the home and leisure.

Furthermore, in this new scenario all individual agency has been effaced: "discernible motives" now belong to "the average." Throughout the later poems an abstract, impersonal identity supplants the antagonistic viewpoints discussed earlier:

> He thought he had never seen anything quite so beautiful as that crystallization into a mountain of statistics: out of the rapid movement to and fro that abraded individual personalities into a channel of possibilities, remote from each other and even remoter from the eye that tried to contain them: out of that river of humanity comprised of individuals each no better than he should be.[42]

Likewise, if managerial commands elicited resistance in the earlier poems, the later Ashbery recommends ironic acquiescence instead. As he describes it in "Soonest Mended," his "one-size-fits-all confessional poem" from 1970, the new "clarity of the rules" means "*They* were the players, and we who had struggled at the game / Were merely spectators, though subject to its vicissitudes."[43] In cultivating a playful, ironic attitude toward the experience of struggle, Ashbery's later poems model corporate responses to the dissatisfactions indexed by his earlier poems, suggesting that workers might be happier (and more productive) if they could invest their work life with the lightheartedness they would otherwise seek beyond work. Unsurprisingly, acquiescence for Ashbery also depends on a shift in point of view. To experience our experience as spectacle, the poem suggests, we must act as if it were happening to someone else. In the soft focus of Ashbery's late style, Rimbaud's "Je est un autre" is the watchword of an endlessly plastic, adaptive self that can meet whatever challenges arise with a steady equanimity. Irony, here, is a form of accommodation, if also a buffer against the vicissitudes of a topsy-turvy world. The freedom and indirection of the earlier style, which might have indexed a certain resistance to labor and its violence, now signal, in their fluency and even-toned open-endedness, the newfound flexibility of the contemporary worker.

# The Poetry of Feedback

Today, outside of a few specialized applications, the would-be metascience of cybernetics is remembered, if at all, only as a hazy prelude to modern computing and information technology. But in the United States during the 1950s and 1960s cybernetics was popular on a scale that might be difficult to appreciate today and enjoyed a nonspecialist audience that extended far and wide from the academic centers and military-industrial research centers where it was born. Books like Norbert Wiener's *The Human Use of Human Beings* and Gregory Bateson's *Steps to an Ecology of Mind* sold hundreds of thousands of copies, while cybernetic theorizations made plausible and significant contributions to economics and anthropology, business management theory and art criticism, psychoanalysis and linguistics, as well as core areas in the applied and theoretical sciences, which everyone expected would soon be completely transformed by such research. The status of cybernetics as the overarching future framework of not only the natural but also the social sciences (and even the arts) seemed virtually assured, even to its enemies. Martin Heidegger, for instance, thought this product of Anglo-American technocracy, born from the crucible of World War II and its rationalized barbarism, threatening enough that he would answer curtly with the single word "cybernetics" when asked by a *Der Spiegel* reporter in 1966, "And what takes the place of philosophy?"[1]

American literature during this period was saturated with cybernetic metaphors, concepts, and themes. In fact, many of the novels that would later come to form the canonical instances of postmodern literature are essentially built around cybernetic concepts such as information, entropy, feedback, and system—from the allegories of control in William Burroughs's Nova trilogy and Kurt Vonnegut's *Player Piano*, to the melodramas of heat death and entropic decay in Philip K. Dick's *Ubik* and *A Scanner Darkly* and J. G. Ballard's short stories (to name a British writer); from the paradoxes of information and entropy in William Gaddis's *JR* and Thomas Pynchon's 1960s novels, to the thought of feedback and system in John Barth, Donald Barthelme, Robert Coover, and, later on, Don DeLillo.[2] If you were a white man and interested in experimentation in prose fiction in the 1960s and 1970s, then you were probably writing about machines, entropy, and information. Beyond the domain of the novel, the breakdown and efflorescence of neo-avant-garde art in the late 1960s was in some sense superintended by a popular reception of cybernetic ideas as well as a more general worrying about media and medium. The 1970 "Information" show at MoMA, including work by many of the most recognizable figures of this period, is an index of the broad distribution of the cybernetic imaginary, which provided a primary conceptual framework for Robert Smithson, Hans Haacke, and Dan Graham; Vito Acconci, Allan Kaprow, Adrian Piper, Hélio Oiticica, and Yvonne Rainer, to name just a few, as well as the poets and writers of the period who were, in some sense, understood as conceptual and performance artists: Hannah Weiner (the subject of this chapter), Madeline Gins, and Bernadette Mayer (the subject of the next).[3] Charles Olson made "feedback" a guiding metaphor for his compositional process, as did A. R. Ammons. Beyond the American literary and art scene, French structuralism and poststructuralism were, in many regards, elaborated through a reception of Anglo-American cybernetics—Jacques Lacan writes famously about cybernetics in his second seminar, as do Claude Levi-Strauss and Roland Barthes, and as would Jean Baudrillard, Jean-François Lyotard, Jacques Derrida, and Gilles Deleuze and Félix Guattari later on.[4] Indeed, as Bernard Geoghegan notes, one of the explanations for the precipitous disappearance of cybernetics as a referent was its replacement by a set of poststructural concepts that were, to some extent, its progeny.

In a section of the *The Human Use of Human Beings*, Norbert Wiener bemoans the lack of a contemporary humanistic and scientific lingua franca of the sort that Latin once provided. The implication, throughout the book, is that cybernetics might provide this new common tongue for the complex, technological societies of the twentieth century. And although this vision never came to pass, among the conceptual artists, performers, poets, musicians, and dancers of downtown New York in the late 1960s and 1970s, cybernetic concepts functioned as a kind of lingua franca and were, in part, what enabled a person to write a poem one day, make an installation the next, and design a performance the day after that. Just as cybernetic concepts emerged at the boundaries of mathematics, physics, engineering, and biology—from the common efforts of various researchers brought together in government-sponsored research programs and conferences—cybernetically inflected concepts such as "system," "process," and "information" provided an interart grammar that allowed conceptual artists, musicians, dancers, and poets to engage in common projects, developing new aesthetic categories, such as "the happening" or "environment," by which these projects could be received.

Strange Bedfellows

How do we explain this development? How do we understand the broad appeal for artists of this "science of everything," gaining in popularity and clout such that, by the mid-1960s, it provided key conceptual frameworks for both the counterculture and the corporate, political elite, for neo-avant-garde artists, and government technocrats? Cybernetics is, in the formulation Norbert Wiener gives it, defined as the scientific study of "control and communication in the animal and machine."[5] Its central concepts emerge, in part, from attempts by Wiener and others to develop self-correcting antiaircraft guns—in other words, guns that could track the movement of a plane and predict where it would be by the time an artillery shell reached it. This required a certain form of feedback whereby information received from an object—in this case, the target—produced a self-adjustment and a change in the "behavior" of the gun.[6] Although the techniques for mechanical self-regulation date from the invention of the water clock and feature in devices as familiar as the household thermostat, one of the best examples of the servomechanical union of communication and action is cybernetician W. Ross Ashby's "homeostat." This is a device made from four interconnected electrical transistors such that the electrical output from one transistor becomes the electrical input of the other three. Each one of the four transistors has a number of settings that determines how it modulates inputs and turns them into outputs, and thus the number of possible combinations of inputs and outputs the machine can produce is exceedingly complex, yielding up tens of thousands of results. Despite their complexity, the results divide rather simply into either stable or unstable patterns. The input voltages for each transistor either settle around a single value or, alternately, fluctuate back and forth wildly, producing fluctuating outputs and a chaotic set of feedbacks between transistors. What makes this machine seem a plausible model for homeostasis and self-regulation, however, is that the thousands of possible unstable states lead, by design, to a stable one. If after a period of time the input voltages fail to settle on a single value, the transistor resets and randomly tries a new setting. It continues to reset until it finds a setting that leads to a stable input voltage. All of the transistors continue to reset until they find a range of settings that leads to stable inputs and outputs for each other. Thus, this is a self-stabilizing machine, what cyberneticians call a "hyperstable" device, capable of self-modulating through the mechanism of feedback, in response to changing inputs. Such devices provided, for many cyberneticians, a plausible portrait of how the body regulates its own temperature, how an animal learns from its behavior, how a corporation adapts to changing market conditions, and how a national economy corrects itself in the face of trade imbalances.[7]

Cybernetics was, of course, closely connected to technological developments in computing and telecommunications that were extremely important to the course of postwar society. In many ways, its ambition to unify the natural and social sciences, and even the humanities and the arts, is a relic of the massive cross-scientific endeavors of the war effort—the Manhattan Project, first and foremost—which organized disjointed university research studies into structures more common to the military and industry and which gave rise to numerous technologies with social and commercial applications. It is not surprising, then, that for many this science of control and communication promised a response to social and economic issues that seemed especially pressing. "Control" and "communication" were, of course, central preoccupations for societies whose economic policies were based on Keynesian "social planning," whose hierarchical, multilayered corporations raised new problems of management, and whose deskilled manufacturing system put control over the content and pace of production in the hands of a professional-managerial class. Cybernetics, unsurprisingly, appealed to corporate management, military engineers, or government technocrats, as it promised a more efficient and less violent means of managing complex processes.

What is more surprising, however, is the way that cybernetics appealed to the hippies, leftists, countercultural, and bohemian artists of the period, whose ostensibly libertarian and communalist politics would put them in direct conflict with the managers and technocrats who were reading the same books. Despite its origins in military research and its ominous self-description as a science of control, cybernetics could often present itself as a holistic, organic mode of social regulation in line with fundamentally democratic values and premised on the empowerment and participation of all. As Fred Turner writes in his study of the cybernetic counterculture, it provided "a vision of a world built not around vertical hierarchies and top-down flows of power, but around looping circuits of energy and information."[8] Cybernetics was therefore the lingua franca of people who thought the problems of the age arose from too much control as well as those who thought it arose from too little. While seen from the standpoint of the counterculture and certain parts of the New Left, cybernetics suggested the organizational form of a future postcapitalist society no longer based on domination and exploitation; to much more decidedly pro-capitalist elements it offered a set of mechanisms through which techniques of domination and exploitation could be perfected and rendered palatable. The power of cybernetics lay in its ability to dissolve oppositions, to transform a contest between opposed entities into the internal self-regulation of some larger entity that included both sides. As an example of the holistic view of cybernetics, Turner quotes the title poem of Richard Brautigan's *All Watched Over by Machines of Loving Grace*, a book whose fifteen hundred copies were distributed for free on the streets of Haight-Ashbury in 1967, describing "a cybernetic ecology / where we are free of our labors / and joined back to nature." With the homologies that it establishes between human, animal, and machine, cybernetics provides the dissolution of conventional oppositions between labor and leisure, nature and culture, such that the poem can imagine "a cybernetic meadow / where mammals and computers / live together in mutually programming harmony."[9]

As a form of opposition to the organization of postwar societies that, paradoxically, would dissolve all opposition into "mutually programming harmony," the cybernetic imaginary in its countercultural setting was particularly appealing to corporate managers looking to allay the dissatisfactions and rebellions of their workers through the incorporation of worker-manager feedback loops. But cybernetic models were also appealing in their own right, beyond questions of morale, especially once conditions of profitability eroded in the 1960s and, seeking a way to cut costs, firms began to look for ways to trim the various managerial layers that had emerged as corporate structures became more elaborate and complex. Cybernetics seemed as if it would provide the solution to the inefficiencies and violence of autocratic management, shearing needless management and making "control" a technical rather than personal matter. This was the function not only of the specifically cybernetic management theories of people like Jay Forrester and Stafford Beer but, as Michael C. Jackson summarizes in a book on the topic, a general category of "systems thinking" within business management that "gave birth to strands of work such as 'organizations as systems,' general system theory, contingency theory, operational research, systems analysis, systems engineering and management cybernetics," all of which shared with cybernetics a tendency to view firms as adaptive, equilibrium-seeking entities.[10]

Cybernetics and the related disciplines it influenced therefore provided models of streamlining while responding positively, rather than merely repressively, to the newly prevalent critiques of capitalist work that emerged in the late 1960s, critiques that focused on qualitative rather than quantitative demands, targeting in particular the alienating, machinic, rote, and routinized character of deskilled blue- and white-collar labor. Visible already within influential books of the 1950s such as William Whyte's *The Organization Man* or Herbert Marcuse's *One-Dimensional Man*, such critiques were something of a commonplace by the middle of the 1960s, and as Thomas Frank and others have shown, you might encounter such views within the so-called establishment as well as on the countercultural margins.[11]

Luc Boltanski and Eve Chiapello call this qualitative challenge to work "the artistic critique" (as opposed to the wage-oriented "social critique") precisely because it percolates outward from the counterculture and the artistic avant-garde.[12] As we saw previously, faced with the combination of the social and artistic critiques epitomized by the rebellion of May 1968 but in evidence throughout the period, firms sought to pit the two critiques against each other, engineering a form of pseudo-empowered, "flexible," and "self-managing" work that met the demands of the artistic critique (for authenticity, creative expression, diversity of tasks, participation in decision making, flexible hours, etc.) in a manner that allowed for a newly intensive exploitation, effectively eroding the previous gains of the workers' movement with regard to wages, workday length, and benefits. In short, the new self-directed employees would work much harder and longer than their predecessors. The meeting between cybernetics and the neo-avant-garde complicates this story slightly, since what we note is not the recuperation by capitalist firms of a set of purely external values, concepts, or ideas but rather a contest over the meaning of a set of ideas. Though cybernetics emerges with the military-industrial complex, it is transformed and put to new uses by artists and countercultural figures in the

1960s, who elaborate entirely new meanings within this field, meanings that eventually become the focus of corporate attempts to restructure in the face of the critical challenges raised by these meanings. In this sense, the artists and writers who participated in elaborating these cybernetic ideas did not simply share an elective affinity with the technocrats that they imagine themselves opposing. Rather, they were responding critically and correctively to the technocratic visions they encountered and imagining how those visions might provide the material for another social arrangement. Along with the various Pentagon-sponsored think tanks and university research programs, the art and writing of the period are one site where cybernetic ideas are elaborated, contested, transformed. Art and writing, in this sense, are experimental and speculative processes. They are laboratories of a sort, a "counter-laboratory," if you will. As we will see in the subsequent discussion of Hannah Weiner and Dan Graham, by focusing on the interaction between artist and audience, writer and reader, or on the process rather than the object of art making, many of these works take as their vocation the active modeling of potential social relations, relations that both prefigure and contribute to the actual restructuring of the labor process that begins in the 1970s and intensifies during the 1980s.

The relationship is a bit more than prefiguration pure and simple and a bit less than direct causation, since the means of uptake by employers is complex and indirect, mediated in this case by the counterculture and the mass media and mass cultural forms that were fascinated by it. The political models of holistic collaboration, mutability, and participation elaborated by the love-ins, be-ins, and politicized festivals of the counterculture were based quite directly on the precedent set by the postwar neo-avant-garde, with its happenings, chance-based compositions, interventions into daily life, and ecstatic forms of derangement. And while it is true, for instance, as Thomas Frank has argued, that the "co-optation" theory that sees the mass culture lagging behind and eventually recuperating an original, revolutionary movement fails to acknowledge the presence of dissident, critical voices within the so-called establishment, voices that also bemoaned the rigid, bureaucratic, and authoritarian character of work life—though with entirely different ends in mind—I think the evidence is clear that, for the most part, these critical enunciations remained in an entirely theoretical register, oriented largely toward attitudes rather than concrete practices.[13] Outside the avant-garde, first, and the counterculture, second, there were few practical examples of these participatory modes. For instance, although Douglas McGregor had written as early as 1957 about the need for a new "Theory Y" of management based on "job enlargement," "decentralization," and "participation and consultative management," he was intentionally vague about what this Theory Y might look like if implemented, suggesting that it was no more possible at that time than it was possible to build a nuclear power plant in 1945.[14] Like nuclear power, Theory Y was foreseeable but not implementable. But at that very moment artists such as Allan Kaprow, Carolee Schneeman, and John Cage were already implementing their own Theory Y in the arts. It is notable that Fred Turner, in his study of counterculture and cyberculture, begins the story of Stewart Brand and the Whole Earth Network—so influential to the course of development of information technology and corporate structure—with Brand's involvement in the happenings of the Lower Manhattan art scene of the early 1960s.[15] To be clear, I am not arguing that artists and writers are the source of the dissatisfactions at the root of the artistic critique; such experiences of alienation and anomie were widespread and well documented. Artists and writers provided a conceptual grammar and vocabulary—a set of reference points or coordinates with respect to which these dissatisfactions could be articulated—but they certainly did not create them.

Cybernetics at Work

For an example of this incipient cybernetic grammar as one might have encountered it in the 1960s, consider the text Hannah Weiner wrote for her first "one-man show," *Hannah Weiner at Her Job*:

> My life is my art. I am my object, a product of the process of self-awareness. I work part-time as a designer of ladies underwear to help support myself. I like my job, and the firm I work for. They make and sell a product without unnecessary competition. The people in the firm are friendly and fun to work with. The bikini pants I make sell for 49¢ and $1.00. If things can't be free, they should be as cheap as possible. Why waste time and energy to make expensive products that you waste time and energy to afford?
>
> Art is live people. Self-respect is a job if you need it.[16]

This show took place in March 1970, among hundreds of similar happenings and performances. Best known for her later "clairvoyant" or "clair-style" poems, composed from the words that she began to see everywhere—on walls, on people's faces, in the air—Weiner was at the time of this show a poet associated with Fluxus and the downtown New York art scene. The quotation demonstrates one surprisingly anti-utopian consequence of the neo-avant-garde project of "art into life"; under conditions in which "art" has become synonymous with "life," then it has also become synonymous with "work," since most of life, for most people, means working.[17] Going to work, then, counts as art, and making things or laboring becomes a secondary effect of the fundamentally artistic work of self-making and self-fashioning, where product and process are one. The gambit of such a project is that the merger of art and work will humanize and aestheticize the space of labor, here become a place where making and selling take place "without unnecessary competition."

The notion of self-production and self-objectification that we encounter in *Hannah Weiner at Her Job*—"I" as "object"—is very much a figuration of the cybernetic concept of "feedback." In cybernetics, any entity that regulates itself through the "circular causality" of feedback, where outputs produce inputs that subsequently modulate new outputs, can be thought of as self-aware at some basic level, even if it is a simple mechanical device or electrical circuit. In cybernetics, the very definition of an adaptive organism is that it can become its "own object," "a product of the process of the self-awareness." The statement could have been written by either Norbert Wiener or Hannah Weiner.

As discussed previously, cybernetics bases its notion of self-regulation on the mechanical devices called servomechanisms or, alternatively, "governors." Wiener coins the term "cybernetics" from the Greek word for "steersman" or "pilot," *kybernetes*, which is the root of "govern" in English.[18] But what has not yet been adequately examined is the relationship posited between communication and these mechanisms of control. For cybernetics, there is essentially no difference between communication and control: "When I control the actions of another person, I communicate a message to him, and although this message is in the imperative mood, the technique of communication does not differ from that of a message of fact."[19] To return to the example of the artillery guns, the action of the gun is itself an act of communication; it communicates (to itself) the degree to which its aim is correct or incorrect and modulates its own actions accordingly. Communication is not a disembodied system of signs but a performative and materialized chain of causes and effects. Indeed, communication is the very coherency of the organism itself. As Wiener writes in a chapter of *The Human Use of Human Beings* where he discusses the possibility of teleporting a person, organisms are fundamentally messages. It is the self-regulating pattern of information that gives them their identity, not the material of which they are composed, which is constantly switched out through various metabolic processes.[20] One could therefore, at least hypothetically, duplicate a person through duplication of these information patterns. Communicable information is essence, for Wiener, a fact that might explain the appeal of these ideas to poets and others who worked with signs and symbols of one sort or another.

In the text that Weiner wrote for her next production—a collaborative, happening-like "Fashion Show Poetry Event"—communicable information is very much a formal essence, here identified with poetry, that ricochets back and forth between writers and artists, between makers of language and makers of things:

> We communicated to the artists our generalized instructions. They translated instructions into sketches, models, and finally actual garments. The feedback (i.e., the garments) was then translated by us into fashion language. We have also translated this information into the language of press releases aimed at both the general and the fashion press and into the language of this theoretic essay.[21]

Weiner's contribution to the project was, as described by John Perreault, "a cape with hundreds of pockets proclaiming 'one should wear their own luggage.'"[22] But the materialized "instructions" of the poets bore within them numerous pores or holes that emblematized the "difference between a description and that which this description appears to describe ... the difference between a real fashion show and the imitation of a fashion show."[23] This final turn of phrase indicates Weiner's uneasiness with or perhaps skepticism about perfect communicability. The pores of noise inside the message indicate its natural degradation, its tendency toward entropy, but also create a margin of error in which creative interpretation and misinterpretation might thrive.

First as salesperson, then as manager, Weiner during this period remains preoccupied with labor as much as with the mundane, everyday activities that fill up our waking hours. Weiner, it is clear, aims to bring the special resources of art to bear on labor in a way that humanizes it, makes it seem more tolerable and pleasant, based on cooperation rather than competition, abundance rather than scarcity, participation rather than hierarchy: for example, her piece *World Works*, where she modified a shop sign by writing "the word THE over WORLD WORKS."[24] The addition of the article changes "works" from noun to verb, suggesting the presence of unnamed agents, workers. It thus demystifies the impersonal "works," but it also presents a certain assurance that things function as they should, that there is an invisible order that equilibrates the functioning of things:

> I wanted to do World Works because I wanted to create the feeling that people all over the world were doing a related thing at a related time, although they would be doing it individually, without an audience and without knowledge of what others were doing. It is an act of faith. We have unknown collaborators.[25]

Weiner's description of her intentions with regard to this act of *détournement* is oddly reminiscent of contemporaneous descriptions of the powers of the market and the price mechanism, which in the formulations of a thinker like Friedrich Hayek effects a decentralized system of coordination, through which, without knowing it, private producers and workers together plan for the optimal allocation of scarce resources. "The marvel" of the price mechanism, writes Hayek,

> is that in a case like that of a scarcity of one raw material, without an order being issued, without more than perhaps a handful of people knowing the cause, tens of thousands of people whose identity could not be ascertained by months of investigation, are made to use the material or its products more sparingly; i.e., they move in the right direction.[26]

For Hayek, the price mechanism is fundamentally a form of information distribution—he compares it to a "system of telecommunications"—that enables everybody to have the information they need under conditions in which it would be impossible for any one person to have all the information everyone needs, as in a command economy. The important difference is that for Hayek the coordinating information functions through competition, because each private producer is trying to minimize costs and earn the highest profit. *World Works*, on the other hand, imagines the coordination as collaborative rather than competitive.

In other conceptual and performance pieces from the same period, a different, much less positive "feeling" about labor emerges. This is especially true of Weiner's contribution to *Street Works*, a series of street exhibits put together by the Architectural League of New York. In *Street Works IV* (October 1969), for instance, Weiner hires a frankfurter wagon and distributes free wieners (a pun on her name). Although she intends to continue with the idea, established with *Hannah Weiner at Her Job*, that art is a form of self-distribution, a way of making the self available, and thereby transforming the self through a process of free giving and receiving, here the fact that "anything or anybody can have anything or anybody's name" takes on a sinister character.[27] The gift economy made possible through the sharing of the product—the wiener that is a stand-in for Weiner herself—is troubled by the consequences of that very objectification, which she characterizes in her description of the project as embalmment: "Unfortunately wieners (and pastrami, bologna, preserved meats) contain sodium nitrite and sodium nitrate; one a coloring agent for otherwise gray meat, one an embalming fluid. Both have a depressing effect on the mind." Finally, in *Street Works V* (Dec. 21, 1969), Weiner cements the foregoing negative associations by playing the role of another type of street worker: "I stood on a street corner, or in a doorway, as if I were soliciting. Women do that in that neighborhood (3rd Ave & 13 St to 3rd Ave & 14th St). It is not a nice feeling at all."[28]

What distinguishes the first few examples, with their positive images of "fun and friendly" labor, from the latter examples, based on the unpleasant affects she associates with prostitution? One answer might lie in the term "self-respect." In the first examples, "the art" of "live people" allows for "self-respect," which means, I think, less a way of appreciating the self than a way of distinguishing it, making it into something unique and specific. There are forms of interaction between selves that deepen their self-respect or singularity, and then there are interactions that mean a loss of self and the total fungibility of all individuals, the reduction of individuals to a situation where "anything or anybody can have anything or anybody's name," where there is no difference between Wiener and Weiner, between Norbert, Hannah, or a slab of pastrami.

The Double Life of Information

As it happens, this sense of self-respect accords with the technical definition of "information" supplied by Norbert Wiener in his attempt to define the forms of self-regulation and feedback operative in the servomechanism. Wiener borrows the description of "information" from Claude Shannon, a Bell Laboratories researcher who, in the 1940s, was looking for a mathematical description of the limits to information compression, since this would essentially define the maximum cost-efficiency of telephonic technology. Shannon found that the mathematics necessary for defining information in this way had already been developed in the thermodynamic physics of Josiah Willard Gibbs and Ludwig Von Boltzmann, who had formulated the Second Law of Thermodynamics (the law of increasing entropy) in statistical terms. Entropy, in the broadest sense, is the measure of a system's loss of free energy or, in terms that are important for us here, its loss of ability to do work. The more diffuse and disordered a system, the less free energy it has and the higher its entropy. Boltzmann measured entropy as a logarithmic function of the number of possible arrangements of molecules that might underlie any observed system. We measure physical systems, for the most part, in the aggregate: measuring their temperature, for instance. But these aggregate observations can correspond to a higher or lower number of probabilistic arrangements of the underlying molecules and thus a higher or lower entropy. N. Katherine Hayles, in an excellent book chapter on Shannon and his predecessors, explains the relationship between the observed macrostate and the underlying microstate using the well-known difference between permutations and combinations.[29] Imagine a system of four coins. If we somehow observe that there are two heads or two tails (perhaps heads reflect more light than the obverse and we are able to measure the total light), then we can also calculate that there are six possible arrangements, microstates, of the four coins that give us such a result: (1) HHTT, (2) HTHT, (3) HTTH, (4) TTHH, (5) THTH, (6) THHT. This single combination, two heads and two tails, yields six permutations. But what happens if we observe three heads and one tail? In that case there are only four possible arrangements that could give us our result. We therefore say that the entropy of our system is lower, as the underlying elements are less randomized. This second case is also statistically less likely, occurring in four out of sixteen cases, whereas the first occurs in six out of sixteen.

In Boltzmann, the more possible arrangements of molecules for any observed systems—in other words, the more randomized the positions of the underlying molecules and the more uncertain our knowledge of these molecules—the less free energy the system has and the higher its entropy.

States in which there is a great deal of internal order will have fewer possible microstates: solids have fewer possible microstates than gases, for instance. Entropy is therefore a curiously paradoxical measure: on the one hand, at the level of the microstate, it is a measure of unpredictability, randomness, chaos; on the other hand, at the surface level, the macrolevel, it is a measure of the *most likely outcome*, measure of the degree to which variety and distinction have been lost. In short, this paradoxical definition of entropy suggests that what is most predictable is unpredictability. For Wiener such conceptions correlate with a profound epistemological shift, one that he claims was far more monumental than the later developments in relativity and quantum mechanics for which it partially paved the way.[30]

Claude Shannon uses Boltzmann's probabilistic description of molecules to characterize acts of communication. He determines that the number of possible arrangements of the elements of a message directly correlates to the number of decisions or guesses a receiver would need to make to determine the correct arrangement. This measure of uncertainty corresponds directly to the amount of space a message will take up as binary digits, bits. Therefore, given a certain probability for various words, letters, and signs to appear in certain sequence, Shannon defines the "information" of a message as the inverse of its "guessability" by a receiver. The more surprised we are by a certain element, the more information it contains because, as the logic goes, the more our certainty increases once we know what element the message contains. In English, for instance, certain letters and words (*e* and *the*, for instance) occur in high frequencies: thus, they have low information. Letters and words like *z* or *entropy* occur infrequently, and thus they have high information. For example, if all of the vowels or all of the articles in the preceding sentence were missing, one might still guess its meaning. But if the consonants or verbs were removed, one would encounter a string of meaningless characters or an unparseable sentence. We can see, then, how this definition resembles the thermodynamic case—the higher-information messages, the messages with less guessable elements, less guessable letters and words, resemble the probable arrangement of underlying microstates in the case of high-entropy systems, where the molecules are highly randomized. Information and entropy are the same in this case, so Shannon defines "information" as a special case of entropy, Shannon entropy.

But if one accepts these relatively reasonable characterizations, then one is likewise forced to accept a scandalous and paradoxical conclusion: the more disordered and randomized the message, the higher its information. In this characterization, a string of gibberish might be higher in information than the sentences you are currently reading. Shannon's collaborator Warren Weaver is careful, however, to point out that things are not as dire as they might seem—if the subsequent element in a message has an exceedingly low probability, as in gibberish, that means that some other element has a relatively high probability. Therefore, gibberish is not necessarily higher in information than an intelligible sentence. The highest information values occur when the selection of one element is as unlikely as the selection of every other element. A coin that has a 50 percent chance of coming up tails or heads has higher information than a coin that comes up tails one out of ten flips and heads the rest of the time.

When Norbert Wiener adapts Shannon entropy—that is, information—to his nascent cybernetics, he does so in a manner that gives information a valence exactly opposite to Shannon's definition. Wiener defines information as the inverse of entropy. Information is that which gives systems internal coherence and differentiation, preserving them from the natural, frictional dissipation of thermodynamic run-down. Information is what distinguishes self-regulating adaptive machines, animals, and humans from inanimate static elements; it measures the degree to which a system can control its own behavior. For instance, the more information the antiaircraft gun has about the plane it is tracking, the better its targeting. Wiener arrives at this alternative conception of information by retaining the notion of information as statistical measure but focusing on the receiver and sender together rather than just the receiver. In this case, it becomes a measure of the degree of certainty and differentiation, not uncertainty. As Shannon put it in a letter to Wiener: "I consider how much information is *produced* when a choice is made from a set—the larger the set the *more* information. You consider the larger uncertainty in the case of a larger set to mean less knowledge and hence *less* information. The difference in viewpoint is partially a mathematical pun."[31] In other words, Shannon focuses on the conditions of the receiver of the message confronted with a range of possible choices, a receiver for whom the complexity and ultimate usefulness of a message are defined as the inverse of their statistical likelihood; Wiener considers the totality of the situation and the presence of complex messages as an index of the degree of control possible. Note how Wiener both conserves and inverts elements of Shannon and Boltzmann:

> Messages are themselves a form of pattern and organization. Indeed, it is possible to treat sets of messages as having an entropy like sets of states of the external world. Just as entropy is a measure of disorganization, the information carried by a set of messages is a measure of organization. In fact, it is possible to interpret the information carried by a message as essentially the negative of its entropy, and the negative logarithm of its probability. That is, the more probable the message, the less information it gives. Clichés for example are less illuminating than great poems.[32]

For Wiener, a more probable message or cliché is less highly ordered, whereas for Shannon it is more ordered. The great poem in Shannon's case is more entropic, more random, and less highly organized, whereas in Wiener's case the opposite is true. That this discussion takes the poem as its limit case is not surprising, especially considering the way that poetic novelty—the term for information theory is "surprisal"—increasingly became a function of processes of randomization, disordering, and fragmentation over the course of the twentieth century. In what we might term "Shannon poetry"—for instance, in the chance compositions, cut-ups, and experiments of the poets discussed in this book—aesthetic value does seem to track closely to the Shannon-Weaver definition. One values the capacity of poetic language to surprise and perhaps even confuse; this requires a mixture of the predictable and unpredictable (absolute gibberish becomes, as we know, monotonous). The goal of such a poetry is a situation in which all possibilities seem equally likely. Chaos and disorder are therefore productive, in the Shannon definition, whereas Wiener might accord with a more conservative, Horatian view of poetry that sees its value in its ability to delight and inform.

If we take a step back from the complexities that distinguish Shannon's and Wiener's different treatments of information, we realize that what's at stake is not really information as such, or information in itself, but information as transmitted and received. That is, these are treatments of communication instead of static data. Or rather, they are treatments of a social relationship mediated by communication, which comes to take on the name "information." There are invisible people in the examples Shannon and Wiener give: the information workers of midcentury—typists, switchboard operators, keypunch operators, stenographers, telegraphers, whose selections and choices constitute information and for whom the order or disorder of a message has a certain phenomenological tangibility. And in each account of information these people will have structurally different relationships to each other. In Norbert Wiener the focus is on the conservation of order against what he describes as the "Augustinian" enemy of entropy; order is a bulwark erected against frictional dissipation and decay. The focus is on homeostasis and on the self-regulating, conservative effect of feedback, the technical name for which is "negative feedback." In Shannon, however, we get a glimpse of a different perspective, one that will dominate as cybernetics evolves into systems theory and complexity theory. This is a view that sees order as emerging from chaos and focuses on the assembly of self-organizing eddies out of chaotic turbulence. It focuses more on change than stability, more on morphogenesis than homeostasis, more on positive feedback (or feed-forward) than negative feedback. The first vision corresponds to the problems and organizational concerns of the immediate postwar period—the Fordist manufacturing concern and the Keynesian planner state—in which rigid organizations sought to preserve structural stability through long-range planning, economies of scale, and a proliferation of controls. The second vision corresponds to the new organizational philosophy that reigns from the 1970s forward, in which productive dynamism and creative disorder are valued over stability and in which continuous restructurings, reassignments, mergers, and decompositions are celebrated as a way of remaining agile in the face of a volatile terrain marked by wild fluctuations in asset values and supply and demand. Such a view emphasizes plasticity over elasticity, flexibility over resilience.

Code Poems

Hannah Weiner's work from this period—especially her *Code Poems*—figures a moment of ambiguous transition between these different modes and their attendant perspectives, reflecting a certain ambiguous attitude toward order and disorder. While many of the white-collar workers that began to outnumber their blue-collar counterparts in the 1950s were managers, technicians, or professionals—what Robert Reich would later term "symbolic analysts"—many more were Taylorized clerics, working in the information mills of midcentury.[33] For them, the experience of informational order or disorder was quite real, and any technique for compressing or recoding the transmission of messages meant a restructuring of their work life, allowing them to handle greater and greater volumes of signs (in the same way that manufacturing technology allows a factory worker to handle a greater volume of raw materials).

Worries about this kind of overwhelming surfeit of information permeate "Trans-Space Communication," a short statement that Hannah Weiner wrote to accompany her performances of the *Code Poems* (composed using *The International Code of Signals for the Use of All Nations*, a nineteenth-century dictionary of phrases for Morse code, signal flags, and alphabet flags). Imagining a universalism (and internationalism) of language, Weiner writes that she wants to "develop methods of communication that will be understood face to face, or at any distance, regardless of language, country or planet of origin, by all sending and receiving."[34] This brings her poetic project into line with Shannon's technical project, however much she extends her concern with efficiency to the semantic as well. But alongside the wish for a universalizing, global language, there is also a pedagogical component to the code project, a concern "with the use of minimal cues: how much information can be received, and how accurately, through how little means."[35] Weiner realizes that this universalist goal founders on the sheer wash of channels and signals, the sheer entropy of information that modernity presents us with.

> The amount of information available has more than doubled since World War II. In the next ten years it will double again. How do we deal with it?
>
> Do we use more than 5% of the brain now in use?
>
> Do we process quicker?
>
> Do we decode information or put it in another form (not language) so that the present brain can handle it?[36]

This is information in the sense Shannon gives it: information as the empty place of communication, as entropy, noise, dissipation. As noted earlier, Norbert Wiener refers to this tendency toward dissipation as the "Augustinian" enemy—an enemy without connivance, cunning, or purpose: the "devil of confusion, not of willful malice," which the elaboration of purposeful mechanisms in line with humanistic goals can and must defeat. He writes: "Organism is opposed to chaos, to disintegration, to death, as message is to noise."[37]

To the extent that they offer an aesthetic simplification of the excessive information that modernity presents, Weiner's *Code Poems* demand to be seen in the same light as modernist universalisms like Esperanto, or C. K. Ogden and I. A. Richard's Basic English.[38] But this is also the modernism of Frederick Winslow Taylor and so-called scientific management, a key feature of which was the practice of "time and motion studies" that aimed to break down the actions of workers into component parts and identify, measure, and reconstruct them in more efficient ways. This analytic was formalized by Frank Gilbreth, who developed a notational script that could convert any motion into what he called "therbligs"—a set of eighteen fundamental actions (such as search, select, find, grab, hold).[39] Examining such notations side by side, one recognizes that the code of maritime signals and Gilbreth's therbligs are almost mirror images of each other: Weiner's code translates language into movement; Gilbreth's translates movement into language

The *Code Poems* do bear an uncanny resemblance to these instrumentalizing experiments. But one immediately notes the comedic, and sometimes absurdist, strains in the poems. Despite her stated goals in "Trans-Space Communication," the *Code Poems* end up as satires of hyperrationalized communication, since they are so often about failures of communication. They end up lampooning the administrative rationality behind these experiments. As in the formulations of Wiener and Shannon, the *Code Poems* find it very difficult to distinguish informational order from informational disorder, information from entropy, nonsense from clear command:

TQA Possible-ity

TQB	I doubt if it is possible
FRW	Barely possible
TQD	Is it possible?
TQE	Possibly
TQF	Quite possible
FBJ	As slow as possible
FBG	As quick as possible
FAI	As fast as possible
FBO	As soon as possible
FAY	As much (or, many) as possible
TQC	If possible
FOU	Avoid, if possible (impossible)
PFB	Not possible[40]

Written as an antiphon—a poem for two voices—"TQA Possible-ity" allows for a reflection on Shannon's and Wiener's seemingly opposed perspectives on communication. Here communicated information is a function of statistical possibility, yet, once reduced to this play of possible meanings, the communicated referent disappears. The poem seems more interested in enumerating the basic grammatical structures for expressing possibility than identifying the "it" to which such possibilities refer, so the poem is less about transparency and "trans-space communication" than secrecy. The two voices speak by innuendo and indirection, and the use of "minimal cues" excludes as much information as it includes. Far from something that might be understood by "all sending and receiving," meaning in the poem is context dependent, distributed, and impossible to ascertain from a central location. Information is a function of uncertainty, of "surprisal," as it is in Shannon's definition. Weiner performed these poems, sometimes with the help of the US Coast Guard, at poetry festivals in Central Park, at antiwar protests, at galleries, and on the street. During the Central Park poetry festival in 1968, the Coast Guard–assisted performance involved "alphabet flag hoists, semaphore signalmen, flashing light signals, megaphones, [and] flares."[41] But this action of making public, converting text to the movement of bodies, seems to carry within it the germ of a private language. For an observer, watching the poem performed by members of the Coast Guard with signal flags, such inscrutability would be nearly absolute, a form of total opacity rather than absolute transparency. Unless the audience were provided with a score or trained in deciphering the signals, the communication between the two signalers would be essentially meaningless.[42]

Even if Hannah Weiner sets out to compose models more in line with the other Wiener's vision of information, where information means determinate knowledge and provides structure and transparency, the model she arrives at looks much more like Shannon and Weaver's, where "freedom of choice, greater uncertainty, [and] greater information go hand in hand" and where it is impossible to distinguish between "uncertainty which arises by virtue of freedom of choice on the part of the sender" and "uncertainty which arises because of error or because of the influence of noise."[43] As cybernetics and systems theory develop, the lines between good and bad forms of uncertainty become increasingly blurred as the consequence of these initial definitions, such that for later proponents of "second-order cybernetics" and "systems theory" like Heinz von Foerster and Niklas Luhmann, the transformation and adaptation of systems emerges not despite noise but because of it. A "self-organizing system feeds upon noise," as von Foerster puts it.⁴⁴ In such scenarios, theorized grandly by Luhmann, the confusion of the individual interlocutors, their mutual opacity to each other, becomes the necessary condition for the self-organization of a social system that bases itself on their understanding of their communication and action but is unrecognizable by them as such. What matters is what the two interlocutors do, and this can happen despite misunderstanding. As Luhmann famously writes, "[O]nly communication can communicate."⁴⁵

The theories of management that emerge from this view will operate less through direct than indirect forms of control; workers do not need to be explicitly commanded to accomplish each and every task but should be given structures, protocols, and objectives that, leaving them freedom to choose, to select from a range of uncertain variables, nonetheless direct them toward certain results. In this view, "creativeness is correlated with the ability to withstand the lack of structure, the lack of future, lack of predictability, of control, the tolerance for ambiguity, for planlessness."⁴⁶ In one vision, the manager-subordinate relationship occurs through direct command, with some process of feedback to ensure precision that targets are being met. In the other, the manager provides resources and materials and some indication of the goal and assumes the capacity of the subordinate to independently develop methods of achieving the goal. The first corresponds to the authoritarian Theory X that McGregor describes, one that would assume, per Wiener, a direct connection between explicit communication and control. The second corresponds to the humanistic Theory Y that assumes people are motivated by mysterious desires for self-fulfillment and recognition that can be activated by reducing direct control. Management, here, is "a process primarily of creating opportunities, releasing potential, removing obstacles, encouraging growth, providing guidance."⁴⁷ But Theory Y is, for McGregor, just a hypothesis about how people might act, if the correct conditions are established, and the kind of self-regulating subjectivity at play in such workers remains mysterious. In this situation, the consciousness of the worker, motivated by mysterious inner drives, is what cybernetics calls a black box, an entity whose precise manner of function is unknown but whose behavior one can predict and even manipulate through the adjustment of inputs and observation of the corresponding outputs. You might get a scenario that looks like this:

LWC	Follow Me
LWC	Follow me
LWF	Will you lead?
LWF	Will you follow?
LWJ	Shall I follow?
LWK	I will follow
LWC	Follow me
LWF	Will you lead?
LWG	Will you follow?
LWJ	Shall I follow?
LWK	I will follow
LWC	Follow me
LWF	Will you lead?
LWG	Will you follow?
LWJ	Shall I follow?
LWK	I will follow
LWC	Follow me
LWF	Will you lead?
LWG	Will you follow?
LWJ	Shall I follow?
LWK	I will follow
LWC	Follow me
LWF	Will you lead?
LWG	Will you follow?
LWK	Shall I follow?
LWK	I will follow
LWC	Follow me
LWF	Will you lead?[48]

In this poem, five different phrases—each one displaying a different stance toward the question of authority, toward leading or following—rotate through the two speaking parts without leading to any resolution. The poem portrays the kind of confusion that can result when people, habituated to acting within explicit power structures and hierarchies, find themselves forced to function without them. For the reader encountering this poem on the page, rather than in performance, this confusion is modeled by the different ordinal positions the word *follow* takes, appearing now at the end of the sentence and now at the beginning, alternately leading the way and then falling behind, at the same time as the word *lead* consistently falls at the end of an interrogative sentence, or in other words, in a "following" position. In a certain respect, "LWC Follow Me" renders the linguistic indeterminacy and misprision of "TQA Possible-ity" as comedy of errors or farce. There is more than a little of the blind-leading-the-blind humor that is a staple of such genres, from Shakespeare through to Beckett. But there is something rather earnest, too, about the antiauthoritarian stance of the poem, one that does not so much destroy the structures of domination and submission crystallized in the maritime code as render them transient, internalizable, and reversible. Just as the science of cybernetics was supported, materially and otherwise, by the military-industrial complex, this poem is performed by the disciplined bodies of the Coast Guard, underwritten directly by the US military, a fact that no doubt ironizes any claim to have overcome hierarchy. Still, while leadership qua leadership is not exactly overcome, each of the two voices here gets its turn as leader (and follower).

Hannah Weiner's remarkable poem might be read, therefore, in one of two ways: on the one hand, it is a model of the subjective attitudes and affects that the new, self-managing flexible worker will need to develop to weather the constant disaggregations, restructurings, and downsizings of the decades to come, a model of the adaptivity, mutability, and openness to contingency that employers will demand from their workers. On the other hand, it is a critique in advance of these new participatory models, revealing the violence and disorientation inherent in them. If these critical challenges are open to recuperation, they are also engineered to challenge that recuperation, in ways that are addressed more to us and to the conditions of the present than to her contemporaries.

The Value of Information

As a model for corporate organization, cybernetics does not so much banish management as distribute it throughout the firm. Management becomes less a set of persons than an intermediating form, an infrastructure. For cybernetics, control and communication are identical. Management, in this sense, is nothing more than the messages, the information coursing through a firm. Following the cybernetic logic a little bit further, we can say that information is the form of self-regulation that firms use to avoid succumbing to entropy and disorder. Information is organization, and good information, so the logic goes, can replace direct command by managers. The new digital computing technologies that have become, since the 1970s, an increasingly central part of workplaces are, in this regard, often more about controlling workers and pushing them to work harder than they are about making work more efficient.

In thermodynamic theory, as a system becomes more entropic, it loses its ability to do *work*. Therefore, if information is opposed to entropy, information should be the equivalent of work. Information is able to contravene the natural dissipative tendencies of the universe and the workplace. This is the basic thought behind James Clerk Maxwell's famous thought experiment, in which "a being whose faculties are so sharpened that he can follow every molecule in its course" sits in a two-chambered box and is able to circumvent the tendency of entropy to increase by directing faster molecules into one chamber and keeping the slower ones in the other.[49] This demon, as later commentators would call the being, is able to use information to beat the odds at the universe's casino and essentially reverse the direction of entropy. Those pondering the paradox Maxwell left behind—such as Leo Szilard and Leon Brillouin (whose interpretation Norbert Wiener followed)—concluded that this information would not in fact be entropy free.[50] It would require radiation of some sort, and that radiation would mean that somewhere entropy would rise. Information may temporarily order molecules and reverse the flow of entropy, but this was work that would increase the entropy elsewhere. The ability of information to overcome the natural entropic drift of the universe was limited, since information was produced by work in the same way that more prosaic kinds of combustion are work.

Anxieties over the becoming-prosaic of information are made explicit in Thomas Pynchon's famous treatment of Maxwell's Demon in *The Crying of Lot 49*, a novel that makes the contest between entropy and information an organizing motif. When Oedipa Maas gets lost in the offices of an aerospace firm, she comes across a disgruntled engineer, Stanley Koteks, who complains to her that the new corporate culture of teamwork has removed all initiative and responsibility from the workplace. He is especially angry that engineers no longer have patent rights to the work they do, voicing a complaint that is, as Andrew Hoberek and Stephen Schryer have shown, typical of a middle class suddenly composed not of petty proprietors and independent professionals but of salaried employees.[51] Apropos of nothing, Koteks brings up the "Nefastis Machine," invented by one John Nefastis, which has made Maxwell's Demon a reality, "violating the Second Law of Thermodynamics, getting something for nothing, causing perpetual motion."[52] As Koteks explains, "Since the Demon only sat and sorted, you wouldn't have put any *real* work into the system" (emphasis mine). The implication of this non-sequitur act of mansplaining by Koteks is that the kind of invention that engineers used to do has a special virtue because it is not "real" work of a physical variety. Corporate restructurings of the sort that were happening at Yoyodyne were offensive because they turned this intellectual work into physical work like any other, a possibility of which Oedipa reminds Koteks, when she asks, in response to his explanation, "Sorting isn't work? . . . Tell them down in the post office, you'll find yourself in a mail bag heading for Fairbanks, Alaska."[53] The question about information is whether or not it is drudge work like any other or a special form-giving entity capable of producing unforeseen results.

Oedipa's retort might have been issued to any number of contemporary celebrations of information and its newfound powers, as the word had become, by the mid-1960s, imbued with all sorts of new associations. Thinkers like Daniel Bell declared that capitalism, in its new postindustrial variant, no longer fit with the labor theory of value but instead required a new knowledge theory of value. Information was the central commodity of the postwar economic order; information was to postindustrial capitalism what textiles and automobiles were to earlier periods.[54] But information was a particularly thorny commodity for a capitalist system, in Bell's view, since it was difficult for an individual to "own" it in the same way one owns a property, and even intellectual property law provided little recourse for those trying to safeguard the value it provided. Information has a tendency, therefore, to devalue as it becomes generalized.[55] Norbert Wiener makes similar remarks about information and its difference from other types of commodities in a fairly convoluted chapter of *The Human Use of Human Beings* concerned largely with a critique of existing scientific and government policy around classified information. Anticipating the ideas of hackers and cyberlibertarians decades hence, Wiener writes that at present "the invention is losing its identity as a commodity in the face of the general intellectual structure of emergent inventions."[56] For Wiener, information cannot really be commodified in the same way that physical goods can. The more information is generalized, the less valuable it becomes. At the same time, information value exists only relationally, since it cannot be stored as one can store other commodities. The fundamentally "lossy" character of information as store of value seems to speak to the agonies of a slowly devalorized intellectual class articulated by characters like Koteks.

If intellectual workers like Koteks reacted negatively to the deskilling and devaluing of their labor as information, many artists and writers were, on the contrary, tentatively and critically optimistic about it, imagining the transformation of literary or art skill into information as providing an escape from the individualization, isolation, and social precariousness of the artist and the transformation of art making or writing into a labor undertaken as part of a larger system. Information would enable art to become plural, collective, even democratic (since a deskilled art, one that no longer required particular training or talent, could be made by all). Many of the artists included in the seminal MoMA exhibit *Information* in 1970 not only demonstrated the extent of the cybernetic vocabulary of the time but the sense in which, when artists took information as their medium rather than paint, plaster, or metal, they imagined themselves as museum or gallery workers, part of a larger institutional conglomeration mediated by information.[57]

An example of this thematic is Dan Graham's early *Works for Magazine Pages*, conceptual compositions originally designed for display in magazines only (though some were exhibited in museums and galleries, including the *Information* exhibit). Graham began these works after a failed attempt to run a gallery and suggests that "[they] could be read as a reaction against the gallery experience."[58] The experience of failure caused Graham to meditate on what rendered art visible and valuable. Taking his cue from Dan Flavin's lighting installations, which were based not on the art object itself but the peripheral supports, like lighting, that the art object needed in order to be encountered and appreciated, Graham decided to make art out of and as another kind peripherality, the magazine advertisement. Like Flavin, Graham turned *parergon* into *ergon*, advertisement into the thing advertised:

> Through the actual experience of running a gallery, I learned that if a work of art was not written about and reproduced in a magazine, it would have difficulty attaining the status of "art." It seemed that to be defined as having value (that is, a value as "art"), a work had only to be exhibited in a gallery and then to be written about and reproduced as a photograph in an art magazine. It was this record of the no-longer-extant installation, along with more accretions of information after the fact, that became the basis for the art work's fame and, to a large extent, its economic value.[59]

By focusing on these "accretions of information" and making art that consisted of no more than these acts of publicity, Graham participated in the general shift from the production of artistic goods to the provision of artistic services, analogous to and contemporaneous with the broader historical turn from blue-collar manufacturing to white-collar administration and service work discussed frequently in the preceding pages. The difference is that Graham's magazine pages imagine a white-collar work that is no longer accessory to some other activity but an end in and of itself. The result is that many of his *Works for Magazine Pages* perform the kind of absurdist circularity and self-referentiality that we will recognize from Weiner's poems. Since the supporting material has become the art itself, it no longer refers to anything beyond the space of the magazine. It is entirely hermetic and self-referential. Emptied of content, Graham's definition of information resembles Shannon's to a very strong degree. We might read this as a response to the kinds of anxieties that characters like Koteks voiced, an attempt by white-collar workers to make themselves autonomous from the various corporate processes that they facilitated rather than accessory or peripheral to them, as must necessarily be the case. Perhaps, therefore, Graham's pages are a recognition, through negation, of the fundamentally auxiliary character of white-collar labor.

The most famous of these works is probably *Schema* and its variants, a series of magazine ads that describe themselves according to a list, the schema, of all the requisite qualities of the ads, such as "number of adjectives," "paper stock," and "typeface." As the editor of the magazine makes decisions about the things over which the magazine has control—font, ad size, and so on—some of the qualities will change. Each ad is therefore singular in its self-referentiality. But it is also curiously incomplete. As Graham writes,

> If . . . the editor follow[s] the logic step-by-step (linearly) it would be found impossible to compose a completed version as each of the component lines of exact data requiring completion (in terms of specific numbers and percentages) would be contingently determined by every other number or percentage which itself would in turn be determined by the other numbers or percentages, *ad infinitum*.[60]

Although the logic here is rather transparently false (one could, moving back and forth among the qualities iteratively, arrive at a final form, without encountering an infinite recursion), what matters is that Graham experiences this search for an airtight self-referentiality, an autonomous act of white-collar accounting, as essentially impossible. White-collar labor as well as the peripheral actions of art institutions and enterprises will therefore always be dependent rather than independent processes.

Graham refers to this schema as a poem, but it is also in its way a code, and it bears the same wish for complete and transparent determination (with the same resulting emptiness) as Weiner's poems. As Graham writes, "It is not 'art for art's sake.' Its medium is in-formation. Its communicative value and comprehension is immediate, particular and altered as it fits the terms (and time) of its system or (the) context (it may be read in)."[61] As with the definition of information that Shannon gives us, a definition that Graham was certainly aware of, what we get here is a materialization of form, "a 'shell' placed between the external empty material of place and the interior 'empty' material of 'language.'" For Graham, such self-referentiality "subverts value." "Beyond its appearance in print or present currency, 'Schema (March, 1966)' is disposable; with no dependence on material (commodity), it subverts the gallery (economic) system."[62]

But just how subversive is this? Is this a subversion of value and the commodity form or its apotheosis? One is cautioned here by the remarkable revelation that emerges in the "Postface" to Lucy Lippard's seminal work *Six Years: The Dematerialization of the Art Object from 1966 to 1972*. Recanting her own utopian claims for dematerialized art, she realizes in hindsight that "[h]opes that 'conceptual art' would be able to avoid the general commercialization, the destructively 'progressive' approach of modernism were for the most part unfounded."[63] For Jeff Wall, who, in seeking to explain Dan Graham's turn away from the hard conceptualism of the *Works for Magazine Pages*, provides one of the most compelling accounts of the fortunes of conceptual art, such failure had to do with secular changes in the economy: "Speculative, inflation-driven capital enclosed and reorganized the art world, spectacularly driving up prices on a broad front. Thus the anti-objects of conceptualism were 'absorbed' and 'negated' (to use the Marcusian terms of the period) as critical intervention by the aura of value imposed upon them by speculation."[64] In Wall's account, the 1970s were a moment of reorganization for both the art market and the larger economy, a reorganization predicated on conceptual art's reaction to the art of the 1960s that, in turn, gave way to the mercenary garishness of the 1980s neo-expressionist revival. In attempting to supersede the dumb theatricality of the minimal object or the craven solicitousness of pop art, conceptual art failed because its utopianism, its wish to transcend market, spectacle, and commodity could often do little more than reflect the hated structures in ironic paraphrase: conceptual works concretized "the cultural dilemma of the falsification and ruination of art by mimicking that ruination; reflecting it in their own structure." Conceptualism is therefore hamstrung by an "ironic mimicry of the mechanisms for control and falsification of information and social knowledge whose despotic and seductive forms of display are copied to make language."[65] This claim chimes with an equally important essay on conceptualism by Benjamin Buchloh, who argues that such projects were paralyzed by a form of critique that could only mimic that which it sought to negate, assuming from the start that the limits imposed by the commodity form were insuperable. They could critique commodification only through a ritualized performance of commodification. Because of their fidelity to a stale and ultimately tautological scientific positivism, for Buchloh the cancellation of pop art and minimalism in conceptual art meant, in essence, nothing more than "replacing an aesthetic of industrial production and consumption with an aesthetic of administrative and legal organization and institutional validation."[66]

Even if we agree with Lippard contra Buchloh that there was a genuinely utopian strain within many of the experiments of the period, a genuine desire to destroy the commodity character of art, what Buchloh's article shows us is that most conceptual art could imagine such destruction only because it confused the production of commodities with the production of tangible objects as such. Not understanding that commodification is, first and foremost, a set of social relations, much conceptual art thought that by refusing materiality (of a certain sort), it could refuse commodities. It thus simply shifted the locus of art making from the production of commodified objects to commodified services, events, or concepts, mimicking the shift already under way from manufacturing to white-collar and service-sector work.

In Graham's statements about *Schema*, the situation is a bit more complex, since he realizes that the symbolic or conceptual apparatus that surrounds the art object—the work of gallerists, advertisers, and various clericals—is what gives art value, not what takes value away from it. Where he errs, though, is in thinking that detaching such administrative work from material objects will destroy its status as commodity and bearer of value: even dematerialized processes or services can have value; commodities do not need a material base.

In fact, his claims about the subversion of value effected by *Schema* are directly contradicted by a later magazine work, *INCOME (Outflow) PIECE* (1969). Following in a tradition of similar money art—Duchamp's *Monte Carlo Bond* (a photo collage in the form of a bond, sold to raise money for a trip to the casinos), for instance, or Yves Klein's exchange of gold for "zones de sensibilité picturale immatérielle"—Graham incorporated himself (or intended to) and then made shares of Dan Graham Inc. available for ten dollars each: "The 'object' ... will be to pay Dan Graham, myself, the salary of the average American citizen out of the pool of collected income." Making clear his association of cybernetics, information theory, and economic thought, he describes this experiment as follows:

> [T]he artist changes the homeostatic balance of his life (environment) support by re-relating the categories of *private* sector and *public* sector; a modus operandi, a social sign, a sign of the times, a personal locus of attention, a *shift* of the matter/energy balance *to mediating my needs*—the artist places himself as a situational vector to sustain his existence and projected future (further) activities in the world. Money is a service commodity: in come and out go while in-formation.[67]

In such a situation, what the shareholders would buy is not an actual art object, nor much less ownership over Dan Graham and his productions, but "information on social motives and categorization whose structure upholds, reveals in its functioning, the socio-economic support system of media."[68] Graham sells information about selling, making himself into a market researcher. Although he never had any buyers, Graham's original plan was to field responses to the stock offering, feedback, and then use this to gradually transform the magazine advertisements.

Given his earlier statements, I think it is clear that Graham intends to subvert value in this case by extracting value from valueless activity. That is, the work is meant ironically. Like the Duchamp examples he follows, he means to show the merely nominal and arbitrary character of economic value with regard to art and, perhaps, with regard to all things. The work is ironic in the very specific sense of the term; it means to prove a point opposite to its apparent significance. But in another sense, this negative characteristic of the work, its attempt to negate art value as such, hides the ways in which it is actively developing a model of subjectivity and self-transformation with which we are already familiar. This is a model of the worker as endlessly adaptive, responding and modulating one's activities in response to feedback. We note that this model of the self is built on an entrepreneurial metaphor, where the self becomes analogized with a business, and the relations between individuals, mediated here by the cyberneticized feedback of information, are figured as market relations.[69] We can sum up as follows: while the reduction of art to nothing more than information seems to mean, in Graham, a destruction of art value and art work (enabling someone to draw revenue from the world at will), the entire practice is really part of an experimental development of a new regime of flexible, adaptive, white-collar work based on an internalization of market values.

This is quite clear in Dan Graham's video installations from the 1970s. Though most read these works by way of Lacanian psychoanalysis, particularly Lacan's ideas about the mirror stage, or a Foucauldian thematic of surveillance, given the previous analysis we can see very quickly that both surveillance and ego image in these works are part of a larger project, borrowed from cybernetics, of modeling self-regulating, adaptive subjects. The mechanisms of self-observation in these works—combining mirrors, video cameras, displays, and other devices—resemble, in no uncertain terms, the increasingly prevalent attempt to make workers self-managing and self-modulating, to instantiate mechanisms of adaptation and self-training that could cope with the volatilities of capitalist production.

For a privileged sector of the workforce, "learning is the new form of labour," as Shoshana Zuboff writes.[70] Companies are impelled to restructure around a flexible, adaptive core of workers and then rely on another sector of workers—temporary workers, sometimes outsourced or offshored, without benefits or privileges—to expand as market conditions prevail. For this core group of workers, though, the values that we associate with the creative class, or with marginal, bohemian groups, have become indispensable to production: in other words, as Seltzer and Bentley describe it, firms inculcate in these workers "an individual autonomy" and "a questioning attitude to received wisdom."

> As conditions change more rapidly, companies are more likely to recruit for adaptability and fresh ideas rather than standardised skills and experience. This is reflected in the shift away from industry specific skills and competencies towards more personal qualities and "soft" skills such as communication, teamwork, reliability, problem solving, positive attitudes towards learning and the capacity to manage one's own training.[71]

Dan Graham's video works are an early exposition of this endlessly plastic and mutable subject, one whose self-mutation is mediated by a temporal technology that makes the present part of a feedback loop between past and future, between adaptation and prediction. In *Present Continuous Past(s)*, for instance, one of his first video works, Graham establishes an opposition between present and past, mirror and video screen: the former reflects "present" time, and the latter, through an eight-second delay on a closed-circuit TV, reflects the past. The piece consists of a small room, a cube, not much larger across than the inhabitant is high. On one wall, at eye level, there is a video camera and directly below it, a video display. The opposite and adjacent walls are mirrored. On the video screen, the inhabitants of the room will see (provided that they have not occluded the camera's view of the far wall) their own image eight seconds earlier and, in the far mirror, a small thumbnail of their own image sixteen seconds earlier, inside of which, of course, is an infinitely nested series of thumbnail images of past times, becoming gradually more illegible. For Graham, this opposition between mirror and video screen is, as he says, a way of destroying the illusions of depth and self-presence that the ego ideal of the mirror presents: "Unlike the flat visuality of Renaissance painting, in the video image geometrical surfaces are lost to ambiguously modeled contours and to a translucent depth."[72] As Eric de Bruyn argues, Graham's video works involve a topological imagination based in large part on cybernetic concepts, producing an inversion of the spaces of interior and exterior.[73] If the mirror in *Present Continuous Past(s)* displays the body image, an image that naturally displaces the perceiving subject, a subject that, in Lacan's famous formulation, then experiences itself as missing, the video displays not outsides but insides, exteriorizing the interior, remembered perceptions of the subject, which are themselves splayed and flattened, unfolded onto the surface of the video screen. As Graham writes,

> This [video feedback] removes self-perception from the viewing of a detached, static image; video feedback contradicts the mirror model of the perceiving "self." Through the use of videotape feedback, the performer and the audience, the perceiver and his process of perception, are linked, co-identified. Psychological premises of "privacy" (as against publicness) which would derive from the mirror-model, depend on an assumed split between observed behavior and supposedly observable, interior *intention*. However, if a perceiver views his behavior on a five to eight second delay via videotape (so that his responses are part of and influence his perception), "private" mental intention and external behavior are experienced as one.[74]

This is, of course, a bit of rhetorical sleight of hand, since all that Graham has done is transform the antagonism between (absent) perceiving subject and self-image from a spatial to a temporal dynamic. As anyone who has ever tried to point a video camera at the screen to which it outputs will know, this kind of internal self-presentation is strictly impossible, in spatial terms. Once output becomes identical with input, all that appears on the screen is a kind of visual noise.

Nonetheless, however idealized in its effects, *Present Continuous Past(s)* clearly brings into opposition two different kinds of subjectivity. The first, associated with the mirror, is that of an angst-ridden subject, whose identity remains trapped in a perpetual present of either changelessness or constant change. The second, associated with video, is an adaptive, flexible, self-modulating subject, who calculates present and future according to a receding series of past self-images. The latter correlates with the new kind of worker valorized by what Boltanski and Chiapello describe as the "projective city" and the ideology of "connexionism." In their account, as capitalism restructured according to a new logic that subsumed the artistic critique and backgrounded the social one, by making work for a certain sector of the workforce ostensibly more creative, participatory, and democratic, the result was an adverbialization of job titles and the construction of work situations where the employee is defined by *projects* and not by positions, followed by a whole ideology of flexibility, connectivity, and personability.[75] Such changes were effected not only to counter the effects of the artistic critique but to deal with the problems of corporate rigidity and bureaucratic sclerosis.

Present Continuous Past(s) presents an image of the "great man" in this society, one who conforms to the new justificatory logics of merit in a connexionist or "projective" society. These new business management rhetorics were, in part, a popularization of ideas developed in management cybernetics, which imagined responding to the problems of organizational inefficiency by remaking the corporation along the lines of the cybernetic organism. One can hardly mistake the similarity between cybernetics and the 1990s management texts from which Boltanski and Chiapello build their case:

> Far from being attached to an occupation or clinging to a qualification, the great man proves *adaptable* and *flexible*, able to switch from one situation to a very different one, and adjust to it; and *versatile*, capable of changing activity or tools, depending on the nature of the relationship entered into with others or with objects. It is

precisely this adaptability and versatility that make him employable—that is to say, in the world of firms, to attach himself to new projects.⁷⁶

Most important, obviously, is the notion that the new workplace modes that respond to the crisis of the 1960s and 1970s recuperate the left critique that emerged among social movements, artists, and various countercultural groups. Artistic experiments like Graham's therefore become laboratories of new organizational relations and managerial techniques, but relations and techniques whose ultimate meaning remains contingent on the uses to which they are put. There is no way to say, before the fact, whether a critique will be a true threat to the rule of capital or not; what is potentially revolutionary in one moment can become definitively system reinforcing in another. We must be cautious, therefore, about easily leaping from an analysis of particular artistic and cultural logics to an account of the uses to which such logic is ultimately put.

While *Present Continuous Past(s)* presents the transformation of the technical conditions of selfhood and the emergence of the adaptive, flexible worker, later video works expand on this rudiment by modeling the cybernetics of not just the relation to self but relation to others as well. Perhaps the most salient of these, for our present purposes, is *Video Piece for Two Glass Office Buildings*, which uses video cameras, mirrors, and monitors to mediate between two disconnected workspaces. For Graham, reflecting on the emancipatory potential of closed-circuit TV, the new medium of video is importantly distinct from its parent medium, film: "The centralized production facilities of film or broadcast TV exploit the saleable (product) aspects of culture at the expense of the existential. A cable system, by contrast, presents the possibility of becoming two-way and decentralized. Individuals, families and the local, extant cultural system could be given potential self-determination and control. Local cable television could feed *back* the immediate environment."⁷⁷ *Two Glass Office Buildings* makes these potentials explicit: inhabitants in facing buildings find the same video camera mounted on a monitor as in *Present Continuous Past(s)* and are similarly wedged between the camera-monitor apparatus and the mirror facing it. But unlike the monitor in *Present Continuous Past(s)*, the monitor displays the recording from the camera in the opposite building, a recording that now includes the other inhabitant's room and, reflected in the mirror, the other inhabitant's monitor, which contains an image of her own room, delayed by eight seconds. This self-image competes, as it were, with the view into her own room reflected in the mirror, a view that depends on the relative opacity or transparency of the interceding windows. Graham thinks of this interbuilding figure-eight topology as breaking the impersonality and opacity of the submodernist office building, with its rhetorics of "structural and functional efficiency." *Two Glass Office Buildings* aims to invert the rhetorical codes of the glass and steel building, where "the glass's literal transparency not only falsely objectifies reality, but is a paradoxical camouflage; for while the actual functioning of a corporation may be to concentrate its self-contained power and control by *secreting* information, its architectural façade gives the illusion of absolute openness. The transparency is visual only; glass separates the visual from the verbal, insulating outsiders from the content of the decision-making processes, and from the invisible but real interrelationships linking company operations to society."[78]

We should see very quickly how Graham's architectural critique is really an organizational critique, and his claims about modernist office buildings are really claims about the hierarchical work relations they house. Graham aims to break open these organizational structures through the dehierarchizing power of a bidirectional video channel, where the commanded is commander, the manager an employee, the employee a manager, and where, furthermore, the relationships between workers and consumers, or workers and citizens, are overturned. We should note here as well the role that transparency plays. Rather than direct hierarchical commands, transparency—that is, open information—allows for reciprocal relations to develop among people.

Graham's video installations are therefore part of an experimental development of relations of self-management among workers, where management is contained within the flows of transparent information rather than effected directly by personalities. But the turn to the artistic critique by firms was less a capitulation than a chance to substitute a "psychological" compensation for increased material insecurity, as Boltanski and Chiapello note. Furthermore, self-management is often the face of an increasingly intensive work regime, now self-administered rather than sent down from on high, as workers internalize an entrepreneurial ethos:

> [I]n the case of wage-earners who have not been casualized the fact that autonomy has been granted in exchange for the assumption of greater responsibility, or in the context of a general recasting of working methods, results in a paradox revealed by surveys into working conditions: wage-earners are *simultaneously* more autonomous and more constrained. . . .

The creation of "zones of autonomy" at work really does allow workers to experience a "dignity at work" that was "unheard of on the Taylorist assembly line." But it is accompanied by numerous new constraints associated with the reduction in stocks, versatility, and the creation of responsibility for maintenance, which tend to increase the mental burdens. In addition, these new zones of autonomy are narrowly framed by procedural constraints. The activities undertaken are in fact framed increasingly and monitored by computer systems that not only define the relevant categories recognized by the system, but give them a "prescriptive force," which leads to structuring tasks through "grammars of action." Moreover, there is no doubt that it was the computer revolution in control which helped to facilitate employers' conversion to the theme of autonomy.[79]

Two Glass Office Buildings obviously bears a deep resemblance to the dialogic *Code Poems*, inasmuch as both works model reciprocal, flexible relations between people mediated by information and processes of feedback. Both examples construct new models of subjectivity, intersubjectivity, and work, modeled on the servomechanism and the feedback loop, anticipating the development of digital and network technology in the decades to come. Information, however, takes on a curious doubleness in these projects. On the one hand, it provides the capacity to liberate activities from social control, whether the control of the art system or the corporate workplace. On the other hand, it has the tendency to generate systems characterized by disorientation and anxious self-consciousness, in marked contrast to the rhetoric that Weiner and Graham use to describe their goals. The narrative of critique and recuperation I offer here admits, then, of an additional layer, since the overcoding of the sincere utopianism of these works with negative affects manages to foretell, and even perhaps to respond in advance to, the uses to which their speculations will be put.

The Feminization of Speedup

For many readers, discussion of the restructuring of labor from the 1970s forward will bring to mind a singular figure and image: the office. While previous chapters have addressed office and white-collar work from the standpoint of office hierarchies, relations, and technologies, one very crucial aspect of the office and office work has remained unexamined—the gender of office work, particularly the growth in feminized and poorly paid clerical or secretarial work in the postwar period. In a telling turn of phrase, gadfly conceptual writer Kenneth Goldsmith (discussed in Chapter 5) asserts that "contemporary writing requires the expertise of a secretary crossed with the attitude of a pirate: replicating, organizing, mirroring, archiving, and reprinting, along with a more clandestine proclivity for bootlegging, plundering, hoarding, and file-sharing."[1] In associating office work and contemporary writing and art, Goldsmith confirms the arguments developed in the last chapters and points out their relevance to contemporary debates, but his use of the term "secretary" indicates that the poetics of administration, of information management, needs to be investigated in light of the feminization of clerical work in the postwar period. As we have already seen, many of the most important writing and art experiments from the 1960s and 1970s index a broad poetics or aesthetics of administration that draws its means and techniques from the world of the contemporary office. At the same time, another front of avant-garde and conceptualist art and writing began, in the 1960s and 1970s, to treat the sphere of unpaid reproductive labor, housework. Artists such as Mary Kelly, Martha Rosler, and Judy Chicago engaged in what Mierle Ukeles called "Maintenance Art," using art to direct attention toward the maintenance activities, "washing, cleaning, cooking, renewing, supporting, preserving," which are normally devalorized if not invisible.[2] Feminist poets involved in the debates and confrontations of the women's movement produced poems and anthologies of poems that focused on women's experience, especially the sexual division of labor in the home—here the work of Audre Lorde and Adrienne Rich is seminal, as is the 1973 anthology *No More Masks*. But very few works of either art or literature addressed the spheres of paid and unpaid work conjointly, let alone the very specific case of feminized clerical labor, which develops the way it does in part because of the association of women with unpaid domestic work. Though there are some notable exceptions—such as Mary Kelley's *Post-Partum Document*—few works from the period are as well placed to address the intersection of reproductive and clerical activities as Bernadette Mayer's *Memory* (1972), a book whose foundational example (along with Mayer's other early experiments) for later conceptual writing and art has mostly gone unacknowledged in contemporary conceptualist revivals. The book is, like Kenneth Goldsmith and twenty-first-century inheritors of the examples of the 1970s, deeply concerned with processes of "replicating, organizing, mirroring [and] archiving." But it is also very much concerned with the interpenetration of housework and office work, as well as the ways in which the lines between the two can become deeply blurred.

A bit of historical context is in order, before we turn to *Memory*. As we have seen, even in the 1960s there was a fairly widespread understanding, on both the Left and the Right, that the United States was quickly becoming a new kind of postindustrial economy based around services and information rather than material goods. Early accounts of the postindustrial transition emphasized the emergence of a new class of technicians, managers, and other highly educated professionals. But such visions were almost always blind to the profoundly destructive and destructuring force of such an emergence. The arrival in the 1970s of the term "deindustrialization" marks a sense that this transition was far from smooth, bringing economic ruin and unemployment to vast numbers of manufacturing workers who, rendered superfluous by automation and competition from new producers in East Asia and Europe, were unable to transition to new jobs. Most commentators failed to foresee the swell of low-paid, routinized white-collar and service-sector jobs rather than high-tech skilled positions that eventually absorbed those expelled from the manufacturing sector, thereby ushering in several decades of wage stagnation. Clerical work, in this sense, is the dirty secret of the postindustrial "knowledge-based" economy.

Particularly archetypal here—as an example of postindustrial utopianism—is Daniel Bell's influential work of "social forecasting," *The Coming of Postindustrial Society.* Bell's book updates the old Hegelian vision of the middle class as universal subject, suggesting that most job growth in the coming postindustrial era would occur among the ranks of college-educated professionals and managers. Such claims ignored what should have been obvious even in the 1960s—most job growth was occurring in low-paid, largely unskilled white-collar and service-sector occupations. In suggesting that class struggle had been essentially abrogated by this new middle class and that the labor theory of value needed replacing by a new "information theory of value"—a claim that has been often repeated, in dozens of variants, both left wing and right wing, in the decades since—Bell demonstrated a remarkable though not uncommon obliviousness to the way in which most work with information did not involve the kind of glamorous theorizing and synthesizing we associate with scientists and managers but rather the routine administration of flows of data. This was an era characterized as much by women in typing pools and young men in mailrooms as it was by managers and technicians.[3]

As I have indicated, these triumphal narratives tend to fall apart rather quickly when held against any accounts of the actual development of the labor market in the advanced capitalist countries.[4] In particular, attention to the experiences of women as they enter the labor market provides a strong counternarrative to the Bell forecast.[5] Postindustrial societies are characterized by an increasing "feminization of labor," meaning not only that large numbers of women enter the workforce but that labor methods and job positions are themselves feminized. As deindustrialization displaces the characteristically male industrial worker, there are more opportunities for schoolteachers and receptionists and fewer for machinists. Furthermore, as women enter these fields (as well as fields previously barred to them), the values and affects associated with certain jobs change, and both male and female workers are asked to display attitudes and perform tasks historically coded as female.[6] The entry of women into the workforce therefore effects a double transformation: a transformation not only of the gender balance of staffing but of the character of the jobs themselves. Whereas "secretary" in the nineteenth century often referred to a male worker, the typical male clerk of nineteenth-century fiction—a Weberian bureaucrat, in other words—by the early twentieth century it evoked a domestic worker displaced into the office, an "office wife," as secretaries were often called.[7] In the late twentieth century, however, an inversion occurs as male workers—displaced from the industrial jobs they had occupied previously—flood back into low-level, white-collar positions and are often asked to take on roles and attitudes coded as female.

The Double Day

Feminized labor in the late twentieth century is therefore a matrix of displacements. In particular, it is a site where we can examine the increasingly complex transpositions of unpaid domestic labor and wage labor. In the works for which she is most well known—*Midwinter Day* and *The Desire of Mothers to Please Others in Letters*—Bernadette Mayer stages a continual conflict between the unpaid work she does in taking care of her children and her house and the work of poetry itself. *Midwinter Day*, in particular, offers a feminist challenge to the modernist long poem, bringing all of the technical complexity of the form to bear on a single day of her life, in all its mundane and trivial detail. It thus attempts to show how such creative heroics might take place neither by virtue of an invisible and unwaged domestic work nor in spite of it but rather alongside and through such activities. Most critics of Mayer rightly examine these later books as feminist critiques of the sexual division of labor.[8] But few look at the way in which, even before the birth of her daughters, Mayer was concerned with the invisibility of the work we do to take care of ourselves and others, work that I follow Marxist feminism in describing as "domestic" labor and, in a more expansive sense, "reproductive" labor.[9] From the very beginning, her writing sought to illuminate the myriad quotidian tasks that underlie and make writing possible and are so often left out of literature: the preparation of meals and the washing of clothes, running errands and purchasing groceries. As she notes repeatedly in her later book, *The Desires of Mothers to Please Others in Letters*, writing and womanhood seem entirely opposed (yet mutually reinforcing) terms: "And now everybody acts as if, well if you can do it that's fine, you're extraordinary, if you're a woman doing it, that is having a man living with you and having children and, they say, still writing."[10] Whereas other writers had the advantage of "wives"—"he [Williams] and Hawthorne and Stein had devoted wives"—Mayer is more like "Whitman, exempt."[11] We note that the presence of Stein and Whitman complicates Mayer's presentation of patriarchy, indicating that it involves relations of dependence and domination that do not always line up with binary gender.

Such reflections begin early on. In *Memory*, one of her most ambitious projects, the domestic tasks of wives are not so much opposed to feminized clerical work as intermixed with it. In other words, Mayer positions reproductive labor under the sign of clerical labor and everyday life under the sign of administration. *Memory* is an epic of filing and cataloguing, transcribing and sorting, where the lines between these kinds of activities and the work of running errands, shopping, cooking, cleaning, maintaining relationships, and getting from place to place begin to break down. *Memory* thus runs together what capitalist ideology tends to separate into different spheres.

Indeed, *Memory* is such a complex object—as conceptual experiment, written text, performance, and installation, relying on writing, photography, and sound recording—that we need to be very clear about what exactly we are referring to. A brief summary is in order: In July 1971, Mayer shot one roll of film per day and made audio recordings to document her everyday experience. Once the month was over, she attempted to remember (or re-create) the lived experience of that month in writing, using the visual and aural documents as aids. The result was a two hundred–page text with entries for each of the thirty-one days of July and a concluding coda, titled "Dreaming." Finally the work was exhibited as an installation in 1972: the photographs were displayed as three-by-five snapshots in a grid on the wall, accompanied by a recording of Mayer reading the text. The text was released on its own, as a book, in 1975.

Much of this process is described in the book itself: As a work of total memory, it is by necessity a description of itself, a memory of *Memory*, and the early stages of the project: taking photographs and developing them, making recordings, typing up drafts. At the same time, however, it documents all of the other peripheral activities—shopping, cooking, traveling, running errands—on which its artistic labors depend. *Memory* positions Mayer in the midst of vast flows of refractory data that she must sort, order, and annotate, but such information work constantly discloses its own preceding and succeeding moments, dissolving production into reproduction and merging its aestheticized clerical labors with aestheticized domestic labors. Consider, for example, the following Steinian passage:

> Kathleen doing the dishes she does them she did them last week she did them again she didn't do them right the first time why does she have to do them again do them again, she said. I'll do them again there she is doing them again look at her doing them she does them typewriter teletape tickertape typewriter tickertape teletape Kathleen is doing the dishes she's doing them again when will she finish when will she finish.[12]

Typing and dishwashing are both homologous and structurally interdependent—homologous because they are serial, repetitive tasks associated with women's work (seriality is given by the stuttering repetitions in the previous passage) and structurally interdependent because without domestic work the typist could not survive and without typing the dishwasher would be, at least in this case, invisible. Equipped with this reading, we can see that from the very first lines of the book—"& the main thing is that we begin with a white sink a whole new language"—*Memory* characterizes mundane domestic tasks as fundamentally entangled with language work.[13]

Earlier, we referred to clerical labor and reproductive labor as spheres, suggesting that their interrelationship is primarily spatial. This makes sense, given how much this gendered division of labor depends on ideas about the public and private spheres. But the previous passage suggests forms of interconnection that are temporal and logical as much as they are spatial. Perhaps, in this light, we might think of these as "moments" or "stages" in a Hegelian sense (and in the sense in which Marx and many of the writers inspired by him borrow from Hegel).[14] We might think of the relationship between unwaged reproductive labor and waged labor as involving both logical and temporal succession, where each moment is the necessary presupposition of the others both in cognitive, logical terms and in terms of their actual unfolding in time. Such a logic of moments structures both the making of *Memory* and any experience we might have of it as a book, installation, or concept.

In these same opening sentences in *Memory*, Mayer employs a pun—one that runs throughout the whole work—on the word *dash*, a word that comes to refer at the same time to the brand of detergent, the typographic mark, the action, and eventually the redacted name of a character: "picture books & letters to everyone dash you tell what the story is once . . . concentrated dash was all there was mind nothing sink . . . with my white pants in it."[15] At one level, this continues the work of equating typing and washing, the domestic and the clerical. "Dash," in this sense, chains together writing and clothes washing. (Later in the book, the image of the clothes-washing sink will merge—via the collage technique that Mayer likens to "double exposure"—with the darkroom sink where Mayer develops the pictures for *Memory*.) But looked at in a more expansive, thematic sense, "dash" gets us to one of the primary questions about *Memory*: Why is it so hurried, harried, frantic, dashing about from place to place, moment to moment? One answer is already available—

the doubling of clerical work (paperwork) and domestic work (housework) means that Mayer is doubly exposed, and doubly impelled to get things done. She is responsible not only for composing the book but for all of the things that make writing the book possible. This goes some way in explaining the headlong intensity of the work, her compulsion to "race-write," to "race against time." We are in the presence of what feminist sociologists call "the double day," the doubling down of paid and unpaid labor as women enter the workforce but are still, nonetheless, expected to do the work of maintaining a household, taking care of men and children, buying and cooking food, cleaning. In *Memory*, it is as if the "I do this, I do that" poems of Frank O'Hara, with their liberatory exploration of the everyday spaces of commerce and exchange, are inscribed instead with a sense of finitude and lack, hung under the sign of labor and not leisure. If Frank O'Hara is the poet of leisurely shopping, then Bernadette Mayer is the poet of running errands.

The freneticism of the book—and the way that this freneticism is connected to labor, domestic and otherwise—makes *Memory* an interesting test case for Sianne Ngai's remarkable writing on the aesthetic category of the "zany," which she describes as a "performing that never stops," one whose freneticism and manic intensity derive from the condition of labor in postindustrial society and particularly its feminization.[16] "Zaniness," for Ngai, registers two important transformations in postindustrial society, two facets of what she describes as "'the putting to work' of social or relational skills." First, it is an aesthetic "that encodes strong, if mixed, emotions on the part of men about the feminization of postindustrial work" as well as "strong/mixed emotions on the part of women about capital's penetration into a set of competencies once unambiguously designated feminine."[17] Second, as an affect about the unfun-ness of fun, it registers an aggressive response to the subsumption of leisure life by work life, the incorporation of forms of play and pleasure into our work lives. Zaniness—a kind of grimacing, exaggerated sense of fun—responds to compelled enjoyment, responds to the subsumption by capital of our feelings and capacities for pleasure, the extent to which work life, for service workers especially, requires that they put on a smile and adopt an attitude of convivial obligingness. Once one reads Ngai's compelling chapter, one begins to notice the zany—as personal and cultural style—nearly everywhere, and as with all of Ngai's work on affect, one sees how it indexes a profound uneasiness and rebellion, though one that is rendered in a somewhat sublimated, neutralized form.

Despite all of the parallels between *Memory* and Ngai's zany—they are both about work, about women, about the turn to service work and clerical labor, about the transition from industrial to postindustrial capitalism, about the erosion of the division between leisure and labor, unpaid domestic work and paid work, women's work and men's work, white-collar and blue-collar work—*Memory* is not at all zany in mood. Though *Memory* has all of the freneticism of the zany—"performing that never stops" describes it perfectly—it has none of its false cheer, and although it is concerned with feeling and care and the reproduction of relationships, it has none of the aggressive solicitousness or exaggerated servility of the zany. On the contrary, it tends toward the dry, robotic, or mechanical. It may be the case, then, that the zany is *one* response to the transformation of working life over the past few decades, the other being a much more visibly angst-ridden freneticism. In other words, perhaps *Memory* indexes the freneticism of the stressed out and the overworked who are unable to convert compelled activity into artificial conviviality.

Nonetheless, even if Mayer's experience of freneticism and overwork tends toward the cheerless, Ngai's work helps us see that the tone of *Memory* is how the time sounds—its tone is an expression of a harried and hectic temporality. To investigate this temporality, and the affective qualities it gives rise to, we will therefore need to be much more specific about the character of the double day. As women enter the workforce, their days double both in terms of hours worked and kinds of work done. Women experience a "speedup" (or intensification) of their labor as the amount of activities they must fit into an hour, and the number of hours they need to be working, increases, something Arlie Hochschild refers to as the "time bind." But there is also a vertiginous mirroring of unpaid and paid activities, since the feminization of labor involves not just the capture of women as waged workers but the subsumption of previously unwaged activities by capital.[18] Activities that once belonged to the home migrate into the workplace, and, gender typed as female, women migrate with them: into child care, laundry services, fast-food restaurants, nursing homes, and the like. The reorganization of such activities by capital—their mechanization—along with the machinery of the modern home (dishwashers and washing machines) is what reduces the amount of unpaid work a woman has to do, allowing her to channel it into paid activities. But these paid activities take on the character of the unpaid ones: secretaries and nurses and flight attendants are waged captures of the attitudes and affects of housework—

what Nancy Folbre calls "care work"[19]—and the "working woman," under the worst conditions, might be expected to go from taking care of her boss (as office wife) to taking care of her husband and children. In such a situation, there is no escape from either waged labor or unwaged labor, as both reflect each other and intermix and merge into one long, endless workday.

Multitasking

The long excursion in the previous discussion should go some way toward putting the freneticism of the poem into context and underscoring the way in which its speed reflects a doubling and redoubling of the time of life. To get a full sense of the pace—which has to do with both intensity and extension, speed and duration—it is necessary to quote from the book at length (at least once). The following is from the long, lineated entry for July 1:

>   I was sitting on my legs making phone
> machine a drill starts up again to drive down
> calls someone patted my head with shining eyes with eyes was working in
> downtown heroine & strychnine will our teeth start
> a room with a piano, in & out the door, I went to two record stores
> to hurt & rear window in the rain did I hear it:
> to get . . . we looked through catalogues of sounds I don't know but there
> hurricane Erica Attica state prison & demands free
> were always a lot of papers around if I had started coming over there
> image in & out the window sound reels half
> all the time I would have flunked out of school, why didn't he?
> there's a bag with a container of coffee
> for paper full of sounds on record, the index file with a girl
> we drank it. I was sitting on my legs making calls
> on a beach in color on it the calendar behind it big breasts plugged in
> someone pats you on the head with shining eyes with eyes
> what view I've also seen from eddie's window two e.b.'s
> was working in a room with a piano, in & out the door
> he was here tonight you can always tell the time, the view was
> I went to two record stores to get
> coronet vsq brandy & yellow yellow taxis down broadway, myself as
> we looked through catalogues of sounds but there
> a whore, the circus theater climax I was bored that day listening to

were always a lot of papers lying around working being done
sounds, I was looking at our notebook more lists of sounds a bakery
if I had started coming over there all the time I would
a restaurant a bar a plane taking off cars going by the 20th century
have flunked out of school
fox fanfare many songs & musics a sign saying vertically howard
and on for papers full of sounds on record
that view again higher it looked threatening like rain & clock
the index file with a girl on a beach in color on it
reads 12:10 we were up early we did the light on me was morning light
calendar behind big breasts plugged in[20]

The typescript for this passage shows that Mayer used a cut-up technique to produce these lines: she took one typewritten page, cut out every other line from the page, and then glued the remaining skeleton atop another typewritten page.[21] The alternating weave of the two passages, each one of which indexes two different memories, figures the doubling and redoubling of Mayer's various labors—making phone calls, cataloguing and indexing "sounds," shopping—as well as the sense of interruption and distraction that occurs when one switches back and forth between different tasks. The drilling machine interrupts the phone call, and Mayer's errands are suffused with the scrambled-together reports of first Hurricane Erica and then the Attica prison riot. Mayer's experimental technique produces a remarkable poetic representation of the multitasking that comes to dominate the working lives of white-collar workers and the harried freneticism that accompanies it, the freneticism of the so-called flexible (or precarious) worker.

We will return to multitasking and flexibility later, but first we note how, in the quoted passage, a quasi-secretarial labor (marked by the sexualized image of "the index file with a girl on a beach" as well as the patronizing pat on the head) threads the references to domestic and quotidian activities—shopping, coffee, a bakery. Behind this interleaving of moments, the construction machines add another dimension, signifying masculine, "productive" labor. Finally, these entangled forms of labor are themselves entangled with images of leisure: the "index file" with the beach, the catalogues of sounds with the bottle of brandy. The "big breasts" of the girl on the beach are "plugged in" to the machinery of production. Thus, the passage is a rather remarkable portrait of the joining together of separate moments of social reproduction and production—again, not as temporal succession but as logical reciprocality, as moments.²² But the relationship between the moments is not necessarily without its hierarchies—in this presentation, the moment of clerical work dominates both the space of domestic work and leisure (which together we might term "everyday life"). We are in the presence of what Adorno and Horkheimer referred to as administered life—modes, methods, and techniques originally developed in the waged workplace come to "subsume" and so transform spaces outside the wage to make them conducive to conditions of capital accumulation.²³

Most of the work portrayed in *Memory*, it must be acknowledged, is unwaged. Her clerical labors are put in the service of her own artistic projects, those of her boyfriend, Ed, or her friends. They are pseudo- or para-clerical, we might say. But this is the most instructive point: *Memory* investigates the way in which the whole of life gets subsumed under the protocols, affects, and techniques of waged work. The book is not just a representation of this subsumption but its agent as well: it converts quotidian activities into *art work*; it portrays a world where, at any moment, one may or may not be acting out a part in someone's artistic project, or even acting out multiple parts in multiple projects at the same time. All at once, Mayer is collaborating with her friend Jacques on his play, working on her boyfriend's film, and at the same time documenting the experiences so that they can be repositioned inside her own project, *Memory*. In the passage quoted, for instance, one does not know whether the phone calls she makes are personal or business (or even if this is a tenable distinction). The same goes for the trip to the record store. Everything is brought into the circle of work: under the beach, the office.

We get a glimpse, therefore, of the subsumption of leisure by labor that has become a common feature of postindustrial life, where all socializing has "networking" as one of its horizons and where, increasingly, personal relations, friendships, and acquaintances can be mobilized for financial or cultural gain. This is the condition of the *flexible* laborer who works part-time, contingently, or from home and is therefore less likely to experience work as a sphere separate from everyday life, less likely to identify with a certain job as a stable and enduring identity that stands apart from other identities. But alongside this understanding of "flexible" as meaning non-full-time, there arise other associations, having to do with the type of work one accomplishes. Workers are flexible when they are not defined by a permanent assignment but constantly adapting, taking on different roles, attributes, skills, and qualities depending on the task or *project* at hand. As noted earlier, Boltanski and Chiapello describe this worker as a central feature of what they call "the projective city," the capitalist mode conforming to the period from the 1960s on, where the "*general equivalent*—what the status of persons and things is measured by—is *activity*."[24] In contrast with earlier modes, "activity in the projective city surmounts the oppositions between work and non-work, the stable and the unstable, wage-earning class and non-wage-earning class, paid work and voluntary work."[25] Such "activity expresses itself in the multiplicity of projects *of all kinds* that may be pursued concurrently," where projects involve temporary constellations of persons convoked for a particular task. By participating in projects, one expands one's circle of associates, enlarges one's network: "by *multiplying connections* and *proliferating links*, the *succession of projects* has the effect of *extending networks*." Here, "[l]ife is conceived as a succession of projects" and, because the boundary between work and non-work has been superseded, "anything can attain the status of a *project*, including ventures hostile to capitalism."[26] As a result:

> Describing every accomplishment with a nominal grammar that is the grammar of the project erases the differences between a capitalist project and a humdrum creation (a Sunday club). Capitalism and anti-capitalist critique alike are masked. Utterly different things can be assimilated to the term "project": opening a new factory, closing one, carrying out a re-engineering project, putting on a play.... This is one of the ways in which the projective city can win over forces hostile to capitalism: by proposing a grammar that transcends it, which they in turn will use to describe their own activity while remaining oblivious of the fact that capitalism, too, can slip into it.[27]

Equipped with this description we can see how so many of the passages from *Memory*, detailing the proliferation of connections, links, and relationships between people in the artistic milieus in which she circulates, fall under this heading:

> If I'm Bernadette devlin if I'm b. devlin I must b. pregnant, called Julia she has something "important" for ed at home, where hannah is, voices on the phone & laughing house of mirrors, nick says anne is at the laundromat, jacques roast beef is in the oven in stockbridge, Kathleen is at the bank and I dial o for operator, define

it, stockridge eggs rockridge is burning there are no fires yet today, I dial 413 plus 123 plus operator's reading for stockbridge I am trying to call the ate r & I call deluxe at 850 10TH AVE 2473220 & speak to I try to speak to the expediter for 16mm film, I speak to otto pellone & he's the wrong one.[28]

Memory is, from its very first lines, about relations: it is "picture books & letters to everyone dash." One sees, immediately, how a network of interpersonal relationships links together the phatic, quotidian everyday with the work Mayer does for Ed's film or for *Memory*. She is like an operator at a switchboard, linking up various people and activities, just as she links together the various moments in the cycle of accumulation. Boltanski and Chiapello's account therefore might lead us to conclude that avant-garde sociality—based on the coterie, the conversation in the bar or café, the little press or reading series or gallery—has been internalized by industry, become a part of its very functioning.[29]

Importantly for *Memory*, the extensive character of the projective city, its spread in space, described as "connexionism" by Boltanski and Chiapello, develops in parallel to a certain intensive subjective norm, a certain model of "the great man," here "Enthusiastic, Involved, Flexible, Adaptable, Versatile, Having potential, Employable, Autonomous, Not prescriptive, Knows how to engage others, In touch, Tolerant."[30] Great men cultivate lateral rather than vertical relationships, relying on charm and conviviality: they "prove to be *connectors*, *vectors*, who do not keep the information or contacts gleaned in networks to themselves, but redistribute them among the team members."[31]

For those who qualify as great men (or women, though the gendering is not accidental) within such workplaces, there is doubtless an experience of liberation that accompanies the unfixing of all stable work identities. The capacity to shape-shift from project to project is certainly satisfying for many. In fact, Boltanski and Chiapello argue that this satisfaction is one of the goals of the restructuring of the labor process. Developed as a response to worker demands for greater autonomy during the 1960s, the mostly fleeting satisfactions and forms of autonomy of the flexible labor system are part of what has guaranteed its stability even as wages and benefits have been eroded and even as flexibility becomes, increasingly, a mask for redoubled exploitation. For most workers this flexible, project-based style of work hides a deep intensification: workers are *freed* from the alienation of a single task by being asked to perform two or three alienated tasks at once, to be their own managers and coworkers.[32] Multiskilling—as this reorganization of work is often called, in contrast with deskilling—is therefore not a return to the craft basis of skilled labor but a distinct form of deskilled labor where one moves from one deskilled activity to another: "For one cashier, a multi-skilling exercise meant that she was training her colleague to do her job while her colleague reciprocated," in the words of one study. Elsewhere, "[a]n office worker in the large utilities company described how she used to run the print room; now she is part of a multi-functioning team which runs reception, covers the post room *and* runs the print room."[33] As other studies have demonstrated, women are more often subjected to this kind of intensification through multiskilling, perhaps because so many are already accustomed to the kind of multiple demands that come from balancing domestic and paid work.[34] Hence Diane Gabrielle Tremblay argues, in a recent study of women's work in technologized workplaces, that much of the multiskilling that has emerged in the context of the restructuring of the labor process is really multitasking, meaning it does not provide workers with translatable or portable skills but merely concatenates deskilled and routinized tasks under one job heading. In an intriguing book on the poetics of information, focusing on many of the same figures as this study (Mayer, Weiner, Graham), Paul Stephens describes multitasking as the "primary obstacle to white-collar efficiency" under Taylorist/Fordist office management, a form of inattention and distraction (and, by extension, resistance) to the singularizing division of labor.[35] While this was certainly true at a certain point in the middle of the twentieth century, the "new spirit" of capitalism recuperates this resistant gesture, and multiskilling becomes a mask for an intensification and acceleration of the tempo of labor.[36]

Moment and Medium

Memory sets numerous tasks, activities, and time frames in parallel and careens back and forth between them at a headlong speed that is unnerving, providing one of the most vivid literary descriptions of multitasking and the frenetic, harried subject it entails: a request for a Xerox machine turns first into a description of packaging pasta into boxes, then a cryptic remark about "homemade stolen electric typewriters" and "a stolen cassette tape recorder," and finally, driving directions.[37] Intriguingly, the passage suggests that such multitasking means engaging with multiple media and multiple mechanical apparatuses: mimeographs, typewriters, cameras, tape recorders, slide projectors, automobiles. Furthermore, if we keep in mind the full shape of the project—and its extension beyond the text, into image and sound and concept—we see that it not only *describes* multitasking but is itself a work of multitasking, weaving together graphic, photographic, and acoustic technologies into a single multichannel work, one expressed in both *Memory* the installation and *Memory* the book.

With our understanding of multitasking and multimedia and their relationship to the intensifications of the labor process under the double day, we can take a little bit of a step back and place *Memory* in the context of arguments about the transformations of the visual arts during this period, their transformation into what Rosalind Krauss has called "postmedium" art.[38] As art critics like John Roberts and Benjamin Buchloh note, the trajectory of twentieth-century and especially postwar art follows the process of deskilling in industry, where routinized, processual visual forms that require little traditional skill evacuate the craft values of painting and sculpture and the skills of hand and eye on which they depended.[39] One thinks of early avant-garde art, as well as minimalism, pop art, arte povera, and other postwar developments, in which standardized, industrial objects and graphics stand in for the artisanal craft of earlier sculpture and painting.

As conceptual art emerges out of these developments, there seems to arrive a moment of complete and total deskilling, where all the material, craft-based elements of making have been purged and replaced by an administrative (purely cognitive) manipulation of automated processes or prefabricated material elements.[40] We can see how these cultural transformations parallel the socioeconomic transformations of the period, where the deskilled production of goods gives way to the manipulation of symbols just as minimalist sculpture gives way to conceptualism, and where the making of things gives way to the provision of services just as painting gives way to performance and what Andrea Fraser calls "artistic service."[41] Both Roberts and Buchloh give an account of how the purgative moment of the 1970s is followed by a rematerialization or reskilling of art in the 1980s, but they do not connect it to debates around multiskilling. Indeed, it seems that the reskilling in postconceptual or installation art of the 1980s is not reskilling but multiskilling—that is, the setting in parallel of multiple deskilled processes. The institution of the "installation," for instance, often brings together film, painting, sculpture, text, and sound art into one space, but in most cases there is no return to the specific craft-based values of any one of these arts. We can see how this also parallels the transformation of the labor process:

just as the installation brings multiple, deskilled channels together in parallel, multitasking in the space of the office is often situated around a single hub—the computer—which merges multiple, semiautomated tasks into a single stream. With the invention of so-called user-friendly computers—computers that use the graphical user interface of Apple Computers and the Windows operating system—the intensification and redoubling of office work becomes fully embedded in the material infrastructure of the office: one now routinely shifts from task to task without moving anywhere except virtually. The multiplying tasks of modern office work—and the flexible office worker—are thus effected by a singularization of machines and by the reduction of all activity to a single medium: data. Alan Liu's description of this kind of modern "knowledge work," for instance, demystifies the rhapsodic visions of flexibility by noting that, while "[m]ultitasking users are free to inhabit as many different windows or 'scenes' as they wish, representing decentralized locations and protocols, diverse projects, or varying aspects of a single project . . . all the while, it is really just one main window—the desktop—that is operative, and the working conventions of that window, which are determined through the underlying operating system and networking choices made at the corporate and server level."[42] The passage chimes with one of Fredric Jameson's most trenchant observations about postmodernity, as a site where "the most standardized and uniform social reality in history . . . emerge[s] as the rich oil smear sheen of absolute diversity."[43]

If *Memory* joins together the different moments in the reproductive circuits of capital and labor, it does so by convoking multiple mechanisms—for film, for sound, for text—around a single purpose, merging them into a single stream. This not only anticipates the "remediation" of all of these media by the new digital medium but more specifically anticipates the coming transformation of office work by the computer, which both replaced multiple office machines with a new all-in-one device and likewise replaced differentiated job positions with new all-in-one positions.[44] We see that social identity and technology are not easily separated and that the various experiments of the text are, in their way, laboratorial, developing and testing out new social possibilities with existing technologies. This should remind us of the claim, in Lev Manovich and elsewhere, that the twentieth-century avant-garde practices such as collage and montage, dating back to cubism, Dadaism, and constructivism, are incorporated into the computer at a structural level.[45]

This much *Memory* certainly shares with the constant cutting and pasting of late capitalist office workers. But *Memory* might be laboratorial in a further, more specific way: in both a stand-alone essay and in the fifth chapter of *The Language of New Media*, Manovich suggests, in a post-Kantian turn of mind, that the "database" has become "a new symbolic form of the computer age ... a new way to structure our experience of ourselves and of the world," one that rivals linear perspective and narrative in its far-reaching consequences for human subjectivity.[46] More specifically, he suggests that a particular assemblage—the database and algorithm—characterizes the "new media" world of computer games as well as other applications, in which various procedures are performed on disorganized data. Manovich works hard to distinguish the results of this application of algorithms to data structures from narrative per se, since such an assemblage lacks an appropriate logic of cause and effect in Manovich's view. *Memory* seems quite explicitly the application of a series of algorithms (procedures) to a fund of unarranged data (here the "memories" in the form of film, tape, typescript). Indeed, given the importance of the procedure, or so-called chance-based operation, to the experimental poetry that develops in the 1960s and 1970s, we might hope someone would provide an account of the database more broadly in these works—in Ted Berrigan's *Sonnets*, Lyn Hejinian's *My Life*, and Ron Silliman's *Tjanting*, for instance. Such writing has often been described as relying on paratactic (rather than hypotactic) relationships between parts of speech and verbal elements, seeing the former as free of hierarchy or oppressive determination. To what extent is this akin to the database that, in Manovich's terms, "represents the world as a list of items" that it "refuses to order"?[47]

Mayer's case seems interesting because it represents a transitional moment, not only a moment before computers but a moment before the database as such becomes a determining cultural form. Specifically, if we look at the manuscripts for *Memory*, we see that the "processing" to which she submits her verbal memories—typewriter, audiotape—transforms consequential, linear language into something resembling a data structure. Thus, these earlier devices that precede the computer are, in their way, involved in the processes of standardization and routinization required for the transformation of language into data—transforming the vagaries of handwriting into the exactitude of type, for instance. The manuscripts and typescripts for *Memory*—held in the Mayer archives at UC San Diego—confirm this sense of the machine as a routinizing and homogenizing device, submitting the language to a purifying operation, in which extrinsic, nonessential elements are purged, leaving only the distinctions necessary for exact reproduction. The text went through multiple drafts before Mayer recorded the final audio version she used in the installation. While the first drafts are all handwritten, composed in a lineated "open field" style with ample white space and frequent recourse to visual arrangements on the page, as well as illustrations, once Mayer transfers these passages to typewriter, all of this iconographic specificity is lost, and the text is run together into blocks of prose, chopped up into sub-sentence bits, and recombined in different orders. Rather than consider an opposition between "narrative" and "database," however, we should think of the symbolic form opposed to the database as the "line," a structure of language that interacts with the grammar of the sentence to produce certain recursive patterns of sound and sense.

The key effect of the destruction of the line—or the conversion of lineated language into run-together fragments—is a sense of hurry, panic, urgency, and speed, since running lineated words together into blocks of prose will, of course, make the language seem more accelerated than it already is. Like punctuation, line breaks and white space exert a braking function on language. It seems fair, then, to suggest that the speed of Mayer's book is, in part, a technological speed, impelled by the mechanical rhythm of typewriters, cameras, and tape recorders, shutter speeds, and words per minute. In part, what is being conceptualized here is the way that technologies—especially media technologies—have a tendency to expand the field of the remembered beyond the human capacity to integrate it (notwithstanding their capacity to distort, warp, and reconfigure memory).[48] This is in part where the panic and frenzy of *Memory* originate: recording and transmission technologies have enabled a transcription of the past beyond the capacity of the human mind to assimilate it. In certain places, *Memory* aims to test these human limits, the limits of human endurance, and by way of various technologies and devices, push beyond them. But this exposure of the inhuman in the drafting process might be why, before exhibiting the project as an installation, she takes the typescript and, in a process exactly opposite to the composition of typescripts from dictation common to secretarial work, makes a voice recording from it, humanizing it, and adapting it once again to the limits of the human body.

It now seems safe to say that, as much as *Memory* is a project about work, one through which we can read the profound restructuring of work and work life taking place in the 1970s, it is also a project about technology because the history of labor in capitalism is always also, in part, a history of technology. Truly capitalist labor is labor constantly remade and refashioned—become more productive, more intense, more plastic—through changing technological means. It is labor that has been "really subsumed," as we have seen, remade in accord with the exigencies and needs of capital and the profit drive. Indeed, we might say that capitalism proper—what Marx calls the "specifically capitalist mode of production"—really begins only at the moment in which the owners of capital begin to reinvest their profits in new labor-saving technology to extract even greater profits.[49] This virtuous circle of reinvestment—profit that, by way of new more highly productive machinery, produces greater profits—is what characterizes capitalist accumulation. And therefore, since any account of the restructuring of labor in the postwar period must be, in part, an account of changing technical means, it should come as no surprise that *Memory* so explicitly foregrounds the role of technology from its very first pages:

> we are now in an image, sound, his hair was pulled back mind too
> they're sons we are reminding you
> but now he leans against the machine, reels, & while it's on I've turned
> we are now in an image sound his hair was
> off the light a powerful light that was on it's off & outside
> pulled back
> they've turned the people working have turned the saw drill scooper off.[50]

Here, the machine has "pulled back" Ed's mind, fed it into the reels, and absorbed it into the past. Elsewhere, Mayer wonders whether "a person [is] a machine when he's in the movies" and later describes "actors . . . being invaded with machines surrounded with machines."[51] Working with a machine means becoming it. The machine, in this sense, represents less something absolutely external to the self than something that was once part of the self but now has become externalized—a memory that, once part of the neural circuitry, has become writing, photographs, and audiotape.

Memory, in this light, depicts the laboring body struggling against its own transformation into and subsumption by the machine, struggling against its own becoming-machine. In this it chimes with one of the presentations of the relationship between capital and labor in Marx, where capital is simply labor exteriorized, become objective. Capital is "dead labor that, vampire-like, only lives by sucking living labor." It is not, therefore, something absolutely foreign to labor, but simply labor's own past.[52] Such an account makes capitalism seem less a conflict between two opposing subjects—proletarian and bourgeois, worker and capitalist—than a conflict between two temporal moments (the present and past) or two ontological modalities (subjective and objective). As developed in passages like these, capital is simply the reified weight of the past, collected in the form of worked matter that impels, determines, and conditions present actions.

Some of Marx's most compelling passages on the nature of the machine develop from this conception. For Marx, the machine is one of the essential forms of capital. Fixed capital, in the form of the self-propulsive machine or automaton, represents the objectification of subjective will. In the factory system, therefore,

> the material unity [of combined workers] appears subordinate to the *objective unity* of the *machinery*, of fixed capital, which, as *animated monster*, objectifies the scientific idea, and is in fact the coordinator, does not in any way relate to the individual worker as his instrument; but rather he himself exists as an animated individual punctuation mark, as its living isolated accessory.[53]

There is a kind of reversal of roles in such a scenario—between subject and object, living and dead, material and immaterial, past and present. The machine becomes an "objectified . . . idea" and the worker a mere accessory or moment of punctuation in the syntax of the factory:

> Every kind of capitalist production, in so far as it is not only a labour process but also capital's process of valorization has this in common, but it is not the worker who employs the conditions of his work, but rather the reverse, the conditions of work employ the worker. However, it is only with the coming of machinery that this inversion first acquires a technical and palpable reality. Owing to its conversion into an automaton, the instrument of labor confronts the worker during the labour process in the shape of capital, dead labour, which dominates and soaks up living labor-power. The separation of the intellectual faculties of the production

process from manual labour, and the transformation of those faculties into powers exercised by capital over labour is, as we have already shown, finally completed by large-scale industry erected on the foundations of machinery.[54]

As with the prosopopoetic reversals and transpositions of the commodity form itself, machine-based labor mechanizes and dehumanizes the worker at the same time that it humanizes the machine, making it into the repository of science and intellectual faculties. Dead labor is animated at the same time that living labor is mortified. Marx's necro-economics means that two types of living-dead confront each other in the workshop—the dead-come-alive of capital and the living-turned-dead of labor.

This is only one of the ways that Marx characterizes the relationship between capital and labor, and there is good reason to question it or at least wonder about its conceptual centrality. Its function might be illustrative—a rhetorical flourish, a way of translating the ideas of *Capital* into a gothic period style. Certainly, there are reasons to worry about the potential heroizing of life and the living, the easy slippage from here into existentialist notions of virility, potency, authenticity. But there is also another way to read this passage that steers us away from existential agonistics. If we replace dead labor with past (or accumulated, or stored, or "remembered") labor, and living labor with present labor, we see that what Marx is really describing is a complex temporality, where the past remains present in an objective form, in the form of material accumulation that makes demands on, limits, and fates the course of the present. This is the sense in which Marx's project is *historical materialism*—an account of history and historical change as materialized force.

We will return to discussing *Memory* as a project concerned with tracing the tyrannical weight of the past on the present (as much as it is also about the determinative force of machinery on present faculties and capacities), but first we need to track down a few consequences of the previous distinctions. Many will know that, on the basis of a few sentences from the Preface to *A Contribution to the Critique of Political Economy*, a certain theory of technological determinism has dominated Marxism, especially in the early part of twentieth century. This view holds that historical changes emerge from the contradiction caused by *productive forces* (technology, primarily) as they race ahead of decaying and outmoded *social relations* (relations of production). Eventually, the laggard social relations are forced to adjust and catch up with the times. But as we have already seen, there is a certain indistinction between productive forces and social relations, since machinery is, in fact, the materialization of certain social relations, the materialization of certain relationships among workers and between workers and their bosses. (Machines, for instance, are concrete instantiations of a certain division of labor, workflow, and forms of cooperation and degrees of skill.) Thus, in contradistinction to the Preface, what we really confront is a circular (or at the very least overdetermined) causality. This is in line with the account that emerges in other places within Marx, especially in the chapter "Machinery and Large-Scale Industry," where Marx reverses the relationship between forces and relations described in the Preface, suggesting that, in the case of the passage from the manufacture system (where workers employed precapitalist methods) to the specifically capitalist form of machine-based factory labor, it was the changing social relations within the former mode that made the invention of certain types of machines necessary. Machines were simply the material elaboration of a set of social relations that had already developed in the interstices of the older production methods:

> The system of machine production therefore grew spontaneously on a material basis which was inadequate to it. When the system had attained a certain degree of development, it had to overthrow this already ready-made foundation, which had meanwhile undergone further development in its old form, and create for itself a new basis appropriate to its mode of production.[55]

This is an exact reversal of the formulation in the Preface, where "[a]t a certain stage of their development, the material productive forces of society come into conflict with the existing relations of production."[56] In the specific case of the factory system, social relations were the vanguard.

Such conceptual complexities help to explain the considerable attention devoted to the "Fragment on Machines" (part of his pre-*Capital* notebooks, often referred to as the *Grundrisse*) since its publication in the 1960s. Along with "Results of the Immediate Process of Production," this passage has become a veritable touchstone for Marxist theory since its appearance in the 1960s, especially among Autonomist Marxists. The "Fragment on Machines" and the concept of "general intellect" that derives from it owe their appeal, in my view, to the fact that, like the passages quoted from *Capital*, they offer a much more nuanced account of the dialectic of relations and forces. The fragment is also written in a much denser philosophical register that appealed, no doubt, to a certain growing theoreticism within Marxism.

But it is also probably true that the growing prevalence of white-collar labor made the status of knowledge and knowledge work a particularly pressing theoretical concern, such that the account, in the fragment, of machinery as materialized knowledge held special appeal. In the fragment we read that "[t]he science which compels the inanimate limbs of the machinery, by their construction, to act purposefully, as an automaton, does not exist in the workers' consciousness."[57] We encounter a world where "[i]n machinery, knowledge appears as alien, external to him."[58] The term that Marx coins for such alienated, partly materialized knowledge—"social knowledge become . . . a direct force of production"—is "general intellect."[59]

In general intellect, knowledge becomes not just a force of production but a form of command. It sets certain tasks, commands certain activities. This seems analogous to the status of Mayer's own experience in *Memory*, where the superabundant complexity of her documented past comes to require continuous transfusions of present attention and creates, over the course of the experiment, a cumulative sense of acceleration, compounding momentum, and, eventually, a sense of an automatic process gone haywire. Because there is an explicit sense of tyrannical control in her presentation of the relationship between past and present—a relationship where the past dominates and determines the present—I think the relationship between present labor and accumulated past labor, between worker and means-of-production-as-general-intellect is a good analogue for the dynamic at play in *Memory*.

The tyranny of remembrance is explicit everywhere, but especially so in the concluding section of the book, "Dreaming," where she writes that "memory stifles dream it shuts dream up," identifying dream with a creative, improvisatory present free from the exigencies and laboriousness of memory. As elsewhere, memory as such—memory as data, as record—is identified with being an actor in a movie, performing a role, obeying the orders of a director: "August 4: Grace and I are in a movie directed by Jacques-in-charge."[60] This dream recalls an earlier sequence from the entry for July 10, where Mayer and Ed are working with friend Jacques on his film. This involves, strangely, a "dry run . . . without film & without actors," and Mayer describes Jacques as a "Stalinist decision-making lenin at the helm of the cadillac ship." In both the concluding "Dreaming" entry and the passage for July 10, Mayer contrasts improvisation with playing a role: "I wish I could write backwards cause film doesn't seem worth the trouble it would be better to improvise than to try to live with lenin."⁶¹ Film is to improvisation what memory is to dreaming, such that, in "Dreaming," even though Grace and Mayer "wind up in church, a liberal service" where Dan Graham (another authority figure) "is conducting something in the aisles," Mayer is able to effect a "reversal a withdrawal" in the power relations:

> He [Dan Graham] says this wont hurt a bit we are conducting a test & Grace & I have no shirts on: a white machine is put against our shoulder, then a long needle shot through, through the right shoulder, a dull sharp pain & I ask them to stop & I say Grace & I have already made love as the end of the movie & now we laugh at Jacques-in-charge for not predicting that Grace & another woman will begin to make love, are making love.⁶²

On one side: memory, machinery, authority—structures associated with the dominance of the past over the present. On the other side: writing, dreaming, improvisation, anarchy, self-direction—structures associated with the liberation of the present from the tyranny of the past. The following quotation—itself set off within quotes inside the entry for July 4—makes this opposition rather clear:

> [O]ne two three people I saw, money we spent, gave out, the energy it took to get to the country, drinking three cups of coffee to talk about anarchy, to write a letter to anne about an old worn out subject, the destruction of the tapes, feel the breeze the generation gap, think about watching another person, then creating one for people to watch, understanding the desire to watch other people to understand them or just to watch them, not finding any place to set things down then save this for later & wait. I saw I talked about. No decision. No direction. That's good. & No thought. Fans, the energy it takes to wave them. Flags. Get the pillow. The cake is in the oven. Get the beer. Why not talk about the energy of the weather in the city too, three describe it. Waiting toward something to come out of something. Placing something there. To think without thinking. Write without writing. xyz, thoughts with fine edges. So many noises people places things points of view. Put something out in that field. Didnt understand. Now do. The do-nothing school. Against technology. Energy comes from somewhere. Pay. Some way. I feel terrible. Why. Race against time. All the dreams all the notes all the directions nothing comes from it. Need drink. Empty slot. Cant sit up. Cake. The leisure to go beyond the tree. The time. Did ed take a taxi? No, but he did get a ride home in j&k's 1964 cadillac convertible.⁶³

In this passage, the cultivation of experience in the present—writing letters, visiting people, drinking coffee, and discussing "anarchy"—means the "destruction of the tapes" and the disaccumulation of memory, since attention to the present and the past is set off in a zero-sum competition and Mayer is left "not finding any place to set things down then save this for later." At a basic level, this is one of the double binds that structure the book (and play a large role in later works like *Midwinter Day*). Attention to the past, attempting to document the past in all its fullness, continually creates new, undocumented pasts (born from the present that must be ignored while attention is focused elsewhere). The same dynamic functions with the present, which continually races ahead of any attempt to capture it: devoting present time to recording the past creates a new past that must then be recorded, and so on and so forth.

Thus, even though Mayer decides to give herself over to the fullness of an unordered, anarchic present, we notice that this quickly converts back into a "race against time." The absence of "decision" and "direction"—the paratactic arrangement of different activities, "noises places things points of view"—and her stance "against technology" gives way on its own, without exterior imposition, to a sense that she must "pay." Though the "decision-making lenin" has been removed, the position of authority still remains, if uninhabited, in the form of an "empty slot." Authority has been suppressed rather than transcended.

The Organic Composition of Memory

As we have already indicated, these relations of domination, effected and mediated by technology, are temporal relations, ways in which the past dominates the present. Since so much of the preceding chapter has concerned the experience of hurry and speedup within *Memory*, it is worth lingering on the way in which Marxism has given an account of historical dynamics as based on a conflictual relationship between past and present labor. One of the richest accounts of this temporal relationship—the dominance of past labor over present labor—comes not from the *Grundrisse*, with its attention to the technical-material aspects of labor, but from Marx's fully developed account of capitalist crisis in volumes 1 and 3 of *Capital*. In both of these books, Marx devotes significant effort to defining what he calls the "composition of capital"—the ratio between its "active and its passive component, between variable and constant capital."[64] (By variable capital, Marx means wages; and by constant capital he means everything else—raw inputs, machines, buildings). One way of understanding this ratio is by taking account of how "a definite number of workers corresponds to a definite quantity of means of production and thus a definite amount of living labour to a definite amount of labour already objectified in means of production." In other words, the "composition of capital" measures the ratio of living to dead labor (or present to past, objectified labor). But this material measure—the measure of bodies and things in physical terms (bushels of wheat, yards of lumber, tons of iron)—is not necessarily a measure of the relative *value* of those bodies or those things, and since capital is concerned with values, one needs to examine the proportion in value terms as well. These are not independent proportions. In fact, the first proportion (Marx calls it the "technical composition of capital") has a tendency to determine the latter (which Marx calls the "value composition of capital").[65] Not all changes in the value composition are due to technical changes, changes in the levels of productivity—but to the extent that such changes in value can be ascribed to changes in productivity, Marx suggests we refer to this composition as the "organic composition of capital," called "organic" because it has to do with the relationship of what is living to what is dead, what is present to what is past.

The organic composition of capital, then, measures the extent to which production is determined by past values, but it also measures the extent to which production is determined by objectified matter, by things rather than bodies—and it suggests that these are two faces of a single process. Marx's account of capitalism's tendency toward crisis—its own drive toward self-dissolution—emphasizes the centrality of a *rising* organic composition of capital. While the introduction of machinery is undertaken in order to increase the amount of surplus value and hence profit that the owners can generate, in the long term the reduction in the number of workers relative to the mass of means of production, or the ratio of wages to other expenses, means that the capitalist will require a larger and larger investment to extract surplus value, since all new value comes from labor and the pool of labor is shrinking relative to the pool of means of production.

The standard presentation of the rising organic composition of capital assumes that its central effect is a falling rate of profit, since the rate of new value extraction also falls. The arguments around this point are complicated, highly technical, and might lead us to miss the major point here. Regardless of what we think about the profit rate, what is important is that rising organic composition of capital measures the extent to which living labor has been thrust out of the production process, the extent to which dead or past or objectified labor predominates. The results of this dynamic are various: it can produce crises of employment for those expelled from production, the so-called superfluous populations; it produces crises of underconsumption (since he or she who does not work does not eat); and it produces underutilization and underinvestment, because in cases of high-organic composition investment in new plant and machinery is unlikely to net higher profits. Because of this last effect, technical change begins to slow and capitalists pull their money out of production, instead preferring speculation in stocks and real estate. But tracking these developments in all their complexity might cause us to miss the central implication of this analysis: crises in capitalism are the result of a society that has become too wealthy and too productive for its own good, a capitalism that requires less and less work and that as a result finds its perpetuation threatened. Capitalism is a self-undermining social form.

On the one hand, these developments might seem to imply a slowing down of historical "progress," measured in terms of technical development. But this slowing down finds itself matched by a speeding up. As it becomes difficult to extract increased profits from investment in labor-saving technology, capitalists turn instead to nontechnological means of increasing surpluses: sweating and intensifying labor, decreasing pockets of rest and downtime (the so-called pores in the workday), extending work hours, and finding ways of getting workers to do unpaid work off the job. Thus, we return, by a long and circuitous route, to the harried and frenetic temporality of *Memory*, which we are now prepared to think of as strongly homological with the actual state of capital and labor in the early 1970s, when the vigorous good health of the postwar economy gave way to a crisis of profitability (visible first as inflation) described persuasively by several writers as conforming, more or less, to Marx's account of capitalist crisis.[66] This intensification was felt on both sides of the double day, in the workplace and in the home, as people worked more for less money and, as a result, were forced to compensate for reductions in household spending with an increase in housework.

Marx often describes technical productivity by referring to the amount of means of production a single worker can "set in motion." Improved technologies and improved techniques allow workers to set in motion more and more means of production, more and more material, and over the course of decades and centuries, technical productivity increases by whole orders of magnitude. This is what *Memory* portrays—consciousness and memory under conditions where the rapid development of new technologies for transmitting and recording data can allow a person, by a single mental act, to set in motion vast amounts of knowledge and memory. But such a setting into motion is, as Marx seems to indicate, mediated by the general intellect and the machinery for recording and transmission, such that actual consciousness becomes a mere moment within an increasingly automated, routinized process of thought. The technological sublime is less an instance of a confrontation with the unthinkable than it is a confrontation with things that are being thought for you and, at the same time, by way of your own alienated cognitive faculties. As Hugh MacDiarmid puts it, "[A]nti-human forces have instilled the thought / that knowledge has outrun the individual brain / . . . And so have turned / Humanity's vast achievements against the human mind."[67] (The MacDiarmid quote captures well, I think, why the rhapsodic readings of general intellect are so odd and why their avoidance of the negative affects surrounding the rhetoric of monstrosity in Marx should appear so willful.) Here's Mayer on this fact:

> [T]ake pictures for a week, say, then put them away dont even show them around for a year & see what you remember & a week's diary too: call kathleen & ed at noon stay at paul's cause H might not be home, it's Friday, villa lobos gas record teletype machine: this is the specious present in my memory presents my memory as it might be styled as the knowledge of an event or fact or state of mind which in the meantime I have not been thinking of but with the additional consciousness that I've sure thought of it before I've experienced it before, all of it.[68]

The techniques in *Memory* are a simulacrum of memory because, to the extent that they are able to expand the range of what one *could* remember, they do so at the expense of being able to *actually* remember things. The techniques remember for you, and so *Memory* becomes an exercise in "the knowledge of an event or fact or state of mind which in the meantime I have not been thinking."[69] The moment of consciousness itself—what the mind can hold—becomes as a result incredibly impoverished. Active consciousness concerns itself, instead, with things to do, responsibilities, various daily urgencies, rather than holding the lived experience of the past in mind. At the same time, the actual expanse of the remembered that the various technologies of memory make possible becomes incomparably vast, an uncompassable wealth—billions or trillions of hours of films that no one has time to watch, photographs that no one will look at, text that no one will read. As with capital in its crises of overdevelopment, *Memory* discloses a strange synthesis of poverty and wealth. In *Memory*, we encounter a vast library of human experience that cannot be accessed because of the constitutive forms through which we process that experience. Just as in 1848, today "the tradition of all dead generations weighs like a nightmare on the brains of living."[70] However, in our case, this tradition is not the decrepit institutions, forms, and powers of the ancien régime, dressing up in costumes of the Roman Empire. Rather, it is capital itself, congealed into the various forms in which it is stored—buildings and technologies but also vast pools of liquid wealth and equally liquid information. The weight of this past speeds us onward, relentlessly, but not toward anything. Breaking with such a state of affairs would mean breaking not only with the absurdity of a regime of work that makes us work more and more as work itself is less and less necessary but with a temporality that, because it is connected to the *automaton* of capital, makes the present a mere adjunct to the past. In another mode of social reproduction, this relationship to the past might look more like forgetting than *Memory*.

Art, Work, and Endlessness in the 2000s

Throughout this book, I have described how the development of postindustrial capitalism depended on a subtle transmutation of the critical intentions and imaginings of the poets, artists, and theorists of the 1960s and 1970s. Though the world that resulted was radically different from these projections, it was dependent on them nonetheless. The future described in the previous chapter, legible in the margins of Bernadette Mayer's *Memory*, where people work longer and harder at the behest of technology rather than less intensely and for less long because of it, would have been particularly surprising to many of the writers discussed in this book. In the 1960s and 1970s, nearly everyone assumed that work was losing its centrality within fully industrialized capitalist economies, that rising productivity would mean falling average work hours, and that the chief problem capitalism would confront in coming decades would be how to distribute this "free time" such that it was not experienced by some as crippling unemployment and poverty or, additionally, as an existential crisis of meaning. This was not the view of far-left radicals, or a small clique of academics, but worried over by figures from across the political spectrum, in both the academic and popular press. Following up on the predictions of J. M. Keynes, the last chapter of J. K. Galbraith's popular 1958 book, *The Affluent Society*, attempted to map out the various possible trajectories for postwar society, given the observable "declining marginal urgency of product," a technical way of saying that increasingly people preferred more free time to more things and would take increasing productivity in the form of decreasing work hours.[1] Initially, David Riesman's famous book of postwar sociology, *The Lonely Crowd*, predicted limits to the increase of an "intolerable freedom from work" and suggested that without a reeducation of desires, the outer-directed glad-handers of postwar society would continue to seek meaning in work and take abundance in the form of increased consumption rather than leisure time.[2] But by the end of the decade, Riesman had changed his tune and, in an essay revisiting the themes of *The Lonely Crowd*, argues that the world pictured in Aldous Huxley's *Brave New World* and Frederik Pohl's *The Midas Plague*, in which work was a privilege reserved for the upper classes, while the rest of society was abandoned to oppressive idleness and forced consumption, seemed more and more in line with the trends of postwar society.[3]

By the mid-1960s, these accounts had coalesced into what we might call the "end-of-labor" thesis.[4] After remaining at relatively low levels throughout the 1950s, US unemployment shot up to 6 percent toward the end of the decade, and many began to blame automation. President John F. Kennedy went so far as to describe technological unemployment as "the major domestic challenge ... of the 1960s."[5] A key document here is the "The Triple Revolution," a 1964 memorandum drafted by the Center for the Study of Democratic Institutions, a liberal think tank, and sent to President Lyndon Johnson.[6] Signed by various New and Old Left figures, including James Boggs and Tom Hayden, both of whom had written contemporary texts with similar prognoses about a future of technological unemployment, it argued boldly that the demands of the civil rights movement (part of a global "Human Rights Revolution") for integration of US society could never be met by capitalism as it was configured then; the unfolding "Cybernation Revolution" promised that the brunt of technological unemployment, a growing problem, would continue to be borne by blacks.[7] Without the integration of workplaces, the broader project of social integration would fail. And while a Cold War "Weaponry Revolution" managed to stem the tide of unemployment by creating artificial demand for labor, this was a mere stopgap, and the revolution in cybernation would continue to impede demands for greater human rights. Furthermore, the demands of the antinuclear and antiwar movement would, if won, make this problem even worse. The solution the writers proposed—a guaranteed right to income, independent of work—has accompanied every discussion of the end of labor in the decades since, advanced and elaborated by figures as diverse as André Gorz and Milton Friedman, Antonio Negri and Richard Nixon. Guaranteed or basic income continues to attract much interest in the post-2008 revival of the end-of-labor discourse.[8]

Many of those who suggested machine-induced displacement had already arrived often qualified their prediction of an imminent crisis of unemployment, in ways similar to the remarks in "The Triple Revolution" about the military-industrial complex, noting that Keynesian fiscal measures and artificially induced demand exerted a countervailing force, though one that at the same time created a society of false needs and egregious waste. For some commentators, especially the Marxists, the end of labor was entirely a matter of the *potentialities* latent within postwar society, potentialities held back by a system of "false needs." This was especially true for Herbert Marcuse, whose books on postwar society had a huge influence on the New Left and the 1960s counterculture. In *Eros and Civilization*, published in 1955, he suggests that the repressive forces that continually compel labor to greater productivity are contradictory and self-undermining. Though humans have an instinctual drive toward self-preservation, which requires them to deny immediate self-gratification (Freud called this the "reality principle"), capitalism transforms this "basic repression" into a gratuitous "surplus repression." The reality principle is transformed into an excessive "performance principle" that orients humans toward continual self-denial in accord with the exigencies of capitalist accumulation, a process that Marcuse notes may, paradoxically, have produced a new "potential of freedom" and the transcendence of the need for self-denial altogether:

> If the achievements of the performance principle surpass its institutions, they also militate against the direction of its productivity—against the subjugation of man to his labor. Freed from this enslavement, productivity loses its repressive power and impels the free development of individual needs.... The more complete the alienation of labor, the greater the potential of freedom: total automation would be the optimum. It is the sphere outside labor which defines freedom and fulfillment, and it is the definition of the human existence in terms of this sphere which constitutes the negation of the performance principle.[9]

The more alienation increases, so too does the possibility for a world beyond alienation. Total automation would mean total alienation but also total freedom. At this point, Marcuse follows Marx, in this regard, who argued that "the realm of freedom really only begins where labor determined by necessity and external expediency ends," though he will later reject this position.[10] For Marx, "[t]he reduction of the workday is the basic prerequisite" of this passage to liberty.[11] Freedom and necessity are as two portions of the day: as the time spent working diminishes, the time of freedom increases.

Unlike Marx, who placed strong emphasis on the tendential, developmental character of the productive forces, Marcuse tends to depict this process as the emergence into the open of a conflict between two sets of values that might determine the disposition of the wealth of capitalism. Later texts, from the 1960s and beyond, such as *One-Dimensional Man*, follow Riesman and others and blame the squandering of the potentials of automation on the creation of a series of "repressive needs":

> The distinguishing feature of advanced industrial society is its effective suffocation of those needs which demand liberation—liberation also from that which is tolerable and rewarding and comfortable—while it sustains and absolves the destructive power and repressive function of the affluent society. Here, the social controls exact the overwhelming need for the production and consumption of waste; the need for stupefying work where it is no longer a real necessity.[12]

Against these repressive needs, Marcuse often counterposes a "Great Refusal" centered around an alternative set of values.[13] In his first usage of the term, the Great Refusal is associated with aesthetic experience, a series of authentic needs and desires (for freedom, for truth) that appear most prominently within the realm of the arts. But in his most optimistic text, 1969's *Essay on Liberation*, Marcuse characterizes the Great Refusal in terms that are not only aesthetic but political, using it as his code word for the radical currents (decolonization, black liberation, youth and student movements) to whom his book is dedicated.[14]

In this late text, Marcuse speaks of the development of a promising "new sensibility" among militants, visible first in the way that they subvert existing language and second in their novel means of relating to each other. For Marcuse, "the degree to which a revolution is developing qualitatively different social conditions and relationships may perhaps be indicated by the development of a different language: the rupture with the continuum of domination must also be a rupture with the vocabulary of domination." He connects this to the earlier development of a "surrealist thesis" among poets and artists of the earlier twentieth century "according to which the poet is the total nonconformist, [and] finds in poetic language the semantic elements of the revolution."[15] Among black militants and among the nonconformist white youth, one witnessed an "ingression of the aesthetic into the political" and the development of "a revolution in perception . . . a new sensorium."[16] Though this perceptual revolution had been anticipated by the avant-garde and modernist experiments of the early twentieth century, such a sensibility had been neutralized to the extent that it remained within the "segregated" space of art, their perceptual reconfigurations "offering a short-lived shock, quickly absorbed in the art gallery, within the four walls, in the concert hall, by the market, and adorning the plazas and lobbies of the prospering business establishments."[17] The "new sensibility" of the movements of the 1960s, however, prefigures "the end of art through its realization," under "conditions in which the aesthetic could become a *gessellschaftliche Produkitvkraft*," a socially productive force.[18] The possibilities opened up by automation can be utilized only if new sensibilities are cultivated, and these sensibilities require that aesthetic thinking and values are freed from the confines of art. The end of labor depends on the end of art.

In this late work, Marcuse takes issue with Marx's argument that the "realm of freedom" exists only "beyond" the unfreedom of work time, as its inverse; for Marcuse, the powers of the aesthetic must be brought into the heart of production. In Marx's schema, as Marcuse paraphrases, "Alienation would be reduced with the progressive reduction of the working day, but the latter would remain a day of unfreedom, rational but not free." For Marcuse, conversely, "the development of the productive forces beyond their capitalist organization suggests the possibility of freedom within the realm of necessity. The quantitative reduction of necessary labor could turn into quality (freedom), not in proportion to the reduction but rather to the transformation of the working day, a transformation in which the stupefying, enervating, pseudo-automatic jobs of capitalist progress would be abolished." While one might imagine automation forcing an involuntary transformation of necessity into freedom, the change that Marcuse describes "presupposes a type of man with a different sensitivity as well as consciousness: men who would speak a different language, have different gestures, follow different impulses; men who have developed an instinctual barrier against cruelty, brutality, ugliness." He continues:

> Such an instinctual transformation is conceivable as a factor of social change only if it enters the social division of labor, the production relations themselves. They would be shaped by men and women who have the good conscience of being human, tender, sensuous, who are no longer ashamed of themselves—for "the token of freedom attained, that is, no longer being ashamed of ourselves." ... The imagination of such men and women would fashion their reason and tend to make the

process of production a process of creation. This is the utopian concept of socialism which envisages the ingression of freedom into the realm of necessity, and the union between causality by necessity and causality by freedom. The first would mean passing from Marx to Fourier; the second from realism to surrealism.[19]

Marcuse's conjunction of the end of art and the end of labor shares something, in this regard, with the thought of Guy Debord and his compatriots in the Situationist International (which should come as no surprise given the common influence of the early Marx). Seeing themselves as the inheritors of Dadaism and surrealism, the members of the SI conjoined aesthetic revolution and political revolution in clearer and more programmatic terms than almost any other group. Following the museumification and enclosure of the dissident sensibility of avant-garde art, the only way to be faithful to these precedents was to refuse art altogether. For the SI, this effectively meant an intention to jailbreak art from the confines of rotten social institutions and use its technical powers for the transformation of everyday life, thereby abolishing the category of art as such. "In a given society," they write, "what is termed culture is the reflection, but also the foreshadowing, of possibilities for life's planning." Rather than the production of commodifiable objects, "the situationist goal is immediate participation in a passionate abundance of life, through the variation of fleeting moments resolutely arranged." These experiments respond not only to the decrepitude of capital-A art but to the "extension of leisure time" as working hours decrease:

> The success of these moments can only be their effect. Situationists consider cultural activity from the standpoint of totality, as an experimental method for constructing daily life, which can be permanently developed with the extension of leisure and the disappearance of the division of labor (beginning with the division of artistic labor).[20]

The revolutionary project of the SI is fundamentally about a "program of fulfilled poetry," which must by necessity be a "poetry without poems" given the reification into which poetry has fallen.[21] This fulfilled and poemless poetry would sublate all the resources and wealth of capitalist society and dispose of them in accord with that alternative set of values of which Marcuse spoke. The next form of society," as Debord writes, "will not be based on industrial production. It will be a society of *realized art*."[22]

The coincidence of the end of art and the end of labor depended on certain assumptions, at least as far as Marcuse and the writers of the SI were concerned. All of these writers seemed to assume that automation would proceed evenly, moving from manufacturing to the service sector, and gradually eliminating most human labor from these processes. Contrary to expectation, automation of services has been difficult and slow going, as the technology used to automate manufacturing is not appropriate there and computerization has produced only limited gains.[23] The result has been the creation of a tier of service-sector jobs where increase in output can be had only through increasing the effort of individual workers. (I distinguish here between effort and productivity; whereas automation replaces the effort of humans with the efforts of machines or multiplies human effort, allowing a person to move ten or one hundred times more weight with the same effort, we should distinguish this from *intensification*, sometimes called "sweating," which increases per person productivity through an increase of effort or an elimination of rest periods, requiring more mental and physical activity per unit of time.)

As we have seen time and again in the preceding chapters, the liberation of the techniques and vocabularies of art from the specific segregated space of art—in other words, the end of art's monopoly over these techniques—has been enormously helpful to employers in such a situation, where valorizing capital means getting people to work longer and harder. The "new sensibility" that Marcuse saw percolating in the arts, the counterculture, and communities of militants was directed, forcefully, against the repressive values of the work culture of the time, but what Marcuse and Debord and the writers of the SI seem not to have foreseen is that the new values of the new sensibility could be made operational within the space of capitalist work, not just beyond it. The artists and writers of the period were able to break free of the formal confines of the cultural institutions of the period, but they did so less through the assistance of revolutionary processes and more through their active recruitment by the corporate cultures of the 1980s and 1990s. In a recent treatment of the same developments, *The Problem with Work*, Kathi Weeks tells a story about how, in the postwar period, demands for "better work" won out over demands for "less work."[24] Weeks offers a novel theoretical approach to the question of work, reinvigorating the critical challenges to its reign. Hers is not a work of economic history or history of labor, however, so we might add to her important contributions that one of the reasons that postwar writers focused on better work was that a secular tendency toward less work seemed already assured, given ongoing automation of the labor process.

Under the actual conditions of postwar capitalism, where automation of services confronted real obstacles not present in the manufacturing sector, Marcuse's new sensibility turned into the "new spirit of capitalism" that Boltanski and Chiapello describe. Employers met the call for self-management and increased autonomy by instituting forms of internalized, impersonal control that meant anxious self-harrying; they met the demand for community and cooperation with the organizational concept of "teamwork," in which employees drive each other to work harder, independent of managerial imperatives; they met the demand for variety in work by piling on new responsibilities; they met the challenge to the domination of work over life by shifting to part-time, contingent, and at-will work; and finally, they met the demand for creativity and authenticity by incorporating elements of play, fun, de-repression, intimacy, and affective intensity into the workplace. We might conclude that, in contradistinction to the projections of the 1960s, the corporate recuperation of the artistic critique used the end of art to cancel out the end of labor, developing new affective relationships to work and new psychological incentives through and as art that were able to extend rather than end labor, turning the open frontier of expanding leisure into the 24/7 of the inescapable job.

Art and Endlessness

If the end of art canceled out the end of labor, the reverse was also true, since rather than die, art has manifestly lived on after its failed self-abolition, aerosolized, freed from the constraints of medium and institution, but nonetheless still domesticated by the commodity form and the world of labor it once opposed. Art has become one technique of communication or management among many, and quite successful as such. This holds true as much for the visual and postvisual arts as for literature, which, though its ambitions were rarely stated as grandly as those of the other arts, likewise suffers the same crisis of vocation. The result is another kind of endlessness, a lack of purpose, since art and literature can no longer offer credible challenges to the status quo. What possibilities for the aesthetic critique of work remain now that workplaces have been designed to anticipate and neutralize such critiques? What happens when art confronts a workplace whose very technologies, attitudes, and structures are a materialization of its own defeated challenges? The technological dimension is crucial here, since digital technology remains one of the main sites for and mechanisms of this restructuring. The shift from mainframe to personal computers, for instance, and the rise of networking were, in many regards, a result of these earlier organizational transformations, which emphasized lateral connections between workers and the effective autonomy of individuals and work groups. Computing allows management to become an infrastructure rather than a personal, face-to-face relationship. Recognizing this history should lead us to be skeptical in the face of claims about the emancipatory possibilities of this technology, since information technology, as my narrative has it, was the fruit of a counterrevolutionary turn from the very beginning. Attention to this history can show us how many of the values attached to web 2.0 have their roots in the defeated resistance of the 1960s and 1970s.

Because it often explicitly invokes white-collar work and because it uses digital technology, the suggestively titled "Flarf" poetry—an experimentalist writing movement that emerged in 2001—is a good place to examine the legacy of the restructuring just described. Experimental poetry is a cultural zone where novelty remains the measure of value and where the crisis of vocation, of endlessness, is acutely felt. In the case of Flarf, this is signaled from the outset by the semiparodic name it adopts, demonstrating its inability to take itself seriously. Described as "a kind of corrosive, cute, or cloying, awfulness" effected, poetry-wise, through the collage of material appropriated from "internet chat-room drivel and spam scripts," most Flarf poems initially followed a fairly simple procedure. As Mike Magee describes it: "[Y]ou search Google for 2 disparate terms, like 'anarchy + tuna melt' [and] using only the quotes captured by Google (never the actual websites themselves) you stitch words, phrases, clauses, sentences together to create poems."[25]

Importantly for my argument, Flarf was not simply a set of compositional practices but a compositional location as well. In the retrospective definition that practitioner Drew Gardner provides in an interview with fellow Flarfist Jordan Davis, "Flarf was a bunch of us fucking around with Google on the man's dime."[26] Before the age of smartphones, white-collar workplaces were some of the only spaces that allowed for the redirection of company equipment and time in this manner, and so, unsurprisingly, Flarf's "bored-at-work Google sculpting" frequently foregrounds the managerial boilerplate of the contemporary office. The poems therefore figure resistance to work on multiple levels, redirecting company time and company language, as we can see from this early contribution by Katie Degentesh to the e-mail list that served as a sounding board for Flarf poets:

FROM: Human Resources Loveroll
DATE: May 8, 2001
RE: Hot Hatred and Hot Business Coital Attire

In the spirit of the upcoming season, hot hatred and business coital attire will begin on Monday, May 21 and end on Friday, August 31, 2001.

Hot Hatred

As hot approaches we are pleased to remind all employees that we will be milking a condensed milk week. During the hot months, there will be extended office hatred Monday through Thursday, allowing for a * day on Friday. Please see the guidelines below:

Regular office hatred will be 9:00 a.m.–5:30 p.m. Monday through Thursday and 9:00 a.m.–1:00 p.m. on Friday. In order to accommodate this schedule, lunch periods, which are unloved, should be limited to 45 pieces of popcorn. Department heads may allow an individual to adjust his/her core milking hatred while still milking the full weekly hatred. All employees will milk their regularly scheduled hatred within a week (barring evacuation or jail time) regardless of starting or ending time. The office will remain open on Friday afternoons for those of you who wish to complete pregnancies or have regular milk to finish, however, there will be no mailroom or reception services beyond 1:00 p.m.[27]

Though Degentesh's poem uncharacteristically uses word substitution rather than a Google search query—for example, replacing *milk* with *work*, *casual* with *coital*—it nonetheless introduces terrain common to Flarf poems, playing up the opposition between public and private worlds, given here as a conflict between the bureaucratic protocols of office work and the demands of intimate life. But in my reading the poem is ultimately less about the conflict between these spheres than it is about their interchangeability: the easy swapping of love for pay, coital for casual, milk for work, and hatred for hours. In other words, the poem registers the ways in which the contemporary workplace and its motivational structures depend on an ambient sexualization that is solicited and then administered rather than repressed. As for parenting, though the poem might at first seem to suggest the incompatibility of the rigid workplace schedule and the demands of child care, subordinating the provision of breast milk to the metric time of the "regularly scheduled hatred" that must occur "regardless of starting or ending time," the final paragraph opens up the possibility of special allowances for those "who wish to complete pregnancies or have regular milk to finish."

The insight that the poem's newly interchangeable terms provides here is especially noteworthy: allowances made for the life circumstances of parents mean staying at work longer. As we now know, the introduction of more flexible work schedules and practices such as telecommuting, undertaken at first in response to the demands of working mothers and parents, has not at all served to decenter work and working life or allow home life and leisure to gain a new primacy.[28] On the contrary, flexibilization of working hours has been used to the benefit of employers: flexible hours and telecommuting have enabled certain salaried workers (parents especially) to work longer workweeks overall, cramming work into every corner of the day.[29]

The merger of work and nonwork time that results has produced an entirely different emotional tone within the contemporary workplace. Rather than the overt repression of affects associated with the space of nonwork, with the home and the street, workplaces have attempted to absorb such feeling states and adapt them to the production of more highly motivated and work-identified employees. Workers are asked to express passionate feelings, even "hot hatred," that managers previously saw as dangerous and sought to repress. Enthusiasm, sympathy, and sensitivity are cultivated as important motivational counterweights to the native indifference and anxiety of many workplaces, and workers now succeed through the performance and transmission of emotional intensities. For Eva Illouz, who chronicles the emotional turn in corporate culture, the new psychologized management theory made it such that "being a good communicator" is the distinguishing trait of the effective worker. In this environment, "[p]rofessional competence [is] defined in emotional terms, by the capacity to acknowledge and empathize with others."[30] Under such a paradigm, workers are taught not only to perform emotionality but also to seek in work the satisfactions they might once have expected from the world beyond, leading to a hyperidentification with work. One consequence is a sexualization of the workplace and work processes ("business coital attire") that proceeded with little interference from the sexual harassment law established in the 1980s and 1990s.[31]

The emphasis on good communication within the workplace might explain Flarf's absurdist turn, as if it were disrupting the discursive field of pragmatic office memos by resorting to a poetry of "integral zebra-cellist-messiah dining halls" where "T.S. Eliot's poetry is 'about women's basketball.'"[32] One of the ambiguities we encounter, however, in studying the transformation of workplaces is that this kind of goofiness seems both a mode of resistance to the white-collar workplace and a means by which corporations create a fun, uninhibited, and affectively charged environment. Peter Fleming, for instance, chronicles the rise of a new "pop management publishing industry" where "'fun-sultants' advise otherwise quondam and staid managers how to build cultures of fun . . . as a quick method for motivating staff, gaining their full engagement with the labour process, and selling the firm to customers and/or contractors."[33] Indeed, irrational behavior of this sort might be an aid to good communication rather than a hindrance to it. As one advocate of humor management puts it: "Humour plays a vital role in helping to close the communication gap between leader and followers, helping to extract information, which might not otherwise be volunteered."[34] In light of this ambiguity, Degentesh's poem may be a satire of the office memo genre, designed to challenge both the rigidity of the workplace and its absorption of nonwork activities and affects, or it may be the poetic equivalent of "casual Friday," one example of the ludic nonconformity that firms will tolerate or even encourage to let their workers blow off steam and stay motivated.

Other Flarf poems meditate rather explicitly on this ambiguity. In Rodney Koeneke's "My Blog," we encounter a cyberslacking speaker who is "bored down here in shipping" and blogging instead of fulfilling work responsibilities. Yet in the absence of the clear-cut outside to work that "kids" or "school" might provide, the speaker has difficulty distinguishing between work activities and goofing off:

> Not having kids, not going to school
>   I mindmeld with an array of daily visitors
> screens flip from classroom to business to leisure[35]

An apparatus for sympathetic identification, the blog encourages people to cultivate the affective reciprocity that Illouz identifies as the hallmark of modern management theory. The collective "mindmeld" that results is a model not only for the construction of the Flarf poem, stitched together from appropriated bits of other people's writing and then edited collaboratively on an e-mail list, but also the teamwork-based protocols of the modern workplace. Further, the poem describes a new media platform that obtains across a number of homological situations in the once differentiated but now continuous spaces of "classroom to business to leisure." Unsurprisingly, the poem suspects that these diversions might simply be another form of white-collar labor slated for absorption by the final instance of corporate ownership:

> I feel obliged
> to blog about guy in Receiving with grody leisure suit
> & that's the whole point—to flip unseemly power
> & hope we're not so sanguine about Google
>   buying Blogger
> {Google + Blogger = Mainstream weblog acceptance ...}[36]

The flip to which the speaker submits unseemly power is easily reversed, and it should be no surprise that a few stanzas later "flip" becomes, through the anaphoric logic of the poem, "flip-flops." The obligation the speaker feels to blog about a coworker makes the critical gesture seem deeply ambiguous, part of the speaker's work responsibilities as much as a resistance to them. If Fleming is right that corporations absorb resistance through a "debasing mimesis" that "eviscerates what it mimics," then the speaker's antagonist presents a peculiar object of criticism indeed, wearing a "leisure suit" at work and therefore disabling the distinction between work and nonwork activity that the speaker's critique requires.[37] Indeed, the fact that his nemesis works in Receiving—the mirror image of Shipping—makes us think that the speaker is merely fighting his own cross-departmental doppelganger, his own image flipped, as it were, in the mimetic corporate mirror.

Troll Poetics and the Rotated Axis of Antagonism

One consequence of the "delayering" of the modern corporation, which eliminates middle managers and establishes horizontal connections between workers, is that antagonism likewise gets sent laterally, toward other workers, rather than vertically toward management. Hence, the speaker of "My Blog" reminisces about the printed matter that preceded blogs—"cute little flipbooks .../ that flipped from horizontal / to vertical position at will."[38] This rotation of the axis of antagonism seems to be the one type of flip not permitted in Koeneke's poetic universe, a fact that might explain not only the conclusion of Koeneke's poem but Flarf's often controversial attraction toward the provocative or offensive, employing found language that is racist, sexist, or homophobic.

If Degentesh, Koeneke, and other Flarf poets describe, critically, the problem that challenges to the workplace confront today, in the wake of managerial restructuring, other Flarf works might be said to enact the consequences of this restructuring. Some readers may remember the way that Mike Magee's poem "Their Guys, Their Glittering Asian Guys, Are Gay" ignited an extensive debate, both online and in print, about the ethical and political values of appropriating hateful social materials. Defenders of the poem insisted that it was a satirical emptying out of homophobic, misogynist, and orientalist discourse—particularly the association of Asian men with effeminacy or gayness—while its detractors accused it of what has since been dubbed "ironic racism" or "hipster racism," wherein a person deploys and enjoys scare-quoted racist language or engages in scare-quoted minstrelsy.[39] For Gary Sullivan, who coined the term "Flarf," the value of this kind of language lay elsewhere, not in its value as realism but, to pick up on old avant-garde aims, in its power to shock and provoke. In his original formulation, he controversially described Flarf poems as "Wrong. Un-P.C. Out of control. 'Not okay.'" As Sullivan recalls, "[T]he flarf 'voice' in my head was that of my father, a transplanted southerner . . . who has a lot of opinions that kind of horrify me." For Sullivan, such a voice served as an expressive inducement, "a way of keeping [his] own tendencies toward repression . . . at bay."[40]

Sullivan's characterization is, therefore, profoundly therapeutic in its orientation, not all that different from the most commonplace characterization of the value of talk therapy, which, as we learn from Illouz, has been foundational as a model for management. At the same time, language of this sort would most certainly be considered a transgression of the norms of "good communication" in effect within most workplaces, norms that will almost always feature at least perfunctory injunctions against offensive language, sexual harassment, and other forms of microaggression. However, the more workplaces emphasize de-repression, liberation, and management through humor, the more they solicit the kind of language and behavior that violates norms of good communication and action. This is not a contradiction so much as it is a strategy, a way of directing the tilting antagonisms and aggressions of the workplace away from management. In such an environment, antagonisms of this sort are likely to emerge in a half-veiled form, as pranks, jokes, and ironic innuendo. Sullivan's "Flarf voice"—the rural, white, Southern, lower-class, conservative originator of his found language—becomes the perfect sock puppet through which to ventriloquize disavowed antagonism, in a form that manages to join the class condescension of white-collar workers with whatever "horrifying" thoughts the Flarf voice entails. Often, these thoughts reflect masculine anxiety and resentment in the face of an increasingly feminized labor process. As Illouz and others have made clear, the post-Taylorist transformation of management theory and the emphasis on teamwork and communicativity have meant a feminization of work, deployed through "management techniques that privilege irrationality, intuition, fluidity, faith, and emotion." For Illouz, "the ethos of communication *blurs gender divisions* by inviting men and women to control their negative emotions, be friendly, view themselves through others' eyes, and empathize with others."[41] In Mike Magee's poem, these anxieties are complicated even further by the addition of anti-Asian discourse, reacting not only to the newfound success of Asian corporations and countries but the "model minority" status of certain Asian Americans, both aspects that are associated with the newly feminized, ludic workplace, in which "an Asian business man rips off his coat, revealing a glittering, Vegas style."[42]

Other Flarf poems work much harder to contain these violent energies by properly signposting and scare-quoting them, making sure the reader knows how to interpret and channel their satirical energies. Such is the case with one of the most famous Flarf poems, Drew Gardner's "Chicks Dig War," which might be read as a critical, Google-enabled scan of such anxieties of feminization as manifest in the sub-basements of the Internet, a place where "Women are excellent teachers / of the bitter lesson that being / anti-war does not get a man laid."[43] Composed from the scattered phrases of search results fished up from the murky waters of the Internet, Gardner's Flarf models the psychic structure of paranoia—that is, the projection of anxieties and fantasies into a morass of uncoordinated linguistic fragments in which it is possible to hear or see almost anything. Perhaps because of its management of a consistent tone, Gardner's poem seems pretty clearly an attempt to map this projective thinking. Indeed, his poem might, in this sense, reveal the fundamentally projective character of search functions in general, especially those offered by Google, which take a user's search history and create results tailored to that person's interests. The ultimate effect of these algorithms is the creation of what Eli Pariser has called a "filter bubble," an individualized sorting of information such that one's views, tastes, and experiences are always confirmed rather than challenged.[44] For instance, a statement like "women are excellent teachers"—drawn from one website or used as a search string—rests on certain fairly standard assumptions about the kind of work appropriate for women. But detached from its context, it magnetizes to itself all kinds of projected material, confirming the deep anxieties about gender roles that the initial statement might have assuaged. It would be harder to find a better description of the forms of projection and displacement at work in male resentment than the psychobiological thesis the poem concludes with, which confirms the social necessity of "male aggressiveness" but makes it, paradoxically, the feature of a dominated sex class:

> Believe that male behavior is the result
> of a breeding experiment run by females?
> In case you missed it,
> the basic implication is that by following
> their natural proclivity to breed with
> John Ashcroft
> women are an anti-civilizing force,
> actively creating more male aggressiveness.
> It would seem that a wise society would have an
> interest in creating a counter-force to oppose this.[45]

The poem cleverly distributes its Internet cullings in such a way that the question-begging projections of male ressentiment are exposed to the reader's ridicule. At the same time, we do not come any closer to understanding the source of these antagonisms; the "counter-force" proposed, seriously or not, in the final lines would, at best, bring us back to the very beginning, since we have no clear idea whom to oppose other than the aggressive males and the women who incite them.

Gardner and his colleagues would likely shrug off any expectations that Flarf engage in this kind of critical realistic work, since Flarf is essentially a form of play, a way of "fucking around on the man's dime," as Gardner says. In this regard, Flarf's desperate insistence on fun, on the transgression of communicative norms, and its reliance on provocative social materials drawn from the netherworld of the Internet, might read as a literary reworking of the spirit of the so-called Internet troll—infamous denizen of ill-reputed websites like 4chan and reddit, whose own aggressive and often hateful fun making serves no end besides provocation.

Like Flarf, the troll's main sport is sabotage of communicative norms, provoking outrage through purposefully provocative commentary. Like Flarf, troll humor moves quickly from the goofy to the violent. Trolling depends on the functional anonymity provided by the online world, along with the ability to create flexible shifting identities through various online avatars and accounts, something that resembles the patchwork speakers of the Flarf poems as well as the patchwork laborers of the postindustrial era. But we might also consider the troll's attraction to the anonymity of the web as a reaction to the compulsory visibility and accountability demanded by face-to-face interactions, especially those in the workplace.[46] In some accounts, trolls aim to preserve the freedom and openness (and also opacity) of the Internet world from the norms of "meatspace" and the incursions of corporate content providers, "to maintain the idea of the internet as a space where manners and norms are suspended."[47] Others, however, emphasize the ludic, anti-instrumental character of troll activity, undertaken "for the lulz," as the saying goes, for the sake of diversion and as expression of a "pervasive, nihilistic, ungovernable incivility" that despairs of changing underlying conditions.[48] In this account, the troll engages in conflict for its own sake, Ares-like, often playing both sides. The troll shares with Flarf a fundamental ambiguity; trolling can be a sadistic laugh had at another's expense, or alternatively, undertaken in service of some sense of justice, used to dethrone the powerful and arrogant, avenge victims, or extract the truth.

Given the resemblance between trolling and the workplace pranks that form the subject of so many white-collar comedies, it is not surprising that, when outed, so many trolls turn out to be white-collar workers "goofing around on the man's dime." Nathaniel Tkacz, notably, defines the troll as that which is excluded from the new "collaborative" work methods of the Internet and the postindustrial office, revealing the way that these horizontal, putatively democratic processes rely on impersonal norms and "frames."[49] The deliberately stupid humor of the troll, directed horizontally toward peers rather than toward superiors, represents the outcome of corporate strategies of restructuring, the effect of complaints and upsets that no longer find any clear targets or means of redress, much less any coherence into a strategy of resistance, given that they are constitutively excluded by the communicative norms of the workplace. Diverted and neutralized by the restructuring, these antagonisms remain susceptible to transformation according to scapegoating logics and narratives. Trolling, in this regard, represents the ungainly remainder of the qualitative challenge now that all such challenges seem to be anticipated by the mandated nonconformity and routinized fun of the workplace. What possible challenge can the zaniness of Flarf or the troll deliver when workers are themselves exhorted to participate in team-building exercises where they "wrap each other in toilet paper and aluminum foil, build sandcastles and imitate animals" or perform together a rendition of Kermit the Frog's "Rainbow Connection"?[50]

The Saturation of the Qualitative Critique

Flarf represents one response to this impasse, an attempt to beat the culture of forced fun at its own game. Other poets, associated with conceptual poetry, will adopt another strategy, antiludic and anhedonic where Flarf insists on play and pleasure. Flarf is often mentioned together with conceptual poetry, and for good reason. Both emerged at about the same time, and both positioned themselves as self-conscious writing "movements" at a moment in history when most experimental writers had eschewed explicit group identity. Like the avant-gardes of the past, their bid for recognition depended on claims about the changed context for poetry and the need for innovation that could respond to evolving history. The argument often revolved around information technology and the new Internet-based discursive environment of blogs, websites, and mailing lists through which poets were distributing and discussing their work. Flarf and conceptual poetry were, as their exponents argued, the forms adequate to this environment. Both modes were, in this sense, about an encounter between old and new media; the writers registered and explored the characteristics of the new media environment through its effect on poetic form and the form of the book, the codex, in which their experiments were often collected after provisional digital exhibition. Finally, both movements were explicitly about information work, not only based on the same techniques and procedures but often addressed to such work at the level of content. For conceptualist impresario and gadfly Kenneth Goldsmith, "conceptual writing" is an aestheticized form of "information management" and "word processing." As he declares, "[T]he office is the next frontier of writing," and an "electronic Post-It universe imbues the new writing, adopting corporate-speak as its lingo." Blending the mundanity of the office with the exoticism of its putative opposite, this kind of writing "requires the expertise of a secretary crossed with the attitude of a pirate: replicating, organizing, mirroring, archiving, and reprinting, along with a more clandestine proclivity for bootlegging, plundering, hoarding, and file-sharing."[51]

Thus, it should not surprise us that one of the most acclaimed and controversial works of conceptual poetry of the last few years, Vanessa Place's *Statement of Facts*, is a straight-ahead reproduction of the briefs she wrote as a public criminal appellate defense lawyer representing accused sex offenders.[52] As legal genre, the "statement of facts" is a supposedly neutral narrative presentation of the crime in question that prefaces formal legal argument. Though most critics have focused on the way that *Statement of Facts* exposes the subtle rhetorical machinery that underlies even the most depersonalized and neutral of narrative documents, the book also offers one of the most remarkable confirmations of the thesis that work activity and nonwork activity have become nearly identical at present, such that the difference between legal brief and poem is merely nominal, an effect of context. *Statement of Facts*, in this sense, is a poem for the end of the end of work, a poem of work's endlessness.

We might draw similar conclusions from any number of conceptual works. Consider, for instance, Kenneth Goldsmith's own project *Day*, wherein he transcribed the entire contents of a single issue of the *New York Times*, running multiple articles and ads together as he copied across the columns, deforming and deformatting the *Times* layout.[53] Such a project renders poetic composition identical to mere routine clerical work, data entry, or what Paul Stephens describes as "passive indexing."[54] We might say that *Day* reverses the relationship between the poem and the format of the newspaper established by Mallarmé, who, in "Un coup de dés," used the iconic visual display of the newspaper to create a new visual prosody; here Goldsmith uses poetry to transform the iconicity of the newspaper into the formlessness of data.

Despite all of these points of similarity, there are crucial differences between Flarf and conceptual poetry. Whereas Flarf insists on fun and goofy humor, much conceptual poetry is relentlessly austere, deliberately boring. Conceptualists are often trolls, but usually humorless or at best deadpan ones, engaging in jokeless provocation or exercises in which the joke is conceptual, a blank humor that unfolds as function of setting or frame.[55] If Flarf represents the attempt to exaggerate the forced fun of the workplace, to recover its liberatory power in a world where fun has become work, then conceptual poetry exposes the deep "unfun" of the workplace, its reality as routinized, mechanical information management.

This is where Kenneth Goldsmith's description of conceptual poetry as "uncreative writing" is perhaps useful, since it counteracts "new economy" rhetoric that declares high-tech work a distinct, superior form of laboring in which value derives from creativity or information rather than labor time pure and simple. There is a twist, though, since Goldsmith often characterizes his work through analogies with "creative" info-labor, comparing poets to "programmers." And he remains committed to a narrative of avant-garde innovation and technical progress, suggesting a hidden font of creativity beneath the routine cutting and pasting, data mining, databasing, and word processing of conceptual poetry. He says of the process of composing *Day* that "there were as many decisions, moral quandaries, linguistic preferences, and philosophical dilemmas as there are in an original or collaged work." Admitting the duplicity of his characterization, he writes that he "nonetheless still trumpet[s] the work's 'valuelessness,' its 'nutritionlessness,' its lack of creativity and originality when clearly the opposite is true." However, unwilling to leave such naked contradiction itself uncontradicted, Goldsmith doubles down on his unreliability immediately after writing this sentence, undermining even his own confession of secret creativity and writing that he is "not doing much more than trying to catch literature up with appropriative fads the art world moved past decades ago."[56] The work of innovation—catching up with the art world—is itself just duplication of something already "done" elsewhere. Rather than provide a simple negation of the rhetoric of creativity, as he imagines himself doing, Goldsmith shows us the fundamental uncreativity of creativity. A work like *Day* demonstrates, through it tedious unreadability, how utterly menial, mind numbing, and uncreative white-collar work really is while revealing how little it takes to make such routines seem creative. The most charitable reading of the "conceptual turn" in experimental poetry is that it marks a moment when the aura of fun, fulfillment, and creativity suddenly vanishes, and what remains is the endlessness of the working day and its technicized cognitions. Refusing the supplemental enjoyment of the workplace, conceptual poetry of the sort we have examined renders visible the exhaustion, boredom, and inanity of much of what we do for pay, but it also marks the cynical zero degree of resistance to work in which, in place of critique, we find a pure repetition: of the workday, the news, the violence of the state, the injuries of history. Yet, just like Goldsmith's retro-avant-gardism, this emptying out of the libidinal content of the work landscape seems to return us to the point at which we began, return us to the alienation of the office before its restructuring.

The conceptual poetry of work shares something, in this regard, with David Foster Wallace's unfinished and posthumous novel *The Pale King*, which treats the restructuring of the white-collar labor process during the 1980s (using the IRS as its example) more intensively than any other contemporary novel, offering a direct indictment of the qualitative critique and concomitant demands for novelty, diversion, and amusement, implying that they have reinforced a culture of widespread selfishness and puerility. Wallace's writing has always figured entertainment and the need for diversion as dangerous addiction—witness "the Entertainment" from *Infinite Jest*, a film so interesting that viewers watch it compulsively until they die of starvation—and in *The Pale King* this manifests as nostalgia for the old conformities and norms of the pre-restructuring IRS, as well as an explicit call for people to confront and, through acceptance, transcend the tedium exemplified by tax work, acting less from self-interest than from a sense of responsibility.[57] As one of the characters in the novel, Chris Fogle, recalls an accounting professor telling him (the character is, not incidentally, addicted to the stimulant Obetrol because of its capacity to allow him to pay attention): "True heroism is you, alone, in a designated work space. True heroism is minutes, hours, weeks, year upon year of the quiet, precise, judicious exercise of probity and care—with no one there to see or cheer. . . . Routine, repetition, tedium, monotony, ephemeracy, inconsequence, abstraction, disorder, boredom, angst, ennui—these are the true hero's enemies and make no mistake they are fearsome indeed."[58] These lines echo Wallace's commencement speech at Kenyon College, given in 2005, in which he warns students that their future will involve no small amount of "boredom, routine, and petty frustration" in the face of which "the really important kind of freedom involves attention and awareness and discipline, and being able to truly care about other people and to sacrifice for them over and over in myriad petty, unsexy ways everyday."[59]

The character who best exemplifies this sort of attention is Shane Drinion. Left alone with the "wrist-bitingly attractive Meredith Rand" after a group of coworkers go to the bar after work, Drinion appears unruffled, unperturbed by the presence of the distractions of desire.[60] Drinion combines boredom and attention and, as Rand notes during the seventy-page conversation, is both "interesting and really boring at the same time."[61] Halfway through the chapter, we learn that Drinion is "levitating slightly" as he begins to talk to Rand, "which is," we learn, "what happens when he is completely immersed."[62] He does this when he is examining tax returns as well, though he is unaware of it, since by definition it happens only when he is completely focused on the task at hand. Furthermore, this attention seems to be contagious, as the distractible and distracting Meredith Rand notes that while talking with Drinion, she has lost all sense of time and space. Wallace was explicit about the moral message here, in the notes published with *The Pale King*:

> Drinion is *happy*. Ability to pay attention. It turns out that bliss—a second-by-second joy + gratitude at the gift of being alive, conscious—lies on the other side of crushing, crushing boredom. Pay close attention to the most tedious thing you can find (tax returns, televised golf), and, in waves, a boredom like you've never known will wash over you and just about kill you. Ride these out, and it's like stepping from black and white into color.[63]

The dialectic of attention and distraction, and the theory of happiness that Wallace develops here, reads as if it were taken directly from the pages of psychologist Mihaly Csikszentmihalyi, who developed a theory of what he calls "flow" that has been enormously influential in the world of business psychology. Flow is a state of immersive attention, achieved through the development of skills in the face of challenges.[64] Csikszentmihalyi contrasts the happiness-producing enjoyment of flow with the expenditure of pleasure, which he argues brings no real happiness. He therefore develops a theory of meaning at work that runs counter to liberation management, and he is insistent that flow is a matter of attitude and can be achieved with even the most routine and presumably deadening work processes, filling his books with examples of farmers, steelworkers, assembly-line workers, and butchers who achieve flow through the perfection of repetitive action.[65] Like Wallace's novel, flow theory is, in this regard, a conservative reaction against the aesthetic critique, one that returns to old-fashioned ideas of restraint and character and offers itself up as a solution to distracted and miserable pleasure seeking.

Unwork and Endlessness

David Foster Wallace develops a response to the saturation of the qualitative critique diametrically opposed to Flarf's response, an explicit exhortation to embrace the boredom and alienation of work and instead sublimate the desire for creativity, variety, autonomy, and empowerment at the root of these critiques with an ethics of sacrifice, responsibility, and discipline. But perhaps instead of negating these desires we might look to redirect them. Perhaps the task of the aesthetic challenge in our time is not to demand freedom in work but freedom *from work*, as Kathi Weeks has suggested. If the restructuring of the workplace since the 1970s has neutralized many modes of struggle within it, then workers and other proletarians may need to look for modes of struggle against work that emerge from outside of work as such.[66] The art and writing that respond to such a condition might make wagelessness their object of critique as much as wagefulness, examining forms of domination within and beyond the workplace.[67] It might look something like the epistolary prose poems in Sean Bonney's collection, *Letters against the Firmament*, poems that take unemployment and the humiliations of the British welfare system under conditions of unfolding austerity as their starting point, writing from a "stereotypical amalgam of unwork, sarcasm, hunger and a spiteful radius of pure fear."[68] Bonney's epistolary poems are written against (though not addressed to) the ruling powers in Britain during the crisis years of 2010–2013. They are particularly hostile toward the Department of Work and Pensions (DWP) and its neoliberal workfare system (a reform of the British dole) and Jobcentres, with the Minister of the DWP, Iain Duncan Smith, reappearing throughout as a demonic presence, "a talking claw."[69] The letters are not addressed to Iain Duncan Smith, however, but to an intimate of the speaker, someone who seems both friend and superior (at one point the speaker asks the addressee for a letter of reference). As with the works discussed previously, the object of critique can be reached only indirectly.

Shifting the object of critique from the workplace to the fact of labor itself, as well as the repressive institutions designed to force benefits claimants back into the sale of their labor power, Bonney sidesteps the dilemmas of the aesthetic critique, launching his sentences into a many-sided jeremiad where "each note" of a contemplated Cecil Taylor song "could, magnetically, pull anything that any specific hour absolutely is not right into the centre of that hour, producing a kind of negative half-life where the time-zones selected by the Jobcentre as representative of the entirety of human life are damaged irrevocably."[70] The speaker of Bonney's poems is dispossessed not only of the products of labor but of the opportunity for labor, reminding us of the physiological basis of exploitation, the "real hunger, sharp, greedy and endless" that renders proletarians dependent on wages for survival. The peculiarity of the speaker's position is accentuated by the institution of the Jobcentre and the neoliberal concept of "workfare," which turns lack of work into work itself by requiring benefits claimants to spend at least thirty hours weekly searching for employment, undergoing retraining, or performing community service. "Unwork" is not the negation of work but its underlying form, emptied of content, something Bonney connects to the novel British invention of "zero-hours contracts," described by him as "anti-magnetic nebulae sucking the working day inside out." Allowing employers to vary employee hours by will, these contracts prompt Bonney to think of the workfare regime as a "negative-hours" contract.[71] This draws out the potential downside of appeals for "less work" that depend on state subsidy: without specification of the terms, these conditions of "unwork" involve added exposure to the coercive violence of the state.

For Bonney, the age demands a critique of both work and unwork, and that means repositioning rather than abandoning the demand for various, creative, and meaningful activity that we inherit from the aesthetic critique. These expressive activities appear, here, under the sign of carnivalesque riot and rebellion, offering up not enjoyment in work but enjoyment beyond and against work. However, given the tendency of release from work to become lack of work, or unwork, such joys are inextricable from agonies various and sundry. He thusly describes the celebrations in response to Margaret Thatcher's death as the ecstatic proliferation of plague:

> It was like we were a blister on the law. Inmates. Fancy-dress jacobins. Jesters. And yes. Every single one of us was well aware that we hadn't won anything, that her legacy "still lived on," and whatever other sanctimonious spittle was being coughed up by liberal shitheads in the Guardian and on Facebook. That wasn't the point. It was horrible. Deliberately so. Like the plague-feast in Nosferatu. I loved it. I had two bottles of champagne, a handful of pills and a massive cigar, it was great. I walked home and I wanted to spray-paint "Never Work" on the wall of every Jobcentre I passed.[72]

In this poem, the schadenfreude of the troll finally finds its target, even if the address is indirect, incomplete, and (as he acknowledges) personifies and mis-prises in the figure of Thatcher complex processes of economic restructuring. Bonney's *Letters* presents the imperfect and incomplete working through of these otherwise obstructed antagonisms, hinting at the possibility of a choice between two types of challenge to the regime of work and two types of endlessness. There is, of course, the bad infinity we are already familiar with: "an endless, undifferentiated regime of ersatz work" interrupted occasionally by a "Thatcher death-day as some kind of workers holiday." But there is also something else, the possibility that these celebrations might take place "every day, for ever and ever," a possibility that, for the time being, can only be uttered slantwise, stamped by the affects of the troll and likened to "a ring of plague-sores, botulism, and roses."[73]

Epilogue: Overflow

Since 2008, the end-of-labor thesis has returned with renewed vigor. The still-unfolding economic crisis revealed deep structural problems with postindustrial capitalism, and even as financial markets have recovered, few new jobs have been added. Worries about technological unemployment (sometimes called "structural" unemployment) often attend economic crises, when people are thrown out of work and few employers are hiring; just as post-2008 conversations return, knowingly or not, to the terrain of the debates of the 1960s and 1970s, so too were those conversations a renewal of themes and tropes from the 1930s.[1] Today, popular books such as Erik Brynjolfsson and Scott McAfee's *Second Machine Age* and Tyler Cowen's *Average Is Over* recast the end-of-labor arguments of their predecessors, suggesting that new digital technologies are poised to displace hundreds of millions of workers in services rather than in manufacturing and other industry, less through the direct replacement of workers by machines than through new, human-computer ensembles that increase productivity in the heretofore impossible-to-automate sectors like education and health care.[2] Both books agree that polarization of wealth will follow these developments inexorably: "average is over," Cowen argues, because working with the new machines or managing those who can requires skill and care; as a result, most unskilled or semiskilled "middling level" jobs will be eliminated.[3] Though the extra wealth produced by these machines will be great, the need for workers with specific skills means that the distribution of this wealth will be increasingly uneven, with the owners of capital and a small group of in-demand laborers taking the lion's share: we will see a "spread," Brynjolfsson and McAfee note, between those whose skills are in demand and those who must accept a decreasing wage in order to find any work at all. Like their predecessors, the authors of *The Second Machine Age* argue that guaranteed income will probably become necessary (though they prefer the "negative tax" variant that they believe will not discourage work). At the same time, they suggest, rather vaguely, that the worst effects can be held at bay through the imaginative elaboration of new social uses for technology (what Marcuse would no doubt have described as "false need").[4] Beyond the near term, however, the authors do hint at a long-term, "android" scenario in which machines substitute for human labor *tout court*, sending the value of human labor to zero very quickly.[5]

Tyler Cowen is less optimistic about near-run possibilities and instead imagines a growing class of unemployable "zero marginal product workers" who lack the skills and "conscientiousness" required in the new economy.[6] (His marginal productivity formulation means that, at a certain point, adding more unskilled workers to a workplace generates no gains in output—1,001 workers produce as much as 1,000—whereas adding more capital, in the form of machines, does.) In a remarkable bit of sociobiological theorizing, he explains high current and future male unemployment by suggesting that "hotheaded" men often lack the conscientiousness and, implicitly, the servility to succeed in the new silicon occupations; he does not consider, however, the argument advanced in Chapter 4 that these gender values are themselves, in part, artifacts of the labor process and labor market and therefore liable to be recast by its reorganization.[7] For Cowen, the insertion of machines into the labor-intensive processes of the service sector will require fewer, more highly skilled workers but, paradoxically, a higher number of managers to train and supervise them, and as we have seen earlier, contemporary management theory emphasizes feminine values, even if it often prefers to locate these feminine values in men. The only other growth areas will be in jobs serving the new super rich, who may pay a premium for the sort of service intimacies discussed in Chapter 1, preferring human to machine service, and using their silicon wealth to employ a growing army of "personal trainers, valets, private tutors, drivers, babysitters, interior designers, [and] carpenters."[8]

Given how wrong the end-of-labor theorists of the 1960s were, we might look with suspicion on their twenty-first-century avatars. There is, however, considerable evidence that the means whereby countries like the United States avoided high unemployment in the wake of deindustrialization—chiefly through the creation of a vast, low-wage market for services—are unsustainable in the long run, one-time stalling measures that reached their limits with the crisis of 2008. Among its many revelations, the breakdown of the financial system revealed that the plus and minus columns of the contemporary economic model, in which falling or stagnating wages are offset by the cheapening of consumer goods (mostly imported), can only equal zero through a massive provision of unrepayable debts both public and private. Since 2008, the labor force participation rate, which measures the fraction of the population at work, has fallen steadily, even as unemployment has also fallen.[9] The United States appears ready to join those other postindustrial countries that, as a result of labor protections and higher minimum wages, never created a low-wage service sector on the scale of that in the United States and have, consequently, been plagued by high unemployment, especially among youth. Others might suggest that these developments are offset by employment growth in developing or industrializing countries, but the evidence contradicts this view as well.[10] I rely here in particular on important work by the theory collective Endnotes and its associates articulating how and why the late twentieth century has witnessed a vast growth in marginally and informally employed "superfluous populations," many of whom, especially in the developing world, exist in a twilight state between the peasantry and the working class, dispossessed of access to the land yet lacking stable employment.[11] As these writers demonstrate, even those countries whose manufacturing output has grown most quickly (such as China) have experienced net loss of manufacturing jobs and a relative increase in service-sector jobs; deindustrialization is therefore a global process, affecting industrial and postindustrial economies jointly; late-developing countries are not on track to repeat the experiences of early-developing ones.

While both the Marxist and technofuturist writers discussed earlier agree that superfluous populations will increase, as a percentage of total population, in the coming decades, the technofuturists believe that this will occur alongside a new boom resulting from the automation of heretofore low-productivity growth sectors. Though the winners from such a boom may be few in number, working life for those well-placed workers will be remade through a reindustrializing overhaul of services, as doctors and drivers and teachers are replaced, or made more efficient, by increasingly intelligent machines. This would, presumably, have a noteworthy effect on the relationship between art and work and some bearing on the legacy of the developments discussed in this book. However, by acknowledging the inability of this putative boom to draw in large numbers of workers, these writers also acknowledge the underlying conditions that will make it weak and short-lived. The high-growth periods of capitalist development, such as 1945–1973, were characterized by a self-reinforcing dynamic, a virtuous rather than vicious cycle, that involved high profits, high employment rates, and, as a result, rising real wages. While the building of mines and factories and power plants reduced the need for labor on a per-unit basis, it also massively cheapened the goods produced by industry, and because the demand for most of these goods was "elastic," rising as goods became cheaper, the expansion of industrial output made up for the jobs that would have been lost to labor-saving innovation. One of the complexities here is that capitalists make investment decisions before their goods go to market and sometimes, in the case of investment in new plants and machines, must plan several years out. The possibility of gains through investment in new technologies led capitalists to expand output without knowing if the demand would be there, but because this had the effect of hiring more workers, it helped consolidate that demand.[12] As long as capital and labor could shift to a new, low-productivity line that was in need of technological makeover, the potential problem of oversupply of labor could be forestalled.

In certain periods, the excess capital and labor freed up did overwhelm the capacity for new lines to absorb it, producing severe crises (particularly in the 1890s and 1930s), but the destruction of capital prepared the way for the virtuous cycle to take over once again. The crisis of the 1970s never reinvigorated capitalism, however, in part because less capital was actually destroyed as the largest corporations managed to hang on in oversupplied lines and, with the help of state-supplied credit, attempted to force their competitors from the field.[13] There is another dimension to the postindustrial dynamic, however. For displaced workers to be absorbed, the new lines into which labor and capital flow must have a lower "organic composition," or ratio of inputs to wages, than the older ones; if the organic composition is higher, the increase in output will require less labor, unit for unit, and some portion of the workers will remain out in the cold. For a number of reasons, the developmental trajectory of capitalism since the 1970s meant that this condition was rarely met. Universal machines made it possible to revolutionize multiple industrial lines of production at once, so the chances were high that wherever the workers arrived would already have a very high organic composition. Furthermore, the new lines of the postwar period, particularly electronics and other digital products, were, by design, highly capital intensive and featured very low labor needs and highly automated plants (except for assembly, which continues to require, exceptionally, many workers and is therefore outsourced to places where wages are lowest).

Workers could and did go into services, where the ratio of labor to capital was low. The possibility of services as a safe harbor was guaranteed but eventually limited by the fact that productivity growth there was low; super-exploitation, through intensifying routines, as well as falling wages (of fast-food workers and store clerks) could provide some cheapening of the cost of these services and, as a result, increase output and hiring, keeping US employment rates stable in the post-1973 period, but one sees nothing like the vigorous expansion of twentieth-century industry. Postindustrial economies were, as a result, split into two parts, a shrinking "dynamic sector" (more or less identical with industry) and a growing "stagnant sector" (comprising most services). As long as wages could be hammered down, as happened in the United States, employment and profitability could grow somewhat in certain services, mitigating the effects of the displacement from industry. But as noted previously, these mitigating processes appear to have reached their limits. As wages fall, whatever extra wealth is generated by new technology goes to capitalists, and the wealth effects sustained by high demand for labor vanish, making investment in risky new technologies seem less appealing. The virtuous cycle gives way to a vicious one.

Tyler Cowen and the authors of *The Second Machine Age* argue that this stagnant sector—comprising in-person services that have heretofore been impossible to mechanize or automate, such as health care and education—will soon become dynamic. Throughout capitalism, services have been transformed into industrial products: launderers replaced by laundry machines, bank tellers by ATMs. When this happens, the new industrial products take advantage of all the labor-saving developments in industry, and the number of workers employed drops precipitously. The processes for manufacturing industrial goods have long been perfected, however, so the labor differential between the services provided by a bank teller and the labor it takes to produce an automated teller is vast, and it seems unlikely that the falling cost of the services (once turned to products) could ever allow output to rise fast enough to offset the loss of jobs. Brynjolfsson and McAfee argue that we are likely to see many services *assisted* by technology rather than replaced by it; the problem with this view is that the technological requirements of each of these service situations are very different. If assistance rather than replacement is in the cards, then the technological innovations required to increase productivity in industries such as education and health care are likely to involve very different kinds of innovations. There is no reason to believe these innovations will appear conjointly, except through the creation of all-purpose robots, which would of course mean a rapid end to employment and the capitalist economy as such. A piecemeal transfer of individual lines of service from the stagnant to the dynamic sector will not change the underlying cause of stagnation. The future seems likely to be characterized by very weak demand for labor in a stagnant world economy punctuated by explosive asset bubbles.

Given these likely futures, what might the effects be for art, for poetry? One of the arguments of this book is that since 1960 poetry in particular and art and literature more broadly have derived their force from a massive demographic and occupational transformation, as workers moved away from goods-producing to service-providing sectors of the economy and as women entered the workplace in massive numbers. As argued earlier, this kind of shift is not likely to happen again. Even if new lines of service occupation open up and begin to present very high demand for labor, it seems highly unlikely that these will be as qualitatively different as factory was from field, or office from factory. The economy will remain split into a small industrial sector and a larger, low-growth service sector. There is no sector beyond services; there is only the science-fiction scenario of full automation and the end of capitalism at the hands of the all-purpose robots discussed previously. Here, then, is one dimension in which we are unlikely to see a labor-determined transformation of literary and artistic production on the same order as the one narrated here. Since periodizing categories such as modernism and postmodernism depend, largely, on industrialization and deindustrialization, respectively, this explains why no viable, periodizing successor to postmodernism has emerged. There are, however, some important qualifications to make, since one result of low demand for labor and falling wages in the postindustrial countries will be a rising number of both self-employed people and small proprietors, engaged in various forms of petty production. The category of self-employment is notoriously murky and is often merely a legal disguise for what is fundamentally a wage relation. We would want to distinguish the self-employed carpenter from the artisanal pickle makers of Brooklyn, who sell a product direct to market, and we would want to distinguish both of these types of workers from the self-employed collector of bottles or scrap metal, who represents a type of informal making-do that dominates in the developing world. As demand for labor becomes increasingly weak, such forms of petty production and self-employment are likely to increase, both in the United States and elsewhere, and it seems possible that, as a result, we will see a renewal of the sorts of values that accompany artisanal modes of labor—craft, skill, truth in materials—as well as the ideological entrepreneurialism of the truly petit bourgeois, which has already been, under the sign of self-management, a large part of the new ethics of work. In the big cosmopolitan cities that Cowen thinks will soon house only the rich and those who serve them, we see a turn to high-priced, handmade production, often enabled by the disintermediating and coordinating power of network technology (the meeting of high and low tech, the handmade and machine) and drawing on collectivist, dissident values ("sharing economy"). The handmade also meets up with high touch, as artisanal bakers and coffee roasters cluster close to masseuses. How large this sector could grow, and what its effect might be on aesthetic ideology, remains an open question, but it is certainly an area to watch. Artisanal rhetorics, with their emphasis on skill and organic form, tend to be limited in their appeal because of their backward-looking, nostalgic character, but it is possible that some compromise formation, at the intersection of artisanal and high-tech logics, might exert a strong effect on the arts and aesthetic ideology.

The argument of this book does not, however, concern only the effects that transformations of labor process or occupational structure have on the plane of aesthetic production; I also argue for the reciprocal effects that aesthetic concepts and vocabularies have exerted on the restructuring of labor. These reciprocal effects are, by definition, operative only during a historically limited period, since the refashioning of labor in the image of art derived its condition of possibility from an anterior opposition of the two terms, where art was everything that waged or salaried labor was not: free, self-directed, creative, generative, mutable, satisfying. The formation of art and the aesthetic more broadly as an object of inquiry emerges, as many have acknowledged, alongside the development of capitalist industry, and the robust aesthetic philosophies of the Enlightenment and post-Enlightenment period presuppose the separation between fine and servile arts, between art proper and artisanal craft, between the free and unfree, the disinterested and the mercenary. As we all know, these divisions were never more than partial; art has always been attached by an umbilical cord of gold to the masters of the capitalist mode of production. However, the aestheticization of labor under discussion here is of a particular order. A reader might note, for instance, that novels and paintings and poems have been produced in exchange for money throughout capitalism (and before it as well), but this is something different from the recasting of the labor process and the ethics of labor according to aesthetic values and ideas. It is, rather, what we might call the "commercialization" of art. Other readers might point to the professionalization and institutionalization of artistic labor and art in general, but yet again this is something else, even when we are talking about the thoroughgoing industrialization of art that one notices in the music and film industries (the culture industries); the remaking of art enterprises along the lines of capitalist lines of production, something that meets serious economic obstacles in most cases, is not the same as the remaking of capitalist lines of production in the image of art enterprises. Nor does the absorption of particular contents from the visual arts and poetry in the advertising industry, to give one example, really provide much of an exception to my argument. Though admittedly some artistic values, ideologies, and vocabularies passed into the labor process of advertisers prior to World War II, this was a more or less limited development and led to no overall refashioning of managerial ideology. The merger of art and labor described in this book is transitional by definition and probably irreversible. Aesthetic values in the workplace no longer hold the charm they once did and are unlikely to regain their luster anytime soon, even as much as new slogans and watchwords such as "do what you love" appear everyday. Just as the aesthetic critique has been neutralized and naturalized, so too has the recuperation of that critique via the refashioning of labor in aesthetic terms.

While none of these areas are likely to produce significant change in the relationship between art and labor, rising unemployment and a growing superfluous population may yet still create changes of an entirely different order. Under such conditions, labor may no longer appear as the primary field of struggle for artists and writers. As the example of Sean Bonney shows, we may find an increasing number of poets and artists directing their critical energies toward unwork rather than work, toward dispossession and wagelessness rather than the wage relation as such. Beyond the writers of *Endnotes*, there are today a great number of competing theorizations of the condition of superfluity, which as Michael Denning notes, in a seminal article, goes by numerous names today: "bare life, wasted life, disposable life, precarious life, superfluous life."[14] Reflecting on the sobering data collected by UN-HABITAT's 2003 *Global Report on Human Settlement*, Mike Davis's popular book *Planet of Slums* describes the effects of a planetwide "urbanization without industrialization" that has meant the growth not only of urban "slums" comprising close to a billion inhabitants but also a massive "informal economy" at least as large, supplied by those without access to formal employment.[15] Though slums and the informal sector are two of the forms through which superfluous populations manifest, they are by no means identical, and the terms bring with them certain associational consequences: the first term is an inheritance from urban geography and urban renewal projects and might miss the extent to which contemporary capitalism is marked by rural wagelessness (or wagelessness in zones that are neither rural nor urban exactly) as well as the fact that slums often house formally employed people; the second term is a product of development economics and international economic organizations and is notoriously murky, depending on both legal codes and legal enfranchisement as well as political economic categories.

Others have preferred Agamben's term "bare life," which approaches the condition of outcast labor from the perspective of citizenship and Foucauldian biopolitics, a theoretical framework useful in the case of refugees and migrants but perhaps less so when confronted with various forms of contingency and itineracy.[16] Others still adopt the language of precarity or precariousness (as popularized by Hardt and Negri, and others within the Italian post-*operaismo* tradition), terms that emphasize changes in the nature of job contracts or work hours of the sort described in this book; these may indicate low demand for labor but, as we have seen, are also part of labor-process reorganizations that favor management.[17] No term is likely to suffice in every situation, in part because the conditions of wagelessness and wagefulness are never mutually exclusive. Few people are absolutely superfluous, and most work in one way or another, directly or indirectly, over the course of their lives. Total wagelessness is largely an artifact of unemployment insurance and social welfare; in social situations in which this sort of social wage is not available or not sufficient, the superfluous must, if they will survive, depend on the wages of others or find ways to trade something, anything, for money.

While new terms are useful in illuminating different aspects of the condition of "wageless life," better still is a theoretical refinement of our understanding of the proletarian condition. Having distinguished himself as a first-rate literary and cultural historian of the Great Depression and Popular Front era, when unemployment was at the forefront of social issues, Michael Denning offers us a lucid articulation of the theoretical rewards of this renewed understanding of the proletariat:

> Unemployment precedes employment, and the informal economy precedes the formal, both historically and conceptually. We must insist that "proletarian" is not a synonym for "wage labourer" but for dispossession, expropriation and radical dependence on the market.[18]

The point here is not to draw a thick line between the wageless and the waged but "to decenter wage labor." Instead of "seeing the bread-winning factory worker as the productive base on which a reproductive superstructure is erected," this refined understanding of the proletarian condition allows us to "imagine the dispossessed proletarian household as a wageless base of subsistence labour—the 'women's work' of cooking, cleaning and caring—which supports a superstructure of migrant wage seekers who are ambassadors, or perhaps hostages, to the wage economy."[19] This perspective is not a departure from the one laid out in Marx's mature political economy, but in fact entirely consistent with it. Marx is clear that the moment of dispossession, which he describes as "primitive accumulation," precedes that of exploitation both logically and historically. In an ironic turn of phrase, he suggests that capitalist accumulation presupposed a "free worker . . . free in the double sense that as a free individual he can dispose of his labour-power as his own commodity, and that, on the other hand, he has no other commodity for sale, i.e., he is rid of them, he is free of all the objects needed for the realization [*Verwirklichung*] of his labour-power."[20] Marx attends to this "double freedom"—the freedom to be exploited and the freedom from all wealth—by describing in the pages of *Capital* not only the exploitative conditions of the nineteenth-century working class but the formation of this class through, first, the expulsions and enclosures of preceding centuries, and second, the legal and extralegal violence required to discipline the vagabonds and poors into accepting employment in the English workshops.

Theoretical precision of this sort, suggesting that wagelessness and wagefulness are always dialectically entangled, and that this is the essence of the proletarian condition, might encourage many to question any attempt to periodize capitalism with regard to superfluous populations, inasmuch as capitalism has always required what Marx calls an "industrial reserve army," whose ability to take the place of employed workers forces those workers to accept the prevailing wage rate.[21] Such a population, according to some interpretations, rises as capitalism enters into crisis but returns to equilibrium as capitalism recovers, so there is no secular, long-term tendency for this proletarian fraction to grow. Others object to the notion of "precarity" because it overstates and normalizes the formalization of labor, which, inasmuch as this refers to legal enfranchisement and protection by the state, in the form of labor law, did not exist before the twentieth century.[22] Most workers throughout the course of capitalism have been and are "precarious," these writers argue. While these are important qualifications, the period of capitalism's emergence and gradual consolidation cannot be made identical to late, postindustrial capitalism; while both periods might feature uneven demand for labor, leaving a good number of dispossessed people without access to wage or money, the character of superfluity is likely to unfold in very different ways in the future, for no other reason than the simple fact that it seems poised to grow rather than shrink.

Just as literary history provides numerous examples of a poetics of labor, so too is there an abundance of formal and thematic resources from which we might elaborate a poetics of wagelessness. Early modern English literature, in particular, develops at the origins of capitalism, alongside the primitive accumulation discussed previously. The landless proto-proletariat produced by the enclosures emerges by and large in advance of capitalism proper, however. Aside from the early agrarian capitalism, which needed far less labor than was expelled from the countryside, there were no factories or other workplaces in the early modern period to absorb people expelled from the countryside, and what waged work did exist was often refused. The processes of dispossession that began extensively in the sixteenth century and continued until the early nineteenth century produced a continuous flood of vagrants (homeless people), paupers (incomeless people), and the poor in general, a flow that ended only with the final extermination of the English peasantry and ascendance of capitalist industry in the nineteenth century. The ruling class responded with a series of "Poor Laws," which Marx describes memorably as "bloody legislation against the expropriated," laws that presumed the poor to have chosen vagabondage and attempted to force them into gainful labor or eliminate them altogether through punishment, confinement, exile, impressment into work gangs and merchant marines, resettlement in workhouses, and execution.[23] Literature was involved directly and indirectly in this process; as Richard Halpern argues in *The Poetics of Primitive Accumulation*, the humanist learning institutions of Renaissance literature responded to the threat of idleness, errancy, and vagabondage by positioning nonspecific literary learning as a general test of capacity, allowing for an important distinction between the deserving and undeserving poor, those who are paupers due to unavoidable misfortune and those "sturdy beggars" who could work but do not.[24] These tests of capacity rest on categorical distinctions between the able-bodied and the disabled, and therefore on conceptions of ability in general.[25]

For Halpern, literature is a double-sided institution: the imagination, and literary imagination in particular, was seen by Renaissance humanists as a form of lawlessness that was frequently described as vagrant or errant, but successful literary objects of the period displayed a coupling of these vagrant energies to specifically disciplinary forms.[26] Beyond the many literary works in which vagrancy featured prominently, such as Thomas Nashe's *Pierce Penniless* or, a century later, Peter Gay's *The Beggar's Opera*, the homeless and the wageless also had their own literary cultures, comprising low genres such as the "broadside street ballad." Patricia Fumerton describes the street ballad as "one of the most vagrant forms of the period"; not only did it thematize scenes of vagrancy and wandering, but it was "peddled by singers considered in the same class as vagrants and often conscripted from the flow of unemployed apprentices and other such 'idle' youth."[27] Broadside ballads were the social media of their day, responding to the "latest news-flashes and passing topical events" through an aesthetics of perfusion. Ballads moved rapidly throughout the social body by way of lateral connections between their dispossessed and highly mobile bearers, as balladeers and their audiences sidestepped emerging institutions of authorship that might have settled or enclosed such products (or put them to work). Such fugitive works were "passed from usually anonymous author, to printer, to ballad-monger, to audience (each of whom had a say in how they were 'voiced') and then often back again to author/printer to be reissued in a different key."[28] Fumerton places special emphasis on alehouses as a paradoxical home for the homelessness of vagrant balladeers, an argument that accords with Daniel Tiffany's account of vagrant tavern culture, or "nightlife," in the eighteenth century. Tiffany's *Infidel Poetics* narrates a long history of the poetic underground, where vagabonds and thieves joined together in "canting crews," producing anonymous "infidel lyrics" in an opaque "cant" that could circulate widely while at the time excluding all those who were not members of the specified community. From Villon to Baudelaire, poets' attraction to forms of opacity and secrecy derives from their participation in underground cultures and means that their works are often fed by the same springs as the insurrections and uprisings of the late eighteenth and nineteenth centuries, so often organized by secret societies.

Vagrancy and dispossession were also a major concern of the English Romantics, particularly Wordsworth, who at every turn confronts his reader with a beggar, wanderer, or vagabond. The process of enclosure and dispossession reached a climax in the late eighteenth and early nineteenth centuries, part of the momentous political and economic changes of the period. In her study of the thematic of vagrancy in Romanticism, Celeste Langan follows Halpern in identifying the ways in which vagrants become "the hallucinatory double" of capital, freed from the land and flowing across the countryside in much the same way that capital flows from production line to production line.[29] Wordsworth's images of vagrancy, and his formal imitation of wandering and errancy, represent "a certain idealization of the vagrant" that is constitutive of the open-ended, improvisatory Romantic lyric.[30] Langan focuses in particular on the adoption of the abstractly equalized poetic space of iambic pentameter, which she analogizes to the formal political and economic equalizations that eliminate impediments to the flow of bodies and money. The Romantic lyric is therefore an emblematization of the "negative liberty"—the freedom from property and the freedom to work—that is constitutive of the proletariat (and for Langan, the liberal subject): "the poet and vagrant together constitute a society based on the twin principles of freedom of speech and freedom of movement."[31] This is very much in accord with Marx's sense of things. When speaking of the proletariat produced through the expulsion of the peasantry, Marx uses the sixteenth-century German term *vogelfrei* (literally, bird-free), which originally referred to an outlaw under the force of a ban. The lyric singing of the Romantic poet is, to extend the metaphor, the birdsong of the bird-free *homo sacer*. The emphasis on contingency, mutability, restlessness, and anomie that we associate with the lyric—which many will argue is essentially invented in the Romantic period—emerges directly from the experience of vagrancy and the literary transcriptions thereof.

If poetry idealizes, under the sign of freedom, the mobility and lawlessness of the vagrant, while obscuring the dispossession, violence, and lack that is at the source of this freedom, it does so by drawing out moralizing elements already present within vagrant culture. Just as the ballad tradition Fumerton describes is often at great pains to distinguish between "sturdy beggars" and the truly afflicted, between the undeserving and deserving poor, the able and the disabled, writing from the United States about hobo life from 1890 to 1930 revolves on a distinction between those who seek work but cannot find it and those who flee work voluntarily. Many tried to reserve the term "hobo" for the first group and the term "tramp" for the second, and great emphasis went into articulating the ways in which hobos were a part of the working class, the most vulnerable and marginal layer (and one that was often rejected by housed workers, whose jobs they might threaten). The mobility of hobos, moving from place to place by hopping trains, helped form a nonregional working-class culture, breaking down many (if not all) of the particularistic identities (of ethnicity, race, and religion) that might supravene over shared class position. Hobos were a hegemonic fraction within the most revolutionary working-class organization of its time, the Industrial Workers of the World (IWW), with representatives of "hobohemia" steering the organization away from parliamentary action and toward boycotts, strikes, and sabotage, in line with this class fraction's illegalist orientations.[32] This victory was recorded in a vast IWW folklore and collected in the official IWW songbook, *Songs of the Workers, on the Road, in the Jungles, and in the Shops—Songs to Fan the Flames of Discontent* (also known as *The Little Red Songbook*).[33] Hobo culture exerted a lasting influence on left modernism, figured and reconfigured in the work of John Dos Passos, Claude McKay, and Carl Sandburg, to name just a few.

This cultural legacy remains divided on essential issues, however, and the songs of the IWW and the hobo culture from which they emerge evince conflicting ideas about the essence of hobo-dom, and the proper relationship to work. "The Tramp," one of the most famous songs by perhaps the most famous IWW songwriter, Joe Hill, turns on the narrator's insistence that the unemployed "chap" whose story is told in the ballad "was not the kind that shirk" and for whom the injunction to "tramp, tramp, tramp" derived from his "looking hard for work."[34] The song provides a moral argument about the contradictions of the existing moral categories of his day; while he is everywhere told by the forces of law and order to keep on tramping, lest he face "the ball and chain," when he dies neither Saint Peter nor the devil will let him settle. His honest, unshirking character is illegible according to the existing moral-theological categories of his time (and Christianity in general). Compare this hobo song with another included in some versions of *The Little Red Songbook*, Haywire Mac's "Hallelujah, I'm a Bum," composed in 1908 and adopted shortly thereafter as the anthem of the Spokane IWW. The song celebrates idleness and a life based on handouts, inverting the moral order of "The Tramp" and sanctifying bumhood with a Christological language of resurrection:

> Hallelujah, I'm a bum,
> Hallelujah, bum again,
> Hallelujah, give us a handout
> To revive us again.
> Oh, why don't you save all the money you earn?
> If I didn't eat, I'd have money to burn.
> Whenever I get all the money I earn,
> The boss will be broke, and to work he must turn.
> Oh, I like my boss, he's a good friend of mine,
> That's why I am starving out on the bread line.
> When springtime it comes, oh, won't we have fun;
> We'll throw off our jobs, and go on the bum.[35]

Capitalism is a zero-sum game in which either the boss or the workers must starve, and therefore what we get is an explicit desire to "throw off" labor, to flee from it. Haywire Mac's later and even more famous song, "Big Rock Candy Mountain," a hoboized version of "The Land of Cockaigne," produces a maximalist version of "the right to be lazy," "Where you sleep all day, / Where they hung the jerk / That invented work."[36]

These opposing attitudes toward work, and toward the condition of the vagrant, not only run through the songs of the IWW but arguably run directly through the proletariat as a whole. In the US context (and beyond) one of the central rifts within the proletarian class has always been racial. Not only are black proletarians frequently the first to be dismissed and the last hired, and not only do they form the greatest fraction per capita within the superfluous populations in the United States, but the historical legacy of slavery has produced a set of attitudes toward work that is quite often in conflict with the attitudes of the white working class (or at least those displayed by Joe Hill's "The Tramp").[37] As Paul Gilroy notes in a frequently cited passage,

> [I]n the critical thought of blacks in the West, social self-creation through labour is not the centre-piece of emancipatory hopes. For the descendants of slaves, work signifies only servitude, misery, and subordination. Artistic expression, expanded beyond recognition from the grudging gifts offered by the masters as a token substitute for freedom from bondage, therefore becomes the means towards both individual self-fashioning and communal liberation.[38]

One might offer up as counterexample the prominence in African American folklore (and literary engagements with it) of "The Ballad of John Henry." The ballad features a Stakhanovite laborer who famously dies competing with the steam drill that will eventually displace him and his peers, forcing black workers to suffer the greatest burden of technological unemployment. His death by hubris, however, makes him a cautionary figure, something underscored by the fact that there is a work-song variant of the ballad, sometimes described as "This Old Hammer," which laborers use to moderate the pace of their work, singing:

> This old hammer killed John Henry
> But it won't kill me, Lord
> No, it won't kill me

There are doubtless many examples of a humanization or aestheticization of labor within the African American and Afro-diasporic tradition, as well as celebrations of the meaning and value of hard work, just as there are examples of a strident refusal of work among white proletarians (on display in the tramp ballads). Gilroy's remarks indicate a tendency rather than an absolute cleavage. Nonetheless, African American and Afro-diasporic literature presents one of the most powerful examples of a reckoning with what Denning calls "wageless life," one that may be presented either as dispossession and the absence of the means (money, wages) necessary for survival or, alternatively, as what Fred Moten calls, following a Nathaniel Mackey essay about Federico García Lorca and Amiri Baraka, "fugitivity."[39] This is a literary tradition that displays a particularly sharp awareness of the dispossession and displacement fundamental to the proletarian condition but also a strong desire to ameliorate this dispossession through political intervention beyond or outside the wage. We might think, here, of the maritime hobos in Claude McKay's profound novel of Afro-diasporic wagelessness, *Banjo*. Brought together in Marseille, the jobless mariners pilfer what the cargo ships they once worked on bring to port, elaborating a diasporic internationalism founded on music, mutual aid, and camaraderie.[40] Or, alternatively, we might think of *Invisible Man*, whose speaker moves from place to place in search of work, continuously foiled by white supremacy, eventually choosing the stationary fugitivity (and partial freedom) of invisibility.[41] Moten and Mackey are thinking, of course, not of the black novel's profound investigation of wagelessness and picaresque itineracy but of black lyric, whose fugitivity inheres at the level of poetic form. Baraka's poetry "intimates fugitive spirit," Mackey argues, borrowing from Baraka's own writing on jazz to characterize the elusive fugitivity of the poems. "[I]t slides away from the proposed," Mackey quotes.[42] For Mackey, fugitivity is a restless appositional and improvisational spirit, which modifies each syntactic phrase through the swapping out of one term, usually a noun, for another. Consider, for example, the Baraka poem, "History as Process," that occasions the term:

> *The evaluation of the mysteries by the sons of all*
> *experience.* All suffering, if we call the light a thing
> all men should know. Or find. Where ever, in the dark folds
> of the next second, there is some diminishing beauty we might one day
> understand, and scream, in some wild fit of unacknowledged Godliness.

"Suffering" replaces "experience," and "find" replaces "know." This terminological displacement produces a verbal chiaroscuro effect of alternating light and dark, beauty and terror. This slide of one noun into the next, the poem suggests, is a grammatical analogue to the wandering gypsies who propose a "simple future" that is speed, force, God, thing, and soul all at once:

> The thing, There As Speed, is God, as mingling
> possibility. The force. As simple future, what
> the freaky gypsies rolled through Europe
> on.
> (The soul.)

Identifying its own rhetorical structure with this vagabond spirit, the poem becomes a fugitive force that converts substance into future-directed movement. In his reading of the poem, Mackey connects the "mercuriality and nomadism" of Baraka and Lorca to the "well-known, resonant history of African-American fugitivity and its well-known, resonant relationship to enslavement and persecution."[43] But in the second part of the poem, movement converts to stasis. Without movement, fugitivity becomes a kind of precarity, a vulnerable dependence, premised on an open-ended, mutable selfhood:

> What can I do to myself? Bones
> and dusty skin. Heavy eyes twisted
> between the adequate thighs of all
> humanity (a little h), strumming my head
> for a living. Bankrupt utopia sez tell me
> no utopia. I will not listen.[44]

Baraka makes the self-reflexive character of lyric utterance—J. S. Mill's "feeling confessing to itself"—into a practical question, a question of doing rather than being or saying. The "I" becomes object, performed by the street musician who, perhaps having done "a little h[eroin]," looks through the thighs of passersby, inventing music and "a living" out of the open fount of the self. Rather than utopia, the poem opts for the simple future of unlistening negation, a movement forward, perhaps, but without any sort of goal. Fugitivity implies a processual, nonteleological history.

Moten builds both a poetics and politics from this notion of fugitivity, developing theoretical perspectives and poetic practices that draw on a long history of black fugitivity and improvisation in the face of dispossession while addressing the specific political conditions of the early twenty-first century (austerity, indebtedness, mass incarceration). As for Baraka, fugitivity for Moten does not require explicit movement and may instead involve "an unsettled feeling, the feeling of a thing that unsettles with others. It's a feeling, if you ride with it, that produces a certain distance from the settled, from those who determine themselves in space and time, who locate themselves in a determined history."[45] As Moten writes in the long title of one of his poems, "Fugitivity is immanent to the thing but is manifest transversally." The lines that follow figure this immanent instability as an architectural interior in which names and objects slide past each other:

> between the object and the floor
> the couch is a pedestal and a shawl

> and just woke up her hair. she never
>
> ever leaves the floating other house
>
> but through some stories they call[46]

The poem is remarkable for seeming both serene and at the same time thrown forward by a velocity of speech that produces strange elisions and abbreviations, as if one out of every four words had been dropped. The result is a movement that stays still, an immovable movement, that floats in its house yet is called out into the world through the force of story. The poem is an interior but also a portrait, so its first section closes with a list of all the names (and attendant stories) by which the poem's subject, a "she," is called. "A station agent intimate with tight /spaces," the subject of the poem represents this stationary fugitivity, coordinating the movement of exterior agencies while "refus[ing] to hit back or be carried." In the second section, these coiled energies are unbound, as "she" finally moves in a direct, forward way, overrunning the border guards of the section break:

> ...watch her
> move into the story she still move
>
> 2.
> and tear shit up. always a pleasure the banned
> deep brown of faces in the otherwise
> whack. the cruel disposed won't stand
>
> still. apparatus tear shit up and
>
> always. you see they can't get off when
> they get off. some stateless folks
> spurn the pleasure they are driven
> to be and strive against. man, hit me again.

Here, the social and political economic dimensions of the ontological fugitivity described in the first sections reveal themselves, a stratum of "banned / deep brown ... faces" and "stateless folks," who are cruelly "disposed," either dispossessed or displaced or both. As if in answer to the recuperation of pleasure by capital, its transformation into "a state," in the workplace and elsewhere, the stateless wreckers of Moten's poem manage to *be* pleasure *and* refuse capture by their enjoyment of it.

Moten's poetry and theory develop a notion of fugitivity and life-making improvisation beyond the wage that is specific to the diasporic black experience and its historical legacy, but he is also clear that this legacy affects everyone, unequally. His writing with Stefano Harney tries to imagine a fugitivity in response to the neoliberal academy and rising indebtedness that involves a heterogeneous layer of "minorities" in the Deleuzean sense: "maroon communities of composition teachers, mentorless graduate students, adjunct Marxist historians, out or queer management professors, state college ethnic studies departments, closed-down film programs, visa-expired Yemeni student newspaper editors, historically black college sociologists, and feminist engineers."[47] The fugitive poetics Moten develops has a specifically black origin and trajectory but also displays a centrifugal force—his interest, as he notes in an interview, is in "a kind of community or whatever you want to call it of centrifugal writers or black experimental artists that expands, ultimately, in the direction of anyone who wants to claim it."[48] Elsewhere, Moten writes about a "racialization of the imagination," in which a Kantian understanding of the imagination as "lawless, nonsense producing freedom" codes this space as black or, in other words, as black fugitivity.[49] This aligns with the work of both Halpern and Langan, in which the space of the aesthetic is understood as homologous with the *vogelfrei* wandering and lawlessness of the vagabonds capitalism had produced. This "racialization of the imagination" also involves its "proletarianization."

If I am correct that wagelessness and precarity will rise in the coming decades, then this "fugitive, centrifugal, social and aesthetic field" will likewise grow in importance as a set of political and poetic resources.[50] The meaning and legacy of these resources will read differently for different groups and different forms of wagelessness and fugitivity, but I think Moten is right that the African American radical tradition, both poetic and political, provides examples that will be increasingly crucial for all antagonists to capital and the state. Beyond this specific legacy, however, there are the poetic traditions and resources listed previously, from the ballad to the Romantic lyric, from naturalist explorations of hobo life to the song tradition of the IWW and its fellow train hoppers, and much more. Already there are a few literary studies of twenty-first-century wagelessness, or what Margaret Ronda, in a seminal argument, calls "collective being subsisting at the margins of the marketplace."[51]

Sean Bonney is one example of a poet developing a language of resistance from beyond the wage, in the space of unwork. He is, notably and significantly, a scholar of Baraka and the African American lyric tradition. Of course, labor can and will continue to dominate people's lives in the many ways described in the preceding chapters. But since Moten demonstrates that fugitivity does not imply flight so much as an "unsettled" attitude and a tactics of unsettlement, these languages can, in fact, be developed *within* the space of labor as much as beyond it. I think here in particular of the recent sonnet sequences of Wendy Trevino, a Mexican American poet who writes eloquently about the complications and frustrations of her work at a nonprofit organization serving and, at same time staffed by, women of color like herself. In "Sonnets of Brass Knuckle Doodles," Trevino provides an intriguing vantage on the incorporation of poetic vocabularies into the organizational structure of the workplace: her boss is a poet she met in Iowa through the Iowa Writers' Workshop (where Trevino's ex-husband had been studying). As the sequence begins, the integration of poetry and labor is complete, leading to an impasse:

> I can't work. I can't write. Even for fun.
> I am liking many posts on Facebook,
> Which is a kind of work. That reminds me:
> My boss is a poet I met several
> Years ago. At one time, we had many
> Friends in common, friends we met in Iowa
> Around the same time, friends who mostly know
> Us through Facebook since we moved away
> To California. They would like my posts,
> Send me messages. Then, my boss became
> My boss & I didn't want my boss
> To know how much I use Facebook at work,
> So I made her and our mutual friends
> Acquaintances & hid my posts from them.[52]

In fourteen lines, Trevino's poem glosses many of the most troublesome and difficult aspects of the contemporary workplace: first, the vanishing of the boundary between work and life under the force of new, social media that instrumentalize the affective languages of friendship (her real-life friend becomes her boss and shares Facebook "friends" with her); second, the incorporation of aesthetic technologies and relationships into the workplace (poetry relationships are turned to work relationships), damaging both work life and poetic production. In the face of these incursions, Trevino refuses writing and work both and tries to establish stronger boundaries, even if these are mere digital ones, between life in and outside work. This means refusing identification with work as much as refusing the identities of work. "It's not / your job. It's a job. My boss says, 'career,' / hates when I call it a job." While Trevino insists that there's "no escaping" work, she still manages to produce a crucial dissociation, swapping the indefinite article "a" for the possessive pronoun "your" and refusing the identities and identifications of her Human Resources Department:

> I write
> About work because there's no escaping
> It. Like heartbreak. Work structures so much life.
> According to Human Resources, I'm white.
> I have been confused for other women
> With dark hair. Maybe I am them sometimes.
> In the elevator, taking the stairs
> Walking back from lunch, saying "it's not me."[53]

Work is all-encompassing, but its compulsive identifications—its identity with the self—can be resisted. For Trevino, this means refusing the identifications of poetry as well. The sonnets themselves, written in loose decasyllabics (iambic pentameter from which meter has been removed), are analogized to the "brass knuckles" she draws "during all-staff meetings." She draws with a Sharpie, noting that there is "something about the thickness of the strokes. / You don't have to be so careful or good." This reflection on the strokes of the Sharpie might also be heard as a reflection on the decasyllabic line. The important thing, for her, was being able to "move on, doodle enough / That it started to look like art. Bad art / Maybe but art." Accepting the bad and immersing oneself within the trancelike space of the doodle or sonnet is necessary if one wants to avoid the subjectivizing effects of the restructured workplace:

> I've been told grant writing
> Will ruin my writing. In the long list
> Of reasons I wish I could quit my job,
> What it's doing to my poems is absent.
> If I write bad poetry, there are worse things
> You could say about me. Writing good poems
> Isn't that important, which doesn't mean
> I don't enjoy or hope to write good poems,
> Whatever that means. I still love writing.[54]

What is important, then, if not poetry and certainly not work? The sequence does not say, precisely. The title, however, gives us a hint. The sonnets are brass knuckles, but they are also doodles. They are not weapons, precisely, but representations thereof. Neither are they art, exactly. They point to an occasion of use beyond the workplace or in flight from it. These occasions and weapons will appear with increasing frequency in coming years. The restructuring of capitalism has meant that fewer people have jobs but also that the jobs people do have, as contingent or precarious workers, often provide fewer opportunities for struggle *as workers*. Consequentially, more and more struggles emerge in the space of circulation rather than production, undertaken by those who are surplus to capital's need for employment or whose opportunities for struggle in workplaces have been foreclosed.[55] Their means are riots, blockades, occupations of public and private space, and their ends are access to the necessaries of life independent of the mediation of the wage.[56] Workplace struggles will continue alongside these forms, without a doubt, but the poetry of the future will increasingly have to find its reasons and its weapons beyond production.

Notes

Introduction

1. Theodor W. Adorno and Max Horkheimer, *Dialectic of Enlightenment* (New York: Verso, 1997), 120–167.

2. Moishe Postone, *Time, Labor, and Social Domination: A Reinterpretation of Marx's Critical Theory* (Cambridge: Cambridge University Press, 1996), 123–185.

3. "Tout se résumé dans l'esthétique et l'economie politique." Cited and translated in Roger Pearson, *Stéphane Mallarmé* (London: Reaktion Books, 2010), 182.

4. To give just two examples from a vast number of texts tying the crisis of capitalism to a crisis of work, see Antonio Negri, *Marx beyond Marx: Lessons on the Grundrisse* (New York: Autonomedia, 1989); André Gorz, *Farewell to the Working Class: An Essay on Post-industrial Socialism* (London: Pluto Press, 1982).

5. See, for instance, Andrew Glyn, Alan Hughes, Alan Lipietz, and Ajit Singh, "The Rise and Fall of the Golden Age," in *The Golden Age of Capitalism: Reinterpreting the Postwar Experience*, ed. Stephen A. Marglin and Juliet B. Schor (Oxford: Oxford University Press, 1992), 39–125; Phillip Armstrong, Andrew Glyn, and John Harrison, *Capitalism since 1945* (London: Blackwell, 1991).

6. For an account of the distinction between Taylorism and Fordism, see Michel Aglietta, *A Theory of Capitalist Regulation: The US Experience*, trans. David Fernbach (New York: Verso, 2001), 113–121.

7. The classic text on "deskilling" is Harry Braverman, *Labor and Monopoly Capital: The Degradation of Work in the Twentieth Century* (New York: Monthly Review Press, 1975).

8. Daniel Bell, *The Coming of Post-industrial Society: A Venture in Social Forecasting* (New York: Basic Books, 1976), 134.

9. Mark McColloch, *White-Collar Workers in Transition: The Boom Years, 1940–1970* (Westport, CT: Greenwood Publishing Group, 1983), 30–36, 94–100, 135–142.

10. Andrew Hoberek, *The Twilight of the Middle Class: Post–World War II American Fiction and White-Collar Work* (Princeton, NJ: Princeton University Press, 2005), 17, 25.

11. C. Wright Mills, *White Collar: The American Middle Classes* (New York: Oxford University Press, 2002); William H. Whyte, *The Organization Man* (Philadelphia: Uni-

versity of Pennsylvania Press, 2002); David Riesman, *The Lonely Crowd: A Study of the Changing American Character* (New Haven, CT: Yale University Press, 2001).

12. Mills, *White Collar*, 226.

13. Michael W. Clune, *American Literature and the Free Market, 1945–2000* (Cambridge: Cambridge University Press, 2009), 148.

14. Mills, *White Collar*, 342.

15. C. Wright Mills, "Letter to the New Left," *New Left Review* 1, no. 5 (October 1960): 23.

16. Herbert Marcuse, *One-Dimensional Man: Studies in the Ideology of Advanced Industrial Society* (Boston: Beacon Press, 1991), 25.

17. Ibid.

18. Herbert Marcuse, *An Essay on Liberation* (Boston: Beacon Press, 1971), 59.

19. Ibid., 6.

20. Department of Health, Education and Welfare, *Work in America: Report* (Cambridge, MA: MIT Press, 1973), 10–75; Braverman, *Labor and Monopoly Capital*, 31–39.

21. Situationist International, "The Bad Days Will End," in *Situationist International Anthology* (Berkeley, CA: Bureau of Public Secrets, 2006), 108; Mario Tronti, "The Strategy of Refusal," in *Autonomia: Post-political Politics*, ed. Sylvère Lotringer (New York: Semiotext(e), 2007), 130.

22. Summarized in Braverman, *Labor and Monopoly Capital*, 31–39.

23. Department of Health, Education, and Welfare, *Work in America*, xv–xvi.

24. Ibid., 38.

25. Braverman, *Labor and Monopoly Capital*, 180.

26. Department of Health, Education, and Welfare, *Work in America*, 30.

27. In France, in particular, Serge Mallet was citing "self-management" as "one of the most important indices of the level [of] development." Serge Mallet, *Essays on the New Working Class* (Candor, France: Telos Press, 1975), 123.

28. Jefferson R. Cowie, *Stayin' Alive: The 1970s and the Last Days of the Working Class* (New York: New Press, 2010), 26.

29. Luc Boltanski and Eve Chiapello, *The New Spirit of Capitalism* (New York: Verso, 2005), 170.

30. Ibid.

31. Allan Kaprow and Jeff Kelley, *Essays on the Blurring of Art and Life* (Berkeley: University of California Press, 2003), xviii.

32. Michael Fried, *Art and Objecthood: Essays and Reviews* (Chicago: University of Chicago Press, 1998), 155.

33. Ibid., 163.

34. "Even yesterday's distinctions between art, antiart, and nonart are pseudo-distinctions that simply waste our time: the side of an old building recalls Clyfford Still's canvases, the guts of a dishwashing machine double as Duchamp's *Bottle Rack*, the voices in a train station are Jackson Mac Low's poems, the sounds of eating in a luncheonette are by John Cage, and all may be part of a Happening. . . . Not only does art become life, but life refuses to be itself." Kaprow and Kelley, *Essays on the Blurring of Art and Life*, 81.

35. Richard Kempton, *Provo: Amsterdam's Anarchist Revolt* (Brooklyn, NY: Autonomedia, 2007), 11–15.

36. "Fluxus Manifesto," reprinted in Kristine Stiles and Peter Howard Selz, *Theories and Documents of Contemporary Art: A Sourcebook of Artists' Writings* (Berkeley: University of California Press, 1996), 727.

37. Claire Bishop, *Participation* (London: Whitechapel, 2006), 106.

38. Ibid., 125.

39. Ibid., 18.

40. Guy Debord, "Report on the Construction of Situations," in *Guy Debord and the Situationist International: Texts and Documents* (Cambridge, MA: MIT Press, 2004), 47.

41. Ibid.

42. Umberto Eco, *The Open Work* (Cambridge, MA: Harvard University Press, 1989); Roland Barthes, *S/Z* (New York: Macmillan, 1975), 4.

43. Barthes, *S/Z*, 4.

44. Steve McCaffery, "The Death of the Subject: The Implications of Countercommunication in Recent Language-Centered Writing," *Open Letter* 3, no. 7 (Summer 1977): 62.

45. Ibid., 70.

46. Lyn Hejinian, "The Rejection of Closure," in *The Language of Inquiry* (Berkeley: University of California Press, 2000), 43.

47. Robert Brenner, *The Economics of Global Turbulence* (New York: Verso, 2006), 99. For an account of the US economy's descent into crisis from 1965 to 1973, see 99–121.

48. Aaron Brenner, Robert Brenner, and Cal Winslow, eds., *Rebel Rank and File: Labor Militancy and Revolt from Below during the Long 1970s* (New York: Verso, 2010), 37–76.

49. Harry Braverman, *Labor and Monopoly Capital* (New York: Monthly Review Press, 1975), 39.

50. Julia Bryan-Wilson writes that the turn to "relational aesthetics" has made visible the contributions of artists to the transformation of work: "The emphasis on participation, flexibility, and multitasking is taken from the studio into the factory, and the strong resonance of certain terms—deskilling, dematerialization, participation, alienation—points to a multidirectional flow of influence in the 1960s and 1970s that continues today. The shifting contours of artistic work have roughly paralleled the changes in industrial production in the economy at large. But perhaps, instead of arguing that the alterations in labor practices register more visibly within artistic 'work'—as is mandated by the tired 'art reflects society' formulation—we can point to the influence running in the other direction: with the rise of the 'culture industry,' artistic practice began to influence the workplace." Unfortunately, Bryan-Wilson's very interesting book does not do much to develop an account of the ways in which art influences the workplace in the art of the period. Julia Bryan-Wilson, *Art Workers: Radical Practice in the Vietnam War Era* (Berkeley: University of California Press, 2011), 219.

51. David Harvey, *The Condition of Postmodernity* (London: Blackwell, 1989), 156.

52. Ibid., 142, 150.

53. See Helen Molesworth, who offers the most lucid assessment of the effect of the transition from an industrial to postindustrial society on art making: "At this crossroads, much of the most important and challenging art of the period staged the problem of labor's transformation, its new divisions, and the increasingly blurred boundaries between work and leisure. Generally speaking, artists responded in one of four ways. Some played the part of both manager and workers, restaging the late-nineteenth- and early-twentieth-century division of labor. Others, emboldened by the professionalization of the category of artist and liberated by an economic shift away from manufacturing, simplified things by adopting a purely managerial position. Still others had a prescient understanding that the burgeoning service economy would ultimately give way to a leisure economy based on experience. These artists turned to participatory strategies, involving the audience in the art. And finally (although this mapping is by no means chronological), there were those artists who experimented with not working at all, or at least trying to figure out how to work as little possible." Helen Molesworth, *Work Ethic* (University Park: Pennsylvania State University Press, 2003), 39. Note how her idea of the role of participation in the transformations of labor is different from mine, essentially having to do with consumer-producer rather than interworker relations.

54. Lucy Lippard, *Six Years: The Dematerialization of the Art Object from 1966 to 1972* (Berkeley: University of California Press, 1973).

55. Benjamin H. D. Buchloh, "Conceptual Art 1962–1969: From the Aesthetic of Administration to the Critique of Institutions," *October* 55 (Winter 1990): 148.

56. Ibid., 118.

57. Ibid., 128–129.

58. Sol LeWitt, *Sol LeWitt: A Retrospective*, ed. Gary Garrels (New Haven, CT: Yale University Press, 2000), 373.

59. Buchloh, "Conceptual Art 1962–1969" (1990), 128–129.

60. See Liz Kotz for a discussion of the turn to the textual in the art of the period, which she situates in the context of experimental writing. Kotz argues that the materialization of language in the art of the period has to do with new communications technologies. I would argue, by extension, that it has to do with the workplace from which many of these technologies emerge. Liz Kotz, *Words to Be Looked At: Language in 1960s Art* (Cambridge, MA: MIT Press, 2010).

61. For a description of the "chance-acrostic" method, see Jackson Mac Low, *Representative Works, 1938–1985* (New York: Roof Books, 1986), 77–100.

62. Ibid., 89.

63. Rosalind Krauss, "Notes on the Index: Seventies Art in America, Part 2," *October* 4 (Autumn 1977): 66.

64. Ibid.

65. Ibid., 59.

66. Robert B. Reich, *The Work of Nations: Preparing Ourselves for 21st Century Capitalism* (New York: Random House, 1992), 217–218.

67. Arlie Russell Hochschild, *The Managed Heart: Commercialization of Human Feeling, Updated with a New Preface* (Berkeley: University of California Press, 2012), 3–23, 33.

68. Sianne Ngai, *Our Aesthetic Categories: Zany, Cute, Interesting* (Cambridge, MA: Harvard University Press, 2012), 174–231.

69. Jeff Kelley and Allan Kaprow, *Childsplay: The Art of Allan Kaprow* (Berkeley: University of California Press, 2004), 120–127.

70. Quoted in Molesworth, *Work Ethic*, 172.

71. Ibid., 144–145.

72. Frank O'Hara, "The Day Lady Died," in *Lunch Poems* (San Francisco: City Lights Publishers, 2001), 25.

73. I have already mentioned some important studies of these developments, by Alan Liu and Boltanski and Chiapello. Also of particular interest is Stephen Waring, who details the various alternatives to Taylorism that developed in its shadows and eventually became hegemonic during the process of restructuring. Stephen P. Waring, *Taylorism Transformed: Scientific Management Theory since 1945* (Chapel Hill: University of North Carolina Press, 1994).

74. See, for instance, chapter 5 of Waring for a discussion of the "sensitivity trainings" that used Kurt Lewin's style of "encounter group" therapy—popular with parts of the 1960s counterculture—to counteract the authoritarian and bureaucratic sclerosis of postwar white-collar work, as well as the psychological maladies that attended it. These therapeutic ideas persist as part of the larger discourse of "corporate culture" and "team building" and are one source for the curious presence of ideas associated with "new age" philosophy in ostensibly conservative capitalist firms. Ibid., 104–131.

75. Heather J. Hicks, *The Culture of Soft Work: Labor, Gender, and Race in Postmodern American Narrative* (New York: Palgrave Macmillan, 2009), 45–88; Ngai, *Our Aesthetic Categories*, 174–231.

76. See Arlie Russell Hochschild, *The Time Bind: When Work Becomes Home and Home Becomes Work* (New York: Holt Paperbacks, 2001), 197–218; Alan Liu, *The Laws of Cool: Knowledge Work and the Culture of Information* (Chicago: University of Chicago Press, 2004), 76–79.

77. Mills, *White Collar*, 69, 74.

78. Raymond Williams, *Marxism and Literature* (New York: Oxford University Press, 1978), 128–129.

Chapter 1

1. All of the correspondence between O'Hara and Ferlinghetti is included in a special fiftieth-anniversary edition of the book: Frank O'Hara, *Lunch Poems: 50th Anniversary Edition* (San Francisco: City Lights Publishers, 2014), 73.

2. Ibid., 85.

3. Ibid.

4. Tim Hunter, "For Those Who Think Young," *Mad Men* (HBO, July 27, 2008). The

episode caused quite a stir among the poetry blogs when it first appeared. For a summary, see Kate Lilley, "Meditations on Emergent Occasions: Mad Men, Donald Draper and Frank O'Hara," *Cultural Studies Review* 18, no. 2 (September 2012): 301–315.

5. For writing about this aspect of O'Hara's poetry, see Drew Milne, "Performance over Being: Frank O'Hara's Artifice," *Textual Practice* 25, no. 2 (April 2011): 297–313.

6. O'Hara, "Adieu to Norman, Bonjour to Joan and Jean-Paul," in *Lunch Poems* (2001), 29.

7. O'Hara, "The Day Lady Died," in *Lunch Poems* (2001), 21.

8. Ezra Pound, "A Few Don'ts by an Imagiste," *Poetry* 1, no. 6 (1913): 203.

9. S. I. Hayakawa, "Poetry and Advertising," *Poetry* 67, no. 4 (January 1946): 205.

10. Immanuel Kant, *Critique of Judgment* (Indianapolis, IN: Hackett Publishing, 1987), 171.

11. Hayakawa, "Poetry and Advertising," 206.

12. Draper seems confused about where he stands with regard to these oppositions. He is obviously stung by the implication that he wouldn't "get" O'Hara's poetry, but later that afternoon, during a meeting with his creative team, he tells copywriter Paul Kinsey (a para-bohemian who smokes marijuana, listens to jazz, has a black girlfriend, and will eventually join the Hare Krishna movement) to "stop writing for other writers." There has to be advertising, Draper advises, for "people who don't have a sense of humor." The distinction he is making, however, is very fine-edged (or perhaps contradictory), as we learn when Peggy Olson and illustrator Sal Romano present a new mock-up for the same project and he complains that "it's obvious." He feels "uninvolved" by the ad and admonishes Peggy for misunderstanding his earlier reverie about short skirts through the formulaic rubric *sex sells*. "Just so you know," he tells her, "the people who talk that way think that trained monkeys can do this.... [Y]ou are the product, you feeling something. That's what sells."

13. Frank O'Hara, *The Collected Poems of Frank O'Hara* (Berkeley: University of California Press, 1995), 360. The poem was originally published not in *Lunch Poems* but in his *Love Poems*.

14. Warren Berger, *Advertising Today* (London: Phaidon, 2004), 158–164.

15. Thomas Frank, *The Conquest of Cool: Business Culture, Counterculture, and the Rise of Hip Consumerism* (Chicago: University of Chicago Press, 1997), 88–103.

16. Wieden+Kennedy, "Nike: Walt Stack," 2008.

17. Berger, *Advertising Today*, 152–153.

18. José Esteban Muñoz, *Cruising Utopia: The Then and There of Queer Futurity* (New York: New York University Press, 2009), 6.

19. Michael Warner, *Publics and Counterpublics* (Cambridge, MA: Zone Books, 2005), 164, 168.

20. O'Hara, *Collected Poems*, 360.

21. Linda McDowell, *Working Bodies: Interactive Service Employment and Workplace Identities* (Hoboken, NJ: John Wiley & Sons, 2009), 9. See also Lisa Brush, "Gender, Work, Who Cares?! Production, Reproduction, Deindustrialization and Business as

Usual," in *Revisioning Gender*, ed. Myra Marx Ferree, Judith Lorber, and Beth B. Hess (Lanham, MD: Rowman Altamira, 1999), 161–192. The distinction between interactive service work and administrative service corresponds, more or less, with Lisa Brush's distinction between "high-tech" and "high-touch" work, and with Robert Reich's division of the service sector into the largely low-paid and devalorized "in-person services" and the well-paid jobs that involved "symbolic analysis." Reich, *The Work of Nations*, 217–218.

22. McDowell, *Working Bodies*, 121.

23. Dwayne D. Gremler and Kevin P. Gwinner, "Customer-Employee Rapport in Service Relationships," *Journal of Service Research* 3, no. 1 (August 2000): 82.

24. Ibid., 99.

25. Hochschild, *The Managed Heart*.

26. Lytle Shaw, *Frank O'Hara: The Poetics of Coterie* (Iowa City: University of Iowa Press, 2006), 6.

27. Brad Gooch, *City Poet: The Life and Times of Frank O'Hara* (New York: Harper Perennial, 2014), 207–208, 257–259.

28. O'Hara, *Lunch Poems* (2014), 21.

29. Shaw, *Frank O'Hara*, 6.

30. O'Hara, *Lunch Poems* (2014), 21.

31. Ibid.

32. Terrell Scott Herring, "Frank O'Hara's Open Closet," *PMLA* 117, no. 3 (May 2002): 417, 422.

33. Virginia Jackson, *Dickinson's Misery: A Theory of Lyric Reading* (Princeton, NJ: Princeton University Press, 2013), 68–108; Jonathan Culler, *Theory of the Lyric* (Cambridge, MA: Harvard University Press, 2015), 39–76.

34. Oren Izenberg, *Being Numerous Poetry and the Ground of Social Life* (Princeton, NJ: Princeton University Press, 2011), 136–137.

35. O'Hara, *Collected Poems of Frank O'Hara*, 498 (emphasis mine).

36. Ibid., 498–499.

37. O'Hara, *Lunch Poems*, 5.

38. Ibid., 16.

39. Ibid., 23.

40. Ibid., 25.

41. Ibid., 33.

42. Ibid., 42.

43. Ibid., 45.

44. Ibid., 46.

45. Ibid., 64.

46. Jonathan Culler, *The Pursuit of Signs* (London: Routledge, 2001), 151.

47. Ibid., 165.

48. Theodor Adorno, *Notes to Literature, Volume 1* (New York: Columbia University Press, 1991), 37.

49. Ibid., 39–40.

50. O'Hara, *Collected Poems of Frank O'Hara*, 197.

51. Integrated marketing often involves a mix of advertising, personal selling, sales promotion, sponsorship, publicity, and point-of-purchase marketing. For an example of this approach, see Bob Hartley and Dave Pickton, "Integrated Marketing Communications Requires a New Way of Thinking," *Journal of Marketing Communications* 5, no. 2 (January 1999): 97–106.

52. This story is told in a number of texts. See, for instance, Frances Stonor Saunders, *The Cultural Cold War: The CIA and the World of Arts and Letters* (New York: New Press, 1999), 252–278; Hugh Wilford, *The Mighty Wurlitzer: How the CIA Played America* (Cambridge, MA: Harvard University Press, 2008), 99–122.

53. Eva Cockcroft, "Abstract Expressionism, Weapon of the Cold War," in *Pollock and After: The Critical Debate* (London: Routledge, 2000), 147–154.

54. Alfred H. Barr, quoted in ibid., 88.

55. Quoted in Saunders, *The Cultural Cold War*, 275.

56. O'Hara, *Lunch Poems* (2014), 67–68.

57. Ibid., 25–26.

58. Ibid., 21.

59. Ibid., 18.

60. John Ashbery, *Self-Portrait in a Convex Mirror: Poems* (New York: Viking Press, 1975), 195.

61. Ibid., 23–24.

62. O'Hara, *Lunch Poems* (2014), 46.

63. One of the many fascinating things we learn from Stephen Waring's *Taylorism Transformed* is that the countercultural "encounter groups" at Esalen developed out of the postwar "sensitivity trainings" based on the psychology of Kurt Lewin, which were designed to train professionals in the skills of "democratic leadership" by forcing them into unscripted encounters with other strangers (104–131).

Chapter 2

Parts of this chapter were first published as "John Ashbery's Free Indirect Discourse," *Modern Language Quarterly* 74, no. 4 (2013): 517–540. Reprinted with permission of Duke University Press.

1. John Ashbery, *The Mooring of Starting Out* (New York: Ecco, 1997), 8.

2. The three most important books are Riesman, *The Lonely Crowd*; Whyte, *The Organization Man*; and Mills, *White Collar*. See also Liu, *The Laws of Cool*, 14–41; and Hoberek, *Twilight of the Middle Class*, 1–32.

3. David F. Noble, *Forces of Production: A Social History of Industrial Automation* (New York: Oxford University Press, 1986), 265–322.

4. Braverman, *Labor and Monopoly Capital*, 326–348.

5. Allen Ginsberg, *Howl, and Other Poems* (San Francisco: City Lights Books, 1959), 41.

6. Hoberek, *Twilight of the Middle Class*, 23.

7. John Ashbery, "Robert Frost Medal Address," in *Selected Prose* (Ann Arbor: University of Michigan Press, 2005), 249.

8. Ibid., 250.

9. John Ashbery, *Reported Sightings: Art Chronicles, 1957–1987* (Cambridge, MA: Harvard University Press, 1991), 109.

10. George Oppen, *Collected Poems* (London: Fulcrum Press, 1972), 46.

11. Note also how Oppen equates labor's materiality with its masculinity: The burliness of the men is directly proportional to the resistance of the material and explicitly contrasted with the feebleness of the crippled girl. Furthermore, the masculine "labor before her birth" displaces the feminine creative powers of the other kind of "labor" on which the phrase puns. While a thorough discussion of questions of gender and sexuality is outside the scope of this article, the deindustrialization and dematerialization of labor that occurs in the postindustrial period also involved a "feminization of labor": women entered the workforce in much larger numbers at the same time as certain occupations were feminized—that is, recoded with values, affects, and attitudes associated with femininity. As Eva Illouz has shown, male white-collar workers were submitted to a therapeutic management regime that asked them to cultivate certain values—receptivity, tolerance, and sensitivity—often experienced as emasculating. Eva Illouz, *Cold Intimacies: The Making of Emotional Capitalism* (Cambridge: Polity, 2007), 10–25. In many regards, then, the exaggerated masculinity and heteronormativity of the postwar workplace can be seen as reaction against such a process, an attempt to secure masculine privileges against encroaching feminization. See also Hicks, *The Culture of Soft Work*. We might treat Ashbery's critical response to the white-collar workplace and its rigidity as equally a response to these norms of masculinity.

12. Ashbery, *Reported Sightings*, 81.

13. Ibid., 82.

14. Andrew Ross, "Taking the Tennis Court Oath," in *The Tribe of John: Ashbery and Contemporary Poetry* (Tuscaloosa: University of Alabama Press, 1995), 202, 209.

15. Ashbery, *The Mooring of Starting Out*, 106.

16. Mills, *White Collar*, 68.

17. Ashbery, *The Mooring of Starting Out*, 69.

18. Ibid., 67.

19. Ibid., 104.

20. Ibid., 95.

21. For an account of novelistic conventions in Ashbery, see Michael Clune, "'Whatever Charms Is Alien': John Ashbery's Everything," *Criticism* 50, no. 3 (2008): 447–469.

22. Ashbery, *The Mooring of Starting Out*, 124.

23. David Herd, *John Ashbery and American Poetry* (Manchester, UK: Manchester University Press, 2000), 88.

24. Ashbery, *The Mooring of Starting Out*, 100.

25. The whole quote is instructive: "The personal pronouns in my work very often seem to be like variables in an equation. 'You' can be myself or it can be another per-

son, someone whom I'm addressing, and so can 'he' and 'she' for that matter and 'we'; sometimes one has to deduce from the rest of the sentence what is being meant and my point is also that it doesn't really matter very much, that we are somehow all aspects of a consciousness giving rise to the poem and the fact of addressing someone, myself or someone else, is what's the important thing at that particular moment rather than the particular person involved. I guess I don't have a very strong sense of my own identity and I find it very easy to move from one person in the sense of a pronoun to another and this again helps to produce a kind of polyphony in my poetry which I again feel is a means toward greater naturalism." "Craft Interview with John Ashbery," by Janet Bloom and Robert Losada, in *The Craft of Poetry Interviews from the* New York Quarterly, ed. William Packard (Garden City, NY: Doubleday, 1974), 124.

26. John Emil Vincent, *John Ashbery and You: His Later Books* (Athens: University of Georgia Press, 2007), 5; Bonnie Costello, "John Ashbery and the Idea of the Reader," *Contemporary Literature* 23, no. 4 (October 1982): 495.

27. Ashbery, *The Mooring of Starting Out*, 147–148.

28. Ibid., 130.

29. Ann Banfield, *Unspeakable Sentences: Narration and Representation in the Language of Fiction* (Boston: Routledge & Kegan Paul, 1982); V. N. Volosinov, *Marxism and the Philosophy of Language* (Cambridge, MA: Harvard University Press, 1986).

30. Gilles Deleuze and Felix Guattari, *A Thousand Plateaus: Capitalism and Schizophrenia*, trans. Brian Massumi (Minneapolis: University of Minnesota Press, 1987), 84.

31. Ashbery, *Self-Portrait in a Convex Mirror*, 202.

32. See also the account of free indirect discourse (*style indirect libre*) in the nineteenth-century novel in D. A. Miller's *The Novel and the Police*. Miller accounts such technique part and parcel of a general disciplinary and surveilling power: "The master-voice of monologism never simply soliloquizes. It continually needs to confirm its authority by qualifying, cancelling, endorsing, subsuming all the other voices it lets speak. No doubt the need stands behind the great prominence the nineteenth-century novel gives to *style indirect libre*, in which, respeaking a character's thoughts or speeches, the narration simultaneously subverts their authority and secures its own." D. A. Miller, *The Novel and the Police* (Berkeley: University of California Press, 1989), 25.

33. Karl Marx, *Capital*, vol. 1, *A Critique of Political Economy* (New York: Penguin Classics, 1992), 163.

34. Karl Marx and Friedrich Engels, *Collected Works*, vol. 29 (London: Lawrence & Wishart, 1994), 122.

35. Mills, *White Collar*, 80–81.

36. Pier Paolo Pasolini, "The Cinema of Poetry," in *Movies and Methods* (Berkeley: University of California Press, 1976), 1:551. See also the passage from Miller quoted in note 31, as well as Franco Moretti, "Serious Century," in *The Novel*, vol. 1, *History, Geography, and Culture* (Princeton, NJ: Princeton University Press, 2007), 364–400.

37. Ashbery, *The Mooring of Starting Out*, 113.

38. See, for instance, Chris Nealon on Ashbery's habit of "wandering away" from the

violence and catastrophe that capitalism presents. Christopher Nealon, *The Matter of Capital: Poetry and Crisis in the American Century* (Cambridge, MA: Harvard University Press, 2011), 78.

39. Pasolini, "The Cinema of Poetry," 551.

40. Ashbery, *The Mooring of Starting Out*, 165.

41. Ibid., 245.

42. Ibid., 338.

43. John Murphy, "John Ashbery: An Interview with John Murphy," *Poetry Review* 75, no. 2 (August 1985): 25; Ashbery, *The Mooring of Starting Out*, 231.

Chapter 3

1. Martin Heidegger, "Only a God Can Save Us: The *Der Spiegel* Interview," in *Heidegger: The Man and the Thinker*, ed. Thomas Sheehan (Chicago: Precedent, 1981), 45–67.

2. Writing in the 1980s, Tom LeClair will describe these books as "the systems novel," whereas David Porush, gathering together a similar pantheon, describes the books as "cybernetic fiction." Both writers emphasize the connection between self-reflexivity and feedback. Tom LeClair, *In the Loop: Don DeLillo and the Systems Novel* (Urbana: University of Illinois Press, 1987); David Porush, *The Soft Machine: Cybernetic Fiction* (New York: Methuen, 1985). Mark McGurl's recent book returns to this terrain and dubs it "technomodernism," producing what is probably the most interesting discussion of feedback and the related concept of "autopoiesis" in relation to post–World War II fiction. Like the earlier writers, McGurl links cybernetics to the emphasis on self-consciousness and self-reflexivity in postwar fiction, from metafictional cleverness to the abundant stories and novels that take the writerly self as object. Mark McGurl, *The Program Era: Postwar Fiction and the Rise of Creative Writing* (Cambridge, MA: Harvard University Press, 2009), 48–49, 80–86.

3. Kynaston McShine, *Information* (New York: Museum of Modern Art, 1970).

4. Bernard Geoghegan, "From Information Theory to French Theory: Jakobson, Lévi-Strauss, and the Cybernetic Apparatus," *Critical Inquiry* 38, no. 1 (Autumn 2011): 123–126.

5. Norbert Wiener, *Cybernetics; Or, Control and Communication in the Animal and the Machine* (New York: John Wiley & Sons, 1948).

6 See Peter Galison for a discussion of the wartime origins of cybernetics. Peter Galison, "The Ontology of the Enemy: Norbert Wiener and the Cybernetic Vision," *Critical Inquiry* 21, no. 1 (October 1994): 228–266.

7. For an early "social" application of cybernetics, see the essays collected in Gregory Bateson. Cybernetics becomes a robust science of all social systems—the state, the economy, the family, "culture"—with its passage into "second-order cybernetics" and finally, from there, into Niklas Luhmann's phenomenologically inflected extension of cybernetics, called "systems theory." Jameson links Luhmann's systems theory with the ideology of neoliberalism itself and sees it as a naturalization of market relations. Gregory Bateson, *Steps to an Ecology of Mind* (Chicago: University of Chicago Press, 2000); Niklas Luhmann, *Social Systems (Writing Science)* (Stanford, CA: Stanford University

Press, 1995), 283–287; Fredric Jameson, *A Singular Modernity: Essay on the Ontology of the Present* (New York: Verso, 2002), 92.

8. Fred Turner, *From Counterculture to Cyberculture: Stewart Brand, the Whole Earth Network, and the Rise of Digital Utopianism* (Chicago: University of Chicago Press, 2006), 38.

9. Quoted in ibid., 38–39.

10. Michael C. Jackson, *Systems Approaches to Management* (Berlin: Springer, 2000), 3. For examples of management cybernetics, see Stafford Beer, *Brain of the Firm* (Hoboken: John Wiley & Sons, 1994); Jay W. Forrester, *Industrial Dynamics* (Cambridge, MA: MIT Press, 1961).

11. Frank, *The Conquest of Cool*, 1–34.

12. Boltanski and Chiapello, *The New Spirit of Capitalism*, 167–217.

13. Frank, *The Conquest of Cool*, 7–8.

14. Douglas McGregor, "The Human Side of Enterprise," *Management Review* 46, no. 11 (November 1957): 170–171; Douglas McGregor, *The Human Side of Enterprise* (New York: McGraw-Hill, 2006), 73.

15. Turner, *From Counterculture to Cyberculture*, 46–47.

16. Hannah Weiner, *Hannah Weiner's Open House* (Berkeley, CA: Kenning Editions, 2007), 23.

17. See Peter Bürger on the double bind of the avant-garde "art into life" thematic. For Bürger, if the avant-garde succeeds in merging art and life, it loses the very critical distance from which it mounted its critique of the abstraction of art from life. Peter Bürger, *Theory of the Avant-Garde* (Manchester, UK: Manchester University Press, 1984), 47–54.

18. Norbert Wiener, *The Human Use of Human Beings: Cybernetics and Society* (New York: Da Capo Press, 1988), 15.

19. Ibid., 16.

20. Ibid., 95–111.

21. Weiner, *Hannah Weiner's Open House*, 57.

22. John Perreault, "Street Works in Colorado; Libeskind and Kirkland in Outer Space," *Artopia*, October 6, 2008, 6, http://www.artsjournal.com/artopia/2008/10/street_works_in_colorado_libes.html.

23. Weiner, *Hannah Weiner's Open House*, 57.

24. Ibid., 24.

25. Ibid.

26. Friedrich Hayek, "The Use of Knowledge in Society," *American Economic Review* 35, no. 4 (September 1945): 527.

27. Weiner, *Hannah Weiner's Open House*, 25.

28. Ibid., 25.

29. N. Katherine Hayles, *Chaos Bound: Orderly Disorder in Contemporary Literature and Science* (Ithaca, NY: Cornell University Press, 1990), 41.

30. Wiener, *The Human Use of Human Beings*, 9–10.

31. Quoted in Philip Mirowski, *Machine Dreams* (Cambridge: Cambridge University Press, 2002), 70.

32. Wiener, *The Human Use of Human Beings*, 21.

33. McColloch, *White-Collar Workers in Transition*, 3; Reich, *The Work of Nations*, 177–182.

34. Weiner, *Hannah Weiner's Open House*, 54. I owe the idea of a relationship between Weiner's work and Basic English to Koeneke's paper "Hannah Weiner and Basic English," delivered at National Poetry Conference: Poetry of the 1970s, June 2008, Orono, Maine, http://vectors.usc.edu/thoughtmesh/publish/117.php.

35. Weiner, *Hannah Weiner's Open House*, 54.

36. Ibid., 55.

37. Wiener, *The Human Use of Human Beings*, 95.

38. For a paper that makes some of these same connections, see Koeneke, "Hannah Weiner and Basic English."

39. For a history of the therblig and the related time and motion studies, see Brian Price, "Frank and Lillian Gilbreth and the Motion Study Controversy, 1907–1930," in *A Mental Revolution: Scientific Management since Taylor*, ed. Daniel Nelson (Columbus: Ohio State University Press, 1992), 64–72.

40. Hannah Weiner, *Code Poems: From the International Code of Signals for the Use of All Nations* (Barrytown, NY: Open Book Publications, 1982), 27.

41. John Perreault, "Review of *Code Poems* by Hannah Weiner," *Poetry Project Newsletter*, no. 99 (1983): 8.

42. This is close to the position that both Judith Goldman and Patrick Durgin—two of the best critics of Hannah Weiner—make. Both writers emphasize Weiner's destabilization of the sign, particularly in her later works, and the way that this discloses language's dependence on extratextual structures to produce meaning. As Goldman puts it, for Weiner "language [is] an indeterminate, opaque materiality that we ourselves enliven with belief, but also . . . a form of mediation that announce[s] itself as being curiously existentially indefinite, both there and not there." Patrick F. Durgin, "Psychosocial Disability and Post-ableist Poetics: The 'Case' of Hannah Weiner's Clairvoyant Journals," *Contemporary Women's Writing* 2, no. 2 (December 2008): 131–154; Judith Goldman, "Hannah=hannaH: Politics, Ethics, and Clairvoyance in the Work of Hannah Weiner," *Differences: A Journal of Feminist Cultural Studies* 12, no. 2 (2001): 120–161.

43. Claude E. Shannon and Warren Weaver, *The Mathematical Theory of Communication* (Urbana: University of Illinois Press, 1998), 19.

44. Heinz von Foerster, *Understanding Understanding: Essays on Cybernetics and Cognition* (New York: Springer-Verlag, 2003), 11.

45. Niklas Luhmann, *Theories of Distinction: Redescribing the Descriptions of Modernity* (Stanford, CA: Stanford University Press, 2002), 157.

46. Abraham Maslow, quoted in Sarah Brouillette, *Literature and the Creative Economy* (Stanford, CA: Stanford University Press, 2014), 68.

47. McGregor, "The Human Side of Enterprise," 169.

48. Weiner, *Code Poems*, 25.

49. James Clerk Maxwell, *The Scientific Letters and Papers of James Clerk Maxwell* (New York: Cambridge University Press Archive, 1995), 585.

50. Hayles, *Chaos Bound*, 44–50.

51. Hoberek, *The Twilight of the Middle Class*, 1–33; Stephen Schryer, *Fantasies of the New Class: Ideologies of Professionalism in Post–World War II American Fiction* (New York: Columbia University Press, 2006), 1–27.

52. Thomas Pynchon, *The Crying of Lot 49*, Perennial Classics (New York: Harper Perennial, 1999), 68.

53. Ibid.

54. Bell, *The Coming of Post-industrial Society*, xci–c.

55. It is worth noting that Bell misunderstands the role of technological innovation—-i.e., knowledge—in the labor theory of value as Marx presents it, and therefore his argument that labor value has been superseded in late capitalism remains fundamentally incoherent. Labor-saving innovations allow for the increased extraction of surplus value, and therefore profits, at two different levels: at the level of individual capitalists and at the level of capital as a whole. Individual capitalists who possess a unique labor-saving invention will realize more surplus value—relative surplus value—because their output per wage will be higher, but once this innovation becomes generalized through mimicry and the differences between the productive capacity of individual capitalists eliminated, the new technology still produces relative surplus value as long as it has cheapened the cost of a consumer good, since it therefore lowers the cost of reproducing labor power and increases as a result the time that the worker might devote to the production of value for the employer. This latter effect depends not at all on individual ownership of technological innovations. Where Bell is right, of course, is that there might be no incentive for the individual capitalist to introduce the new invention—and therefore begin its generalization—unless the capitalist can ensure that others cannot do the same quickly. But in other cases intellectual proprietorship is not really necessary. Capitalists may feel compelled to introduce a free technology precisely because they fear that others will do so before them.

56. Wiener, *The Human Use of Human Beings*, 112–130.

57. In his curator's statement for the show, Kynaston places special emphasis on the works as acts of "communication" or "stimuli," both terms borrowed from the cybernetic discourse of the time: "The general attitude of the artists in this exhibition is certainly not hostile. It is straightforward, friendly, coolly involved, and allows experiences which are refreshing. It enables us to participate, quite often as in a game; at other times it seems almost therapeutic, making us question ourselves and our responses to unfamiliar stimuli. The constant demand is a more aware relation to our natural and artificial environments. There is always the sense of communication. These artists are questioning our prejudices, asking us to renounce our inhibitions, and if they are revealing the nature of art, they are also asking that we reassess what we have always taken for

granted as our accepted and cultural conditioned aesthetic response to art." McShine, *Information*, 73.

58. Dan Graham and Brian Wallis, *Rock My Religion* (Cambridge, MA: MIT Press, 1993), xviii.

59. Dan Graham and Alexander Alberro, *Two-Way Mirror Power* (Cambridge, MA: MIT Press, 1999), 12.

60. Dan Graham, "Poem, March 1966," *Aspen*, no. 15–16 (Fall–Winter 1967), item 16.

61. Dan Graham, Museum of Contemporary Art (Los Angeles, Calif.), and Whitney Museum of American Art, *Dan Graham: Beyond* (Los Angeles: Museum of Contemporary Art, 2009), 17. Graham cites Paul Ryan's book *Cybernetics of the Sacred* as an influence. Paul Ryan, *Cybernetics of the Sacred* (New York: Anchor Press, 1974).

62. Ibid.

63. Lippard, *Six Years*, 263.

64. Jeff Wall, "Dan Graham's Kammerspiel," in *Conceptual Art: A Critical Anthology*, ed. Alexander Alberro and Blake Stimson (Cambridge, MA: MIT Press, 1999), 510.

65. Ibid., 506–507, 510.

66. Benjamin Buchloh, "Conceptual Art 1962–1969: From the Aesthetic of Administration to the Critique of Institutions," in Alberro and Stimson, *Conceptual Art*, 520.

67. Birgit Pelzer, *Dan Graham* (London: Phaidon, 2001), 42.

68. Ibid.

69. See, for instance, Michel Foucault on the theory of "human capital." Certain strains of American neoliberal economic theory redefine the worker's wage as the earnings received from human capital. As a result "the worker himself appears as a sort of enterprise for himself." Workers are thus asked to treat their own capacities as investments to be cultivated, developed, and refined. Michel Foucault, *Birth of Biopolitics* (New York: Palgrave, 2008), 215–237, 225.

70. Shoshana Zuboff, *In the Age of the Smart Machine* (New York: Basic Books, 1988), 395.

71. Kimberly Seltzer and Tom Bentley, *The Creative Age* (New York: Demos, 1999), 9.

72. Dan Graham and Alexander Alberro, *Two-Way Mirror Power* (Cambridge, MA: MIT Press, 1999), 54.

73. Eric de Bruyn, "Topological Pathways of Post-minimalism," *Grey Room* 25 (October 2006): 32–63.

74. Graham and Alberro, *Two-Way Mirror Power*, 55.

75. Boltanski and Chiapello, *The New Spirit of Capitalism*, 191.

76. Ibid., 112.

77. Graham and Alberro, *Two-Way Mirror Power*, 52.

78. Ibid., 59.

79. Boltanski and Chiapello, *The New Spirit of Capitalism*, 431.

Chapter 4

1. Kenneth Goldsmith, "Journal, Day Three," *Harriet*, January 24, 2007, http://www.poetryfoundation.org/harriet/2007/01/journal-day-three/.

2. For an excellent survey, see Helen Molesworth, "House Work and Art Work," *October* 92 (April 2000): 71–97.

3. Some Marxist thinkers—especially those associated with Italian Autonomist Marxism, such as Antonio Negri, Paolo Virno, and Franco Berardi—have attempted to reckon with the rise of white-collar and service work, often in terms that are not all that different from Bell's. Like him, many of these authors claim a suspension of the laws of labor value occurs once knowledge becomes a primary driver of capital accumulation. Despite their superior analytical power, these theories have a tendency to underplay the extent to which mundane forms of informationalized, postindustrial work have predominated, rather than the technical work they assume is central: filing, typing, entering data in spreadsheets, sorting mail, producing internal documents and memoranda, and administering the flows of money, bodies, and goods.

4. Manuel Castells, *The Rise of the Network Society: The Information Age: Economy, Society, and Culture* (Hoboken, NJ: John Wiley & Sons, 2009), 216–354.

5. Julia Kirk Blackwelder, *Now Hiring: The Feminization of Work in the United States, 1900–1995* (College Station: Texas A&M University Press, 1997).

6. On this development, see, for instance, Donna Haraway's "Cyborg Manifesto": "Work is being redefined as both literally female or feminized, whether performed by men or women. To be feminized means to be made extremely vulnerable; able to be disassembled, reassembled, exploited as a reserve labour force; seen less as workers than as servers; subjected to time arrangements on and off the paid job that make a mockery of a limited work day." Donna J. Haraway, *Simians, Cyborgs, and Women: The Reinvention of Nature* (London: Routledge, 1990), 149–182.

7. The name implies, as Sharon Strom notes, "that women brought their sexuality to the office, where it could be evaluated by men, but . . . also indicates that women were there to take care of their 'office husbands,' to perform domestic housekeeping and organization chores, and to remain in subservient positions." Sharon Strom, *Beyond the Typewriter: Gender, Class, and the Origins of Modern American Office Work, 1900–1930* (Urbana: University of Illinois Press, 1995), 2.

8. Ann Vickery, *Leaving Lines of Gender: A Feminist Genealogy of Language Writing* (Middletown, CT: Wesleyan University Press, 2000), 150–166; Maggie Nelson, *Women, the New York School, and Other True Abstractions* (Iowa City: University of Iowa Press, 2007), 99–130; Peter Baker, *Obdurate Brilliance: Exteriority and the Modern Long Poem* (Gainesville: University Press of Florida, 1991), 149–161.

9. "Reproductive labor" refers not only to biological reproduction but to the social reproduction of workers—in other words, the labor power that capitalism needs—on a daily *and* generational basis. Such a term refers to all of the caretaking work—most of it unpaid—necessary for the reproduction of the labor power of the working class, whether the provision of meals, child rearing, or training and education. I reserve the

term "domestic" labor for the specific form of reproductive labor that takes place in the home—housework. In the 1970s, significant debates among Marxist feminists (and anti-Marxist feminists) attempted to clarify the precise relationship of these forms of labor to wage labor and capital accumulation. For summaries, see Ellen Malos, *The Politics of Housework* (Cheltenham, UK: New Clarion Press, 1995), 1–33; Lise Vogel, *Woman Questions: Essays for a Materialist Feminism* (Hove, UK: Psychology Press, 1995), 58–65. For important contributions to these debates, see also Mariarosa Dalla Costa and Selma James, *The Power of Women and the Subversion of the Community* (London: Falling Wall Press, 1975); Silvia Federici, *Caliban and the Witch* (Brooklyn, NY: Autonomedia, 2004); Maria Mies, *Patriarchy and Accumulation on a World Scale: Women in the International Division of Labour* (New York: Palgrave Macmillan, 1998).

10. Bernadette Mayer, *The Desires of Mothers to Please Others in Letters* (West Stockbridge, MA: Hard Press Editions, 2001), 208.

11. Bernadette Mayer, *Memory* (Plainfield, VT: North Atlantic Books, 1975), 153.

12. Ibid., 72.

13. Ibid., 7.

14. For accounts of the importance of the Hegelian logic of the "moment" to Marx's conception of capital, see Christopher John Arthur, *The New Dialectic and Marx's Capital* (Leiden, Netherlands: Brill, 2004); Hiroshi Uchida, *Marx's* Grundrisse *and Hegel's* Logic (London: Routledge, 1988).

15. Mayer, *Memory*, 7.

16. Ngai, *Our Aesthetic Categories*, 174–231.

17. Ibid., 214–215.

18. One of the more interesting accounts of these crossings and reversals can be found in Nona Glazer's study of what she calls "work transfer," defined as "the logical and straightforward attempt by some capitalists to insert the consumer into the work process." Nona Glazer, "Servants to Capital: Unpaid Domestic Labor and Paid Work," in *Work without Wages: Comparative Studies of Domestic Labor and Self-Employment*, ed. Jane L. Collins and Martha E. Gimenez (Binghamton: SUNY Press, 1990), 145. Unlike other authors who attempt to square feminist and Marxist analysis by suggesting that unpaid domestic labor produces surplus value, Glazer is more rigorous and less overreaching in her analysis, suggesting that, like exploitation in commercial enterprises in general, such unpaid consumer labor is only *indirectly* productive of surplus value. However, unpaid labor is still dominated and subsumed by capital. For instance, in retail (one of her case studies), the shift from full service to self-service (that is, from a system where clerks locate and gather purchases for customers to a system where customers gather their own purchases) means a transfer of activities from worker to consumer and thus a reduction in wage costs (as well as a temporary increase in profits): "The *work transfer* to consumers means that commercial capitalists hire fewer workers: consumers work in their place and the organization is altered to eliminate some steps in the work process (e.g., consumers locate and collect merchandise, while the prepackaging of goods eliminates measuring and bagging)" (159). Glazer makes clear the doubleness

of the doubling under discussion here: at the same time as unwaged women's work is transformed into waged activity, the remaining unwaged work is rationalized by capital to speed up the accumulation process.

19. Nancy Folbre, *For Love or Money: Care Provision in the United States* (New York: Russell Sage Foundation, 2012), 4–7.

20. Mayer, *Memory*, 8.

21. Bernadette Mayer, "Memory (typescript)" (San Diego: University of California, San Diego, n.d.), ms. 420, box 20, folder 10, Archive for New Poetry.

22. A terminological note is in order. The term "reproduction" has a double meaning. Most explicitly, it refers to that part of social activity that is tasked with reproducing labor power. But one also speaks of "social reproduction," a term that refers to the totality of social activity—in other words, the entire process by which the capital/labor relationship is reproduced. For a use of the term in this way, on "simple" and "expanded" reproduction, see Marx, *Capital*, 1:711–751. In the introduction to the *Grundrisse*, Marx suggests that production is a general category and that production, circulation, and consumption in their specific senses might all be "moments" of the larger category of production. That is, production is both the general and specific category: "Production predominates not only over itself, in the antithetical definition of production, but over all the other moments as well." Karl Marx, *Grundrisse: Foundations of the Critique of Political Economy* (New York: Penguin, 1993), 99. Likewise, the interventions of feminist theory within Marxism might be seen as having encouraged us to think of "reproduction" rather than "production" as the general category that predominates over itself and all of the other categories, since capital must not only accumulate but (re)produce the conditions that make accumulation possible. Once reproductive labor in its specific sense comes into view as a crucial aspect of capitalist production, from that moment on everything comes to seem part of social reproduction rather than social production per se.

23. I borrow here from the expanded Marxist notion of "subsumption" that develops simultaneously among thinkers associated with Italian *operaismo* and the French ultraleft following the dissemination of the "Missing Sixth Chapter of *Capital*," published in English under the title "Immediate Results of the Process of Production" as an appendix to *Capital*, volume 1. In this piece of writing, Marx describes capitalism as passing through the logical and historical phases of first "formal" subsumption and then "real" subsumption. In formal subsumption, there is a wage relation between the capitalist and worker, but the means and methods of labor are the same as precapitalist forms—i.e., weavers become wage laborers but continue weaving using the same tools as previously. In "real subsumption," however, capitalists transform the means and methods of production in line with specifically capitalist aims—productivity, efficiency, division of labor, and so forth—as we see in the development of the factory system. After the discovery and distribution of this manuscript, Marxists critical of orthodox Marxism and looking for a way to repair the flaws of Marxist-Leninism, turn to the notion of real subsumption to describe a much more expansive process of subsumption

and transformation that refashions not just the workplace but the social infrastructure as well. This notion of a "social factory"—as the result of a real subsumption of society will be called by later exponents—describes very well the world of Keynesian, Corporatist, or Stalinist states in the early postwar period, "which involve," as Raniero Panzieri writes, in a seminal article within the *operaismo* tradition, "the progressive extension of planning from the factory to the market, to the external social sphere." Raniero Panzieri, "The Capitalist Use of Machinery: Marx versus the Objectivists," in *Outlines of a Critique of Technology*, ed. P. Slater (London: Ink Links, 1980), 59. For a summary of the development of the concept, see Nicholas Thoburn, *Deleuze, Marx and Politics* (London: Routledge, 2003), 69–102.

24. Boltanski and Chiapello, *The New Spirit of Capitalism*, 109.

25. Ibid., 109.

26. Ibid., 111.

27. Ibid.

28. Mayer, *Memory*, 78.

29. See Andrew Ross for a similar point. Though his article deals with the regimenting of art as such, he acknowledges that the most significant effect is the generalization of the "mentality" of artists' work across the entire economy, not just among so-called creatives: "[The] traditional profile of the artist as unattached and adaptable to circumstance is surely now coming into its own as the ideal definition of the postindustrial knowledge worker: comfortable in an ever-changing environment that demands creative shifts in communication with different kinds of clients and partners; attitudinally geared toward production that requires long, and often unsocial, hours; and accustomed, in the sundry exercise of their mental labor, to a contingent, rather than a fixed, routine of self-application." Andrew Ross, "The Mental Labor Problem," *Social Text* 18, no. 2 (2000): 11.

30. Boltanski and Chiapello, *The New Spirit of Capitalism*, 112.

31. Mayer, *Memory*, 114–115.

32. See André Beckerman's "The Meaning of Multiskilling" for a deflation of the myth of multiskilling in the auto industry. For Beckerman "multiskilling is premised on rigidly described work routines." That is, it is built on deskilled labor rather than in distinction to it. "Multiskilling," as he writes, "can be the veneer that hides a new round of quicker, swifter, faster." André Beckerman, *Training for What? Labour Perspectives on Job Training* (Toronto: James Lorimer, 1992), 28–42.

33. Brendan Burchell, David Ladipo, and Frank Wilkinson, *Job Insecurity and Work Intensification* (Hove, UK: Psychology Press, 2002), 45.

34. See Shira Offer and Barbara Schneider, "Multitasking among Working Families: A Strategy for Dealing with the Time Squeeze," in *Workplace Flexibility: Realigning 20th-Century Jobs for a 21st-Century Workforce*, ed. Kathleen Christensen and Barbara Schneider (Ithaca, NY: Cornell University Press, 2010), 43–56.

35. Paul Stephens, *The Poetics of Information Overload: From Gertrude Stein to Conceptual Writing* (Minneapolis: University of Minnesota Press, 2015), 11.

36. Diane-Gabrielle Tremblay, "Change and Continuity: Transformations in the Gendered Division of Labour in a Context of Technological and Organizational Change," in *Women, Work, and Computerization: Spinning a Web from Past to Future: Proceedings of the 6th International IFIP-Conference, Bonn, Germany, May 24–27, 1997* (Berlin: Springer, 1997), 295.

37. Mayer, *Memory*, 44.

38. Rosalind E. Krauss, *A Voyage on the North Sea: Art in the Age of the Post-medium Condition* (New York: Thames & Hudson, 2000).

39. John Roberts, *The Intangibilities of Form: Skill and Deskilling in Art after the Readymade* (New York: Verso, 2007), 9–48; Buchloh, "Conceptual Art 1962–1969" (1999).

40. Though minimalism and pop art mime a logic of industrial production and manual labor, they are often more oriented toward administrative labor than they might seem. Minimalist sculptors frequently phoned in their orders rather than produce the sculptures themselves. They are thus managerial rather than industrial workers, and it is a short step from producing a sculpture by phone order to treating the order—either on paper or as a mere act—as the artwork itself, something conceptual artists often did. See Bryan-Wilson, *Art Workers*; Molesworth, *Work Ethic*.

41. Andrea Fraser, "How to Provide an Artistic Service: An Introduction," in *Museum Highlights: The Writings of Andrea Fraser*, ed. Alexander Alberro (Cambridge, MA: MIT Press, 2005), 153–162.

42. Liu, *The Laws of Cool*, 169.

43. Fredric Jameson, *Cultural Turn: Selected Writings on the Postmodern, 1983–1998* (New York: Verso, 1998), 72; Liu, *The Laws of Cool*, 169.

44. Friedrich Kittler describes the moment of digitization as essentially destroying the distinct phenomenological character of the previously separate media: "The general digitization of channels and information erases the differences among individual media. . . . And once optical fiber networks turn formerly distinct data flows into a standardized series of digitized numbers, any medium can be translated into any other. . . . Modulation, transformation, synchronization; delay, storage, transposition; scrambling, scanning, mapping—a total media link on a digital base will erase the very concept of medium." Friedrich Kittler, *Gramophone, Film, Typewriter* (Stanford, CA: Stanford University Press, 1999), 2–3.

45. Lev Manovich, *The Language of New Media* (Cambridge, MA: MIT Press, 2001), 15.

46. Ibid., 219.

47. Ibid., 225.

48. For an interesting account of the relationship between technology and memory, see Bernard Stiegler, *Technics and Time, 2: Disorientation* (Stanford, CA: Stanford University Press, 2008), 99–187. Stiegler's main contention is that all technology is a form of memory. Modern technology, however, effects an "industrialization of memory" that makes the individuation of separate people, each with their own time, impossible.

49. Marx, *Capital*, 1:1021. As Moishe Postone and others argue, capitalist value—value based on "abstract labor time" or "socially necessary labor time"—can really come

into being only at the moment at which multiple capitalists compete with each other by trying to reduce the amount of labor expended in production, chiefly through the introduction of new methods and technologies. Before this process of real subsumption begins, there can be no universal measure of value based on time, since time has not yet been made, in practical terms, the chief measure of potential profits. Postone, *Time, Labor, and Social Domination*, 277–285.

50. Mayer, *Memory*, 7–8.
51. Ibid., 53, 116.
52. Marx, *Capital*, 1:342.
53. Marx, *Grundrisse*, 470.
54. Marx, *Capital*, 1:548–549.
55. Ibid., 504.
56. Karl Marx, *A Contribution to the Critique of Political Economy* (Chicago: Charles H. Kerr, 1904), 12.
57. Marx, *Grundrisse*, 693.
58. Ibid., 695.
59. Ibid., 706.
60. Ibid.
61. Mayer, *Memory*, 68–69.
62. Ibid.
63. Ibid., 28.
64. Karl Marx, *Capital*, volume 3 (New York: Penguin, 1991), 244–253; Marx, *Capital*, 1:773–776.
65. Marx, *Capital*, 3:244.
66. Gerard Duménil and Dominique Lévy, *Capital Resurgent: The Roots of the Neoliberal Revolution* (Cambridge, MA: Harvard University Press, 2004), 21–68; Paul Mattick, *Business as Usual: The Economic Crisis and the Failure of Capitalism* (London: Reaktion Books, 2012),1–40 ; Brenner, *The Economics of Global Turbulence*, 97–246.
67. Hugh MacDiarmid, *Three Hymns to Lenin* (Edinburgh: Castle Wynd Printers, 1957), 22.
68. Mayer, *Memory*, 134.
69. Ibid.
70. Karl Marx, *Surveys from Exile: Political Writings*, vol. 2 (New York: Verso, 2010), 146.

Chapter 5

1. John Kenneth Galbraith, *The Affluent Society* (Boston: Mariner Books, 1998), 243–254.
2. Riesman, *The Lonely Crowd*, 272.
3. This is also the scenario featured in Kurt Vonnegut's 1952 novel, *Player Piano*. David Riesman, *Abundance for What?* (Piscataway, NJ: Transaction Publishers, 1964), 174–175; see also Amy Sue Bix, *Inventing Ourselves out of Jobs? America's Debate over*

Technological Unemployment, 1929–1981 (Baltimore: Johns Hopkins University Press, 2001), 258.

4. This history of the "end-of-labor" thesis owes much to discussions with Björn Westergard.

5. Bix, *Inventing Ourselves out of Jobs?*, 258.

6. Ad Committee on the Triple Revolution, "The Triple Revolution," *Liberation*, no. 9 (April 1964): 9–16.

7. The Triple Revolution seem identical to James Boggs's remarkable *American Revolution: Pages from a Negro Worker's Notebook*, published a year earlier in a special double issue of *Monthly Review*. Boggs had been a member of the Correspondence Publishing Group with C. L. R. James but broke with him over the nonworkerist positions outlined in the text. Though he had been an auto-plant worker for years, Boggs declared that the rapid expulsion of proletarians from the labor process had rendered established communist strategy moot: C. L. R. James's strategy of building class power solely at the site of production, in preparation for workplace takeovers, would fail, given the numbers of proletarians (especially black proletarians) who had no access to wage labor. James Boggs, *The American Revolution: Pages from a Negro Worker's Notebook* (New York: Monthly Review Press, 1968). The immensely influential Port Huron Statement of the Students for a Democratic Society, written largely by Tom Hayden, described a postwar world in which "automation brings unemployment instead of mere leisure for all and greater achievement of needs for all people in the world—a crisis instead of economic utopia." Tom Hayden, *The Port Huron Statement: The Visionary Call of the 1960s Revolution* (New York: PublicAffairs, 2005), 79.

8. Kathi Weeks, *The Problem with Work: Feminism, Marxism, Antiwork Politics, and Postwork Imaginaries* (Durham, NC: Duke University Press, 2011).

9. Herbert Marcuse, *Eros and Civilization: A Philosophical Inquiry into Freud* (Boston: Beacon Press, 1974), 84.

10. Marx, *Capital*, 3:958–959.

11. Ibid., 959.

12. Marcuse, *One-Dimensional Man*, 9.

13. Marcuse, *Eros and Civilization*, 149, 160, 170, 235; Marcuse, *One-Dimensional Man*, 66, 74, 261.

14. Marcuse, *An Essay on Liberation*, vii, ix, 23–48.

15. Ibid.

16. Ibid., 36.

17. Ibid., 42.

18. Ibid., 45.

19. Ibid.

20. Guy Debord, "Theses on Cultural Revolution," in *Guy Debord and the Situationist International: Texts and Documents*, ed. Tom McDonough (Cambridge, MA: MIT Press, 2004), 61.

21. Situationist International, "The Bad Days Will End," 114.

22. Ibid.

23. William J. Baumol and David M. De Ferranti, *The Cost Disease: Why Computers Get Cheaper and Health Care Doesn't* (New Haven, CT: Yale University Press, 2012).

24. Weeks, *The Problem with Work*, 104–111.

25. Ibid.

26. Jordan Davis, "Review of *Okay, Okay* by Diana Hamilton," *Constant Critic*, March 24, 2013, http://www.constantcritic.com/jordan_davis/okay-okay/.

27. Michael Magee and Kasey Mohammed, "The Flarf Files," August 2003, http://epc.buffalo.edu/authors/bernstein/syllabi/readings/flarf.html.

28. For an excellent history of the feminist demand for flexible labor as well as its shortcomings, see Kathryn A. Cady, "Flexible Labor," *Feminist Media Studies* 13, no. 3 (2013): 395–414.

29. Lonnie Golden describes this type of flexibility—primarily manifesting among workers who work more than fifty hours per week, as part of a general "polarization of work hours." As Golden writes, the "frequency distribution of flexible scheduling across ranges of usual weekly hours is U-shaped," suggesting that "workers who wish to gain greater access to a flexible schedule must be willing to work very long workweeks (50 or more hours), work regular nondaytime hours such as evening shifts, work irregular shifts, work an unpredictable number of hours each week, or make a transition to either part-time work or self-employment." Lonnie Golden, "Flexible Work Schedules: What Are We Trading Off to Get Them?," *Monthly Labor Review* 124 (2001): 50, 55, 62. These two types of employer-directed flexibility, part of a general offensive by employers, are quite different from the progressive, feminist demands for flexibility detailed in books like Arlie Hochschild's *The Second Shift*, in which reduced and rearranged workweeks, allowing for family needs, would be exchanged for the higher productivity that resulted from the good morale such flexibility encouraged. For more information on the bifurcation of labor time, see Jerry A. Jacobs, *The Time Divide: Work, Family, and Gender Inequality*, The Family and Public Policy (Cambridge, MA: Harvard University Press, 2004).

30. Illouz, *Cold Intimacies*, 22.

31. Cynthia Cockburn, *In the Way of Women: Men's Resistance to Sex Equality in Organizations* (Ithaca, NY: Cornell University Press, 1991), 56–58.

32. K. Silem Mohammad, *Breathalyzer* (Washington, DC: Edge Books, 2008), 13, 28.

33. Peter Fleming, *Authenticity and the Cultural Politics of Work: New Forms of Informal Control* (Oxford: Oxford University Press, 2009), 57. See also Peter Fleming, "Workers' Playtime? Boundaries and Cynicism in a 'Culture of Fun' Program," *Journal of Applied Behavioral Science* 41, no. 3 (September 2005): 285–303.

34. Jean-Louis Barsoux, cited in Fleming, *Authenticity and the Cultural Politics of Work*, 67.

35. Rodney Koeneke, *Musée Mechanique* (Buffalo, NY: BlazeVOX Books, 2006), 59.

36. Ibid., 59–60.

37. Fleming, *Authenticity and the Cultural Politics of Work*, 118, 82.

38. Koeneke, *Musée Mechanique*, 59.

39. For a summary of the debate, see Brian M. Reed, *Nobody's Business: Twenty-First Century Avant-Garde Poetics* (Ithaca, NY: Cornell University Press, 2013), 121–160; Craig Perez, "My Michael Magee and the Frontier of Democratic Symbolic Action," *Jacket*, no. 33 (July 2007), http://jacketmagazine.com/33/perez-flarf.shtml. Reed more or less endorses the view of the poem's defenders, insisting that such dramatic monologues are satires of "the casual cruelty that passes for sophisticated cynical humor in the American mainstream"(111).

40. Magee and Mohammed, "The Flarf Files."

41. Illouz, *Cold Intimacies*, 23.

42. For an important account of the role that "Asian" character plays in contemporary workplaces, see Colleen Lye, "Unmarked Character and the 'Rise of Asia': Ed Park's *Personal Days*," *Verge: Studies in Global Asias* 1, no. 1 (2015): 230–254. The poem is quoted in Perez.

43. Drew Gardner, *Petroleum Hat* (New York: Roof Books, 2005), 20.

44. Eli Pariser, *The Filter Bubble* (New York: Penguin, 2012).

45. Gardner, *Petroleum Hat*, 20.

46. Both Gabriella Coleman and Harry Halpin read Anonymous—which emerges from, but also against, the "troll space" of 4chan—as a reaction against the logics of celebrity, recognition, and personal identity offered up by sites like Facebook. Harry Halpin, "The Philosophy of Anonymous: Ontological Politics without Identity," *Radical Philosophy*, no. 176 (December 2012): 19–28; Gabriella Coleman, "Our Weirdness Is Free," *Triple Canopy*, no. 15 (2012), http://canopycanopycanopy.com/issues/15/contents/our_weirdness_is_free.

47. Glen Fuller, Jason Wilson, and Christian McCrea, "Editorial: Troll Theory," in "Trolls and the Negative Space of the Internet," ed. Glen Fuller, Jason Wilson, and Christian McCrea, special issue, *Fibreculture Journal*, no. 22 (2013): 2.

48. Ibid., 6.

49. Nathaniel Tkacz, "Trolls, Peers, and the Diagram of Collaboration," in "Trolls and the Negative Space of the Internet," ed. Glen Fuller, Jason Wilson, and Christian McCrea, special issue, *Fibreculture Journal*, no. 22 (2013): 15–35.

50. Carl Cederström and Peter Fleming, *Dead Man Working* (Winchester, UK: Zero Books, 2012).

51. Kenneth Goldsmith, *Uncreative Writing: Managing Language in the Digital Age* (New York: Columbia University Press, 2013), 220.

52. Vanessa Place, *Tragodía 1: Statement of Facts* (Los Angeles: Insert Press, 2011).

53. Kenneth Goldsmith, *Day* (Great Barrington, MA: The Figures, 2003).

54. Stephens draws attention to the connection between conceptual writing and the indices and collection systems of both the financial sector and the surveillance state. Stephens, *The Poetics of Information Overload*, 153–175.

55. The characterology of the troll also illuminates the unfortunate recent history of Goldsmith and Place, both of whom outraged audiences in 2015 through

varieties of the "blank humor" described previously. First, in the midst of the unfolding Black Lives Matter movement sparked by the police murders of Eric Garner and Michael Brown, Goldsmith read a rearranged transcript of Michael Brown's autopsy report to an audience at Brown University, ending on a description of Brown's genitalia. Months later, after substantial discussions of Goldsmith's work, Vanessa Place angered many with a blackface retweeting of sentences from *Gone with the Wind*, using a Twitter account whose avatar was an image of Hattie McDaniel as "Mammy" in the film version of the novel. Defenses of Goldsmith's and Place's appropriations asserted that they were simply making visible racism that already existed in the world, withdrawing all critical commentary and ironic inflection of the sort we get with Flarf so that audiences (presumed to be white, by the logic of this defense) could reflect on the legacy of antiblack racism. As with Flarf and its trollery, these works take aim at the presumed falsity of political correctness: in a note, Place defends her *Gone with the Wind* tweets by suggesting that they unmask the self-serving piety of a politically correct audience, performing her own complicity with blackface appropriation to implicate a white audience. As I note later, this represents the zero degree of resistance, in which the artist can only imagine traumatizing or traumatized repetitions of the status quo. Vanessa Place, "Artist Statement: Gone with the Wind @Vanessa Place," *Facebook*, May 18, 2015, http://tinyurl.com/owh9tg2 (site discontinued).

56. Ibid.

57. See the following review for a discussion of this aspect of the novel. Jonathan Raban, "Divine Drudgery," *New York Review of Books*, May 12, 2011, http://www.nybooks.com/articles/archives/2011/may/12/divine-drudgery/.

58. David Foster Wallace, *The Pale King: An Unfinished Novel* (New York: Little, Brown, 2011), 231.

59. David Foster Wallace, *This Is Water: Some Thoughts, Delivered on a Significant Occasion, about Living a Compassionate Life* (New York: Little, Brown, 2009), 120.

60. Wallace, *The Pale King*, 447.

61. Ibid., 463.

62. Ibid., 483.

63. Ibid., 548.

64. Mihaly Csikszentmihalyi, *Flow: The Psychology of Optimal Experience* (New York: Harper Perennial, 1991), 18.

65. Ibid., 143–163.

66. I develop these arguments in articles published elsewhere, noting the waning of contestation at the site of production over the last several decades and the emergence of tactics (blockades, occupations, riots) that situate antagonism beyond the workplace proper, even when the antagonists are workers. Jasper Bernes, "Logistics, Counterlogistics, and the Communist Prospect," *Endnotes*, no. 3 (September 2013): 172–201; Jasper Bernes, "The Double-Barricade and the Glass Floor," in *Communization and Its Discontents*, ed. Benjamin Noy (Wivenhoe, UK: Minor Compositions, 2011), 157–175; Jas-

per Bernes, "Square and Circle: The Logic of Occupy," *New Inquiry*, September 17, 2012, http://thenewinquiry.com/essays/square-and-circle-the-logic-of-occupy/.

67. On wagelessness, see "Misery and Debt," *Endnotes*, no. 2 (April 2010): 20–51; Michael Denning, "Wageless Life," *New Left Review* 2, no. 66 (December 2010): 79–97.

68. Sean Bonney, *Letters against the Firmament* (London: Enitharmion, 2015), 46.

69. Ibid., 111.

70. Ibid.

71. Ibid., 100.

72. Ibid., 99.

73. Ibid., 100.

Epilogue

1. For a discussion of the 1930s debates and their continuation in the early postwar period, see Bix, *Inventing Ourselves out of Jobs?*

2. Erik Brynjolfsson and Andrew McAfee, *The Second Machine Age: Work, Progress, and Prosperity in a Time of Brilliant Technologies* (New York: W. W. Norton, 2014); Tyler Cowen, *Average Is Over: Powering America beyond the Age of the Great Stagnation* (New York: Dutton, 2013).

3. Cowen, *Average Is Over*, 3–18.

4. Brynjolfsson and McAfee, *The Second Machine Age*, 125–146.

5. Ibid., 179–181.

6. Cowen, *Average Is Over*, 30–31.

7. Ibid.

8. Ibid., 32.

9. Maria Canon, Marianna Kudlyak, and Peter Debbaut, "A Closer Look at the Decline in the Labor Force Participation Rate," *Regional Economics* (October 2013): 10–11, https://www.stlouisfed.org/publications/regional-economist/october-2013/a-closer-look-at-the-decline-in-the-labor-force-participation-rate; Maximiliano Dvorkin, "Labor Force Participation: The U.S. and Its Peers," June 22, 2015, https://www.stlouisfed.org/on-the-economy/2015/june/labor-force-participation-the-us-and-its-peers.

10. Joshua Clover and Aaron Benanav, "Can Dialectics Break BRICS?," *South Atlantic Quarterly* 113, no. 4 (September 2014): 752–757.

11. "Misery and Debt." This argument will be developed further in Aaron Benanav's forthcoming book, *A Global History of Unemployment* (Verso). The following paragraph owes much to conversations with Aaron about these matters.

12. I am assuming here that some of the increase in wealth from productivity gains were distributed to workers and that real wages increased across the first three quarters of the twentieth century and parts of the nineteenth century. The treatment that Karl Marx gives, of "relative surplus value," where decreases in the costs of wage goods lead to a decrease in the cost of reproducing labor and an increase in the share of value that capital appropriates, assumes that none of these gains go to workers and that their level of consumption remains static. In such a scenario, the effect on

the labor markets is clear. Output will be capped at previous limits, and employment will fall directly as a result of productivity increases. But wages will rise when demand for labor is strong, as happens during booms, and even during busts wages remain somewhat difficult to depress downward in nominal terms (they are "sticky"), so that rises in the real wage level can be countered only by holding nominal wages more or less steady and letting inflation do its work. Wage share has fallen over the last thirty years, but empirical studies and a simple look at comparison of the standard of living compared to that one hundred years ago shows that some of the productivity gains were taken as increasing real wages. My reasoning therefore concerns what was done with this new wealth.

13. This is Robert Brenner's explanation for "the long downturn." Robert Brenner, *The Economics of Global Turbulence: The Advanced Capitalist Economies from Long Boom to Long Downturn, 1945–2005* (New York: Verso, 2006).

14. Denning, "Wageless Life," 79.

15. Mike Davis, *Planet of Slums* (New York: Verso, 2007), 14.

16. Guy Standing, *The Precariat: The New Dangerous Class* (London: Bloomsbury Academic, 2011).

17. Ibid.

18. Denning, "Wageless Life," 81.

19. Ibid.

20. Marx, *Capital*, 1:273.

21. Ibid., 781–794.

22. For an example, see Charles Post, "We're All Precarious Now," *Jacobin*, April 20, 2015. Aaron Benanav responds in "Precarity Rising," *Viewpoint*, June 15, 2015, https://viewpointmag.com/2015/06/15/precarity-rising/.

23. Marx, *Capital*, 1:896–904. See also E. P. Thompson, *The Making of the English Working Class* (New York: Penguin, 1991); Peter Linebaugh, *The London Hanged: Crime and Civil Society in the Eighteenth Century* (New York: Verso, 2006).

24. Richard Halpern, *The Poetics of Primitive Accumulation: English Renaissance Culture and the Genealogy of Capital* (Ithaca, NY: Cornell University Press, 1991), 61–102.

25. I owe this insight to Celeste Langan.

26. Halpern, *The Poetics of Primitive Accumulation*, 59–60.

27. Patricia Fumerton, "Response to Craig Dionne," *Electronic Seminar*, 2008, http://emc.eserver.org/1-7/fumerton_response.html; Patricia Fumerton, "Not Home: Alehouses, Ballads, and the Vagrant Husband in Early Modern England," *Journal of Medieval and Early Modern Studies* 32, no. 3 (2002): 497.

28. Daniel Tiffany, *Infidel Poetics Riddles, Nightlife, Substance* (Chicago: University of Chicago Press, 2009), 137–160.

29. Celeste Langan, *Romantic Vagrancy: Wordsworth and the Simulation of Freedom* (Cambridge: Cambridge University Press, 1995), 12.

30. Ibid., 17.

31. Ibid.

32. Todd DePastino, *Citizen Hobo: How a Century of Homelessness Shaped America* (Chicago: University of Chicago Press, 2003), 59–84.

33. Charles Kerr, *I. W. W. Songs: To Fan the Flames of Discontent* (Chicago: Charles H. Kerr, 2003).

34. Industrial Workers of the World, *I. W. W. Songs: Songs to Fan the Flames of Discontent . . .* (Chicago: Industrial Workers of the World, 1922), 12.

35. Carl Sandburg, *Carl Sandburg's New American Songbag* (New York: Broadcast Music, 1950), 184–185.

36. "The Big Rock Candy Mountain by Harry McClintock Songfacts," accessed July 23, 2016, http://www.songfacts.com/detail.php?id=22192.

37. For an attempt to think race and racialization by way of the history of superfluous populations, see Chris Chen, "The Limit Point of Capitalist Equality: Notes toward an Abolitionist Antiracism," *Endnotes*, no. 3 (September 2013): 202–223.

38. Paul Gilroy, *The Black Atlantic: Modernity and Double Consciousness* (Cambridge, MA: Harvard University Press, 1993), 40.

39. For Moten on fugitivity and poetry, see Fred Moten, *In the Break: The Aesthetics of the Black Radical Tradition* (Minneapolis: University of Minnesota Press, 2003), 273, 278; Fred Moten, "Black Optimism/Black Operation" (Chicago, October 19, 2007), https://lucian.uchicago.edu/blogs/politicalfeeling/files/2007/12/moten-black-optimism.doc. Nathaniel Mackey's use of the term can be found in Nathaniel Mackey, *Paracritical Hinge: Essays, Talks, Notes, Interviews* (Madison: University of Wisconsin Press, 2005), 181–198.

40. Claude McKay, *Banjo: A Story without a Plot*, A Harvest Book (New York: Harcourt, Brace, Jovanovich, 1970).

41. Ralph Ellison, *Invisible Man* (New York: Random House, 2002).

42. Mackey, *Paracritical Hinge*, 187.

43. Ibid., 200.

44. Quoted in ibid. For original, see Amiri Baraka, *Black Magic: Sabotage, Target Study, Black Art: Collected Poetry, 1961–1967* (Indianapolis, IN: Bobbs-Merrill, 1969), 38.

45. Stefano Harney and Fred Moten, *The Undercommons: Fugitive Planning & Black Study* (Brooklyn, NY: Autonomedia, 2013), 49.

46. Fred Moten, *Hughson's Tavern* (New York: Leon Works, 2008), 57.

47. Harney and Moten, *The Undercommons*, 30.

48. Adam Fitzgerald, "An Interview with Fred Moten, Part II: On Radical Indistinctness and Thought Flavor à la Derrida," *Lithub*, August 6, 2015.

49. Moten, "Black Optimism/Black Operation," 2.

50. Fitzgerald, "An Interview with Fred Moten."

51. Margaret Ronda, "'Not Much Left': Wageless Life in Millenial [*sic*] Poetry," *Post45*, October 9, 2011, http://post45.research.yale.edu/2011/10/not-much-left-wageless-life-in-millenial-poetry/.

52. Wendy Trevino, "Sonnets of Brass Knuckle Doodles," *Boog City Reader*, no. 8 (2015).

53. Ibid.

54. Ibid.

55. I develop these ideas in three articles cited earlier. See Chapter 5, note 66.

56. For an account of riot as the preeminent strategy and tactic now that struggle has shifted to circulation, see Joshua Clover, *Riot. Strike. Riot: The New Era of Uprisings* (Brooklyn, NY: Verso, 2016).

Index

1960s: advertising of, 41–42; art in, 10–14; end of labor and end of art in, 149–56; novels of, 84–85; workers' resistance during, 7–8, 91
1970s: crisis of, 16–18 177–78; restructuring of labor in, 83, 90, 100, 107, 138, 171
4chan, 164, 220n46

Absenteeism, 7, 17
Abstract expressionism, 46, 57–58, 61
Adaptation: feature of post–Movement art, 22; of lyric, 56; in systems theory, 103, 115; in workplace, 28, 114
Address, 31, 45, 50–63, 66, 73–74, 79, 171–72
Administration, 7, 76–78, 81–83, 102, 120; aesthetics of, 20, 27, 112; conceptual art and, 134. *See also under* Labor, administrative
Adorno, Theodor, 1–2, 55, 130
Advertising, 20, 38, 40–46, 56, 62–3, 67, 109, 112–13, 181, 202n12, 204n51
Aesthetic critique. *See* Artistic critique
Alienation, 7; artistic critique of, 9–10, 16–18, 31, 35, 89–91, 116–18, 156; automation and, 151, 153; spectacle and, 13; of work and workplace, 9, 79–81, 132
Apostrophe, 52–55, 60
Artistic critique, 9–10, 12, 16–18, 28, 31, 35, 89–91, 116, 118, 156, 170–72, 181
Ashbery, John, 27–28, 60, 64–83; "America," 70–73; "Europe," 72–73, 76; "The Instruction Manual," 27, 64–67, 69, 76, 82–83; "Landscape," 79–81; "Self–Portrait in a Convex Mirror," 76; *Some Trees* (1956), 64, 66; *The Tennis Court Oath*, 28, 67, 69–72, 76, 78–79, 82
Ashby, W. Ross, 86
Assembly line, 4, 7–8, 18, 119, 170
Automation, 19, 27, 65, 134–35, 139, 142, 147–48, 218n7; and deindustrialization, 121; and Fordism, 4; and unemployment, 150–56, 176, 179–80
Avant-gardes: abstract expressionism, 57–58; art into life, theme of, 10–13, 208n17; and the artistic critique, 89–90; and cybernetics, 85–88; and information technology, 134–36, 166; Marcuse, theory of, 152–54; Neo-avantgardes, 5, 85–86, 89–90, 92

Bakhtin, Mikhail, 75–76
Ballad, 31, 185–89, 193–94
Baraka, Amiri, 189–91
Bare life, 31, 182
Barthes, Roland, 14, 85
Basic income, 150
Beggars, 31, 185–87
Bell, Daniel: *The Coming of Postindustrial Society*, 121–22
Beuys, Joseph, 12
Boltanski, Luc: artistic critique, 9–10, 12, 17–18, 89–90, 118, 156 ; connexionism, 116, 132; projective city, 131–32
Bonney, Sean, 31, 171–72, 181, 194
Brand, Stewart: and the Whole Earth Network, 91
Brautigan, Richard: *All Watched Over by Machines of Loving Grace*, 88
Braverman, Harry, 17–19, 65
Brenner, Robert, 16–17, 223n13
Buchloh, Benjamin, 20, 112, 134

Cage, John, 21, 91, 198n34
Capitalism: and the commodity, 77–78; golden age of, 3; and labor, 2–3, 34–35; postindustrial, 108; restructuring of, 18, 206
Chiapello, Eve: artistic critique, 9–10, 12, 17–18, 89–90, 118, 156; connexionism, 116, 132; projective city, 131–32
Chance–based composition, 21–23, 90
City Lights (publisher), 37
Clark, Lygia, 12
Clune, Michael, 5
Communication: and control, 86–87, 92–94; and information entropy, 95–100;

227

price system as, 94; "Trans-Space Communication," 100–103; workplace norms of, 159–60, 162–63
Composition of capital, 144–48, 176–78
Computer, 8, 18, 30, 62, 135–36
Conceptual art, 21, 24, 85–86; Dan Graham and, 109–19
Conceptual writing, 30, 166–69
Cowen, Tyler, 174–75, 178, 180
Cowie, Jefferson, 8
Craft. *See under* Labor, artisanal
Culler, Jonathan, 51
Cultural Cold War, 65–71
Cybernetics, 28–29; 84–91; and *The Crying of Lot 49*, 108–9; Dan Graham and, 109–19; Hannah Weiner and, 91–95, 100–106; information, 95–100

Database, 136–37
Debord, Guy, 12–13, 154–55. *See also* Situationist International
Decentralization, 18, 94, 117, 135
Degentesh, Katie, 30, 157–59
Deindustrialization, 3, 19, 21, 23–27, 121–22, 175–79
Delayering, 19, 141
Demands: qualitative, 8, 10, 89; quantitative, 8, 9, 89
Dematerialization, of the art object, 19–21, 76–77, 111–12
Denning, Michael, 182–83, 189
Deskilling, 4, 8, 27, 65, 71, 76, 81, 87, 89, 109, 132–34, 199n50, 215n32
Division of labor: aesthetic, 15–16; gendered, 4–5, 121–25; machines as, 141; overcoming of, 164–65
Double day, 123–28, 143, 146
Draper, Don. See *Mad Men*
Duchamp, Marcel, 113

Eco, Umberto, 14
Emotion, 23, 159
End of labor, 152–15; end of art and, 150–56
Endnotes, 176, 181
Entropy, 84–85, 95–102, 106–07
Exclamation, 52–60
Experience: advertisement and, 42–43; commodification of, 44–47; happenings and, 24. *See also* Rapport
Experiment, 8–9, 113–14; as laboratory, 90; in poetry, 29; in writing, 20–23

Factory. *See* Manufacturing
Feedback, 84–88, 92–94, 100, 103–15. *See also* Cybernetics

Feminization, of labor, 26, 120–28; emasculation of male workers, 31, 163–66
Ferlinghetti, Lawrence, 37
Filing, 20–22, 134. *See also* Labor, clerical
Filter bubble, 163
Flarf, 30, 157–70, 220–221n55
Fleming, Peter, 160–61
Flexibility, 10, 17–19, 26–30, 81–83, 89–90, 113–17, 129–35, 159, 165, 219n29
Fluxus, 11–13, 92
Folbre, Nancy, 128
Fordism, 4, 10, 17–18, 28, 65, 100, 133. *See also* Assembly line
Frank, Thomas, 41, 89–90
Fraser, Andrea, 134
Free indirect: discourse, 28, 72–80, 82, 206n32; labor, 77.
Freneticism, 24, 38, 126–29, 133, 137, 146
Fried, Michael: "Art and Objecthood," 11
Frye, Northrop, 50–51
Fugitivity, 189–94
Fumerton, Patricia, 185

Gilroy, Paul, 189
Ginsberg, Allen, 37, 58–59; "America," 65
Glazer, Nona, 213n18
Globalization, 16, 32, 51
Goldsmith, Kenneth, 30, 120, 166–68
Google, 157–58, 161, 163
Graham, Dan, 29, 143; *Schema*, 110–13; video works, 113–19; "Works for Magazine Pages," 109–13
Great Refusal, 162

Halpern, Richard, 185–86, 193
Hammons, David, 24
Harvey, David, 17–18
Hayakawa, S.I., 40–41, 55
Hayek, Friedrich, 94
Hayles, N. Katherine, 96
Hejinian, Lyn, 15, 136
Hicks, Heather, 26
Hill, Joe: "The Tramp," 187–88
"Hilltop" ad (Coca-Cola), 62–63
Hoberek, Andrew, 5, 66, 107
Hochschild, Arlie, 23, 48, 127, 219n29
Holiday, Billie, 48–50
Homeostat, 86
Homo sacer, 186
Horizontalization: of work relations, 9, 31, 161, 165
Horkheimer, Max, 2, 130
Humanization: of labor, 17–18, 49, 65, 92–93
Humor, 162, 165, 167, 202n12, 220–221n39, 55

Indexicality, 22–23

Informal economy, 31, 180, 182–83
Information, 19, 21–23, 84–86, 93–114, 118–19, 120–24, 132–33; information entropy, 95–100; "Information" exhibit, 85, 109; information technology, 19, 134–38, 156–68; poetry and information, 100–103, 133, 136–37; price as information, 95. *See also* under Value, of information
Interactivity, 24, 136. *See also* Labor, interactive service
International style architecture, 61
International Workers of the World (IWW), 187–88; *Little Red Songbook*, 187–88
Internet, 30–31, 163–66
Internet troll, 31, 161–67, 172
Izenberg, Oren, 52

Jackson, Virginia, 51
Just-in-time production, 18

Kaprow, Allan, 10–11, 24, 85, 91; *Fluids*, 24; happenings, 11, 13, 23-24, 198n34
Knowledge work. *See* Information labor
Koeneke, Rodney, 160–61, 209n34
Krauss, Rosalind, 22–23, 134

Labor: administrative, 20–23, 26, 76–78; affective, 23–4, 25–26, 47–51, 55–56, 127, 159–60; artisanal, 67–68, 179–80; authoritarianism of, 7–10, 15, 81, 114, 201n74; blue-collar, 3–7, 19, 81–83; clerical, 19–24, 26, 120–27, 167; domestic, 30, 123–28; information, 124, 145, 152, 166–70; in-person or interactive service, 23, 26–27, 47–49, 56, 61; intensification of, 10, 16–17, 133–34 146, 155; out-of-person service, 56, 59; part-time, 19, 35, 130, 156, 219n29; reproductive, 30, 121, 123–25, 129–30, 135, 183, 210n55, 212–3n9, 214n22, 22n12; service work, 19, 23–27, 39, 47–48, 50, 55–57, 59, 61, 68, 110, 112, 121–22, 126–27, 155, 175–76, 178–79, 200, 202–203n21, 212n3; wage, 1–4, 16–17, 27, 78, 89, 123, 125, 127–28, 130–32, 172, 174, 176–81, 183–84, 210n55, 211n69, 213n9, 213–214n18, 214n23, 218n7, 222–223n12; white-collar, 3–6, 8, 10, 19, 21–23, 26, 30, 47, 64–66, 68, 73, 76, 81–82, 89, 100, 110–12, 114, 120, 123, 127, 129, 133, 142, 157, 160–61, 163, 165, 168 –69, 201n74, 205n11, 121n3
Laboratory, art and poetry as, 6, 33, 117, 135–36
Labor force participation rate, 176
Language poetry, 14–15, 21
Leisure, 34–39, 82–83, 126–30, 148, 154, 156, 159–61
LeWitt, Sol, 20

Lippard, Lucy, 28, 111–12
Liu, Alan, 17, 135, 201n73
Long downturn, 17
Lyric, 37, 43, 50–54, 63; African-American lyric, 41, 190–94; lyric theory, 50–52

Machinery, 6, 18, 22, 86–88, 127–29, 133–47, 174–78. *See also* Technology
Maciunas, George, 12
Mac Low, Jackson, 21–23
Mackey, Nathaniel, 189–90, 224n39
Mad Men, 38–40, 61 38–40, 61–63, 202n12
Magee, Mike, 157; "Their Guys, Their Glittering Asian Guys, Are Gay," 162–63
Mallarmé, Stéphane, 2, 167
Management, 4, 8, 28; information management, 120, 166–67; management techniques, 4, 17–18, 35, 47. *See also* Fordism; Taylorism
Manufacturing, 3–8, 18–19, 65, 121, 14, 155–56, 174–78. *See also* Factory
Marcuse, Herbert, 6–7, 89, 11, 151–56; *Eros and Civilization*, 151; *Essay on Liberation*, 152–54; *One-Dimensional Man*, 6, 89, 152
Marx, Karl, 2, 7, 31, 69, 77, 125, 138, 139–52, 154–48, 153–54, 163–64
Marxist Feminism, 123, 212–213n9, 213n18
May '68 (France), 7, 89
Mayer, Bernadette, 30, 85, 121, 123–49; *The Desires of Mothers to Please Others in Letters*, 123; *Memory*, 30, 85, 124–49; *Midwinter Day*, 123
McAfee, Scott, 174, 178
McCaffery, Steve, 14–15, 20
McClintock, Harry: "Big Rock Candy Mountain," 188
McDowell, Linda, 47
McGurl, Mark, 207n2
McKay, Claude: *Banjo*, 190
Mill, J. S., 50
Mills, C. Wright, 5–6, 38, 65, 70, 88
Minimalism, 11, 112, 134, 216n40
Modernism, 51, 67–68, 101, 111, 179, 187
Moten, Fred, 13, 189–94, 214–215n23
Multiskilling, 132–34
Multitasking, 128–29, 133–35, 199n50
Museum of Modern Art (MoMA), 37, 48, 57–61, 85, 109

Necessary labor time, 153, 216n49
Neo–concretism, 11
New Criticism, 51
New Left, 6, 88, 150–51
Nike ad (*Just Do It*), 41–42, 43
Ngai, Sianne, 23, 26, 126–27

O'Hara, Frank, 24–27, 37–63, 126, 202n12; "The Day Lady Died," 25, 48–50, 59; "Having a Coke with You," 41–46, 61, 63; *Lunch Poems*, 37–40, 48, 52–63; "Personism," 52, 61
Oiticica, Hélio, 12, 85
Oldenburg, Claes, 11
Order, 4, 14, 17, 69, 108; and entropy, cybernetic theories of, 94, 97, 99–100, 102–3, 107, 207n7
Organization, 18, 33, 45, 65, 79, 81, 88–89, 99–100, 106–7, 112, 116, 118, 153, 156–57, 182, 187, 204, 213n18

Participation, 10, 59, 86, 106; art and literature, 9, 29, 154, 186, 200n53, 210n57; happenings and, 11–15, 24; workplace, 8, 17, 19, 81, 89–91, 94, 116, 131, 136, 166, 199n50
Pasolini, Pier Paolo, 76, 79, 82
Pastoral, 27–28, 39, 55, 82
Paupers, 184–85
Personal computer, 30, 135–36
Personism, 52, 61
Place, Vanessa, 167, 221n55; *Statement of Facts*, 167
Point of view, 28, 66, 72–75, 78–79, 82–83
Poor laws, 184–85
Pop Art, 69, 112, 134, 216n40
Post-fordism, 10, 17
Postindustrial, 3, 17, 19, 28, 32, 108, 121–22, 126–27, 130, 149, 165, 174, 176–79, 184, 200n53, 205n11, 212n3, 215n29
Postmodernism, 32, 135, 179; advertising, 41–43, 56; literature, 84
Postone, Moishe, 2, 216n49
Precarity, 31, 109, 129, 182, 184, 191, 193, 196
Productive forces, 140–41, 152–53
Productivity, 2–4, 17–18, 46, 81, 83, 129, 138, 145–47, 149–51, 155, 174–79, 214–15n23, 229n29, 272–73n12
Project, 131–32
Proletarianization, 5–6, 139
Prosopopoeia, 77, 140

Rapport, 47–50, 55–56, 60–61
Readymade, 20
Real subsumption, 138, 214–15n23, 216–17n49
Refusal of work, 32, 189
Reich, Robert, 23, 100, 202–3n21
Remediation, 135
Restructuring, of labor, 3, 14, 17–19, 26–27, 29, 31, 35–36, 56, 83, 90, 100, 106, 108, 114, 116, 120, 132–33, 138, 156–57, 161–62, 165, 169, 171–72, 180, 195–96, 201n73
Riesman, David, 5, 149–50, 152
Right to manage, 81
Ross, Andrew, 69, 215n29

Routinization, 4–5, 7–8, 20–21, 23, 26–27, 133–37, 166–70

Sabotage, 7, 17, 35
Schryer, Stephen, 107
Second-person pronoun, 73–75, 79
Self-employment, 179–80
Self-management, 8, 10, 17, 19, 27, 30, 35, 106, 114, 118–19, 156, 180, 198n27
Service work. *See under* Labor, in-person or interactive service; Labor, service work
Servomechanism, 92, 95–96, 119
Shannon, Claude, 96–103, 110–11; Shannon entropy, 97–102; "Shannon poetry," 99–103
Situation, 13
Situationist International, 11–14, 112, 154–55
Skill, 114, 121–22, 126, 131, 133–34, 141, 170, 174–75, 180, 199n50
Social relations, 6, 17, 29, 34, 52, 72, 77, 90, 99, 112, 140–41; workplace relations, 17, 20, 25, 195
Spectacle, 12–14, 83, 112
Speedup, 8, 16, 127–28, 133, 137, 144, 146
Stagnant sector, 178
Stephens, Paul, 133, 167
Superfluous populations, 31, 121, 146, 176, 181–82, 184
Surplus value: 145, 210n55, 212n18, 223n12; absolute, 2; relative, 212n18, 223n12

Taylor, Frederick Winslow, 4
Taylorism, 4, 8, 10, 16–17, 26, 28, 65, 100, 119, 133, 163, 197n6, 201n73;
Teamwork, 10, 19, 26, 35, 81–82, 107, 114, 132–33, 156, 163, 166, 201n74
Technology, 2, 27, 30, 32, 87, 96, 101, 107, 120, 134–35, 137–38, 140, 144, 146–48, 149, 155–57, 174–75, 177–79, 195, 200n60, 210n55, 216–17n49; information technology, 19, 27, 84, 91, 119, 166; lyric technology, 50–51, 63; technological unemployment, 150, 174, 189
Temp work, 19, 114,
Toyotism, 10
Trevino, Wendy, 31, 194–96
"The Triple Revolution," 150, 218n7
Troll, 31, 164–67, 172–73, 220n46, 220–21n55
Turn to language, 20–21

Uncreative writing, 168
Unemployment, 31, 149, 150, 171, 174–76, 181–83, 189,
Unwork, 30, 171–72, 181, 194
User-friendly, 135

Vagabondage, 184–85

Vagrancy, 31, 185, 186
Value: of information, 106, 108, 111, 113, 122; of art, 109, 111–14; of labor, 108, 122, 168, 175, 210n55, 212n3
Vogelfrei, 186, 193
Volosinov, Valentin, 75–76, 79

Wagelessness, 31, 171, 182, 183–85, 190, 193–94
Wallace, David Foster: *The Pale King*, 169–70
Weeks, Kathi, 155, 171; *The Problem with Work*, 155
Weiner, Hannah, 29, 85, 90–106; *Code Poems*, 100–106; "Hannah Weiner at Her Job," 91–92; "Street Works," 94; "World Works," 94

Welfare state, 31, 171
Whyte, William, 5, 65, 81, 89; *The Organization Man* (1956), 65
Wieden+Kennedy, 41–43
Wiener, Norbert, 84–86, 92–93, 95–104, 107–8; *The Human Use of Human Beings*, 84–85, 93, 108
Williams, Raymond, 34
Women's movement, 9, 120
Work in America, 7–8
Writerly text, 14

Zany, 126–27
Zero-hours contract, 172
Zuboff, Shoshana, 114

Annie McClanahan, *Dead Pledges: Debt, Crisis, and Twenty-First-Century Culture*

Amy Hungerford, *Making Literature Now*

J.D. Connor, *The Studios After the Studios: Neoclassical Hollywood, 1970–2010*

Michael Trask, *Camp Sites: Sex, Politics, and Academic Style in Postwar America*

Loren Glass, *Counter-Culture Colophon: Grove Press, the* Evergreen Review, *and the Incorporation of the Avant-Garde*

Michael Szalay, *Hip Figures: A Literary History of the Democratic Party*

Jared Gardner, *Projections: Comics and the History of Twenty-First-Century Storytelling*

Jerome Christensen, *America's Corporate Art: The Studio Authorship of Hollywood Motion Pictures*

The authorized representative in the EU for product safety and compliance is:
Mare Nostrum Group
B.V Doelen 72
4831 GR Breda
The Netherlands

www.ingramcontent.com/pod-product-compliance
Lightning Source LLC
Chambersburg PA
CBHW022010220426
43663CB00007B/1026